LANGUAGE ASSESSMENT IN ACTION

edited by

Geoff Brindley

National Centre for English Language Teaching and Research
Macquarie University, Sydney NSW 2109

Language assessment in action

Published and distributed by the
National Centre for English Language
Teaching and Research
Macquarie University
NSW 2109

ISSN 1035 6487
ISBN 1 86408 058 2

AND GLADLY TECHE

The National Centre for English Language Teaching and Research (NCELTR) is a Commonwealth Government-funded Key Centre of Research and Teaching established at Macquarie University in 1988. The National Centre forms part of the Linguistics discipline within the School of English, Linguistics and Media at Macquarie University.

NCELTR Research Series
Series Editor: Geoff Brindley

This series contains research reports on theoretical and empirical studies of significance to all those involved in the teaching of English as a second language to adults.

Editing, design and layout: Jennie Skinner

Contents

Introduction

In Australia in the 1990s, growing demands are being placed by funding authorities on all sectors of education to provide more explicit and detailed information on program activities and outcomes. English as a Second Language (ESL) programs have not been immune to this trend and as a result, assessment has begun to assume a more prominent role in the ESL curriculum. At the level of the classroom, teachers are increasingly being called upon to monitor and record individual learner progress and achievement in much more systematic ways. Meanwhile, at the broader institutional level, educational authorities have begun to commission the development of standardised tests and assessment tools of various kinds in order to guide decisions on such matters as resource allocation, certification and selection.

The last few years have accordingly seen greatly increased activity in the development of tests and assessment procedures for assessing, monitoring and reporting learners' proficiency, progress and achievement in ESL programs. These range from large-scale standardised proficiency tests and reporting systems to informal monitoring procedures aimed at assisting teachers to keep track of individual classroom learning.

The aim of this volume is to bring together a range of these testing and assessment initiatives and to document the issues, problems and dilemmas which arise as practitioners and language testers attempt to devise systems, instruments and procedures to meet their particular assessment needs. Although the language testing literature now includes a number of useful guides to assessment (e.g. Shohamy 1985; Heaton 1988; Hughes 1989; Weir 1993; Cohen 1994) and authoritative volumes on theoretical principles (e.g. Bachman 1990, Bachman and Palmer, forthcoming), there are relatively few 'case study' accounts of the way in which assessment tools have been constructed to meet the needs of particular groups. It is hoped that this volume will help to fill this gap by providing some insights into the rationale and decision-making processes which have accompanied the development of tests and assessments in both institutional and classroom contexts.

The first three contributions by McDowell, McKay and Mincham describe the development of system-wide procedures for assessing language proficiency and achievement. McDowell's account of the steps involved in the construction of a test for overseas-qualified teachers begins with an overview of the Bachman (1990) model of language ability which provided the starting point for test development. She then illustrates the way in which specifications were established on the basis of analysis of data gathered in the target language use situation, pointing out the inevitable practical limitations on such an exercise. McDowell goes on to describe the components of the test, demonstrating how each one derives from Bachman's model of language ability and reflects the patterns of use language revealed at the needs analysis stage. In the process, she points out some of the difficult design issues involved in constructing communicative language tests which seek to take account of abilities such as pragmatic competence which are neither easy to elicit or to quantify. Finally she discusses issues of test validity and reliability and points to possible directions for future validation research. McDowell's account highlights the necessity for test developers to begin with a clear theoretical conceptualisation of the abilities they are assessing and to 'reality-test' their constructs against data from the target language use situation. Only in this way is it possible to establish a basis for content and construct validity.

A similar concern for construct validity characterises the contribution by McKay, who describes the development of an assessment and reporting package for primary and secondary ESL learners, involving the construction of a set of language proficiency bandscales. Like McDowell, she adopts a theoretical model of language ability — in this case the Bachman/Palmer (forthcoming) framework — as an organising framework for classifying the abilities to be described in the assessment instruments. However, she departs from Bachman and Palmer's ability-based approach to scale construction by including content and context in the band descriptors. This step she sees as necessary in order for the scales to serve as concrete assessment tools for teachers rather than as guidelines for test constructors. McKay then demonstrates how assessment activities were developed so as to reflect directly those aspects of language described in the bandscales. Her discussion of the validation of the bandscales raises some of the issues and problems involved in establishing the construct and content validity of general proficiency rating scales and describes the role that Rasch partial credit analysis can play in investigating the way in which scales are used. She makes the important point that content validity can be improved by ensuring that as many future users of the scale as possible are consulted as part of the development process. Finally McKay addresses the key question of how to implement the bandscales and suggests ways in which they can serve as a starting point for further research into the language development of different populations.

The chapter by Mincham also addresses ESL assessment in the school context. The target group, as in McKay's project, is students from non-English speaking backgrounds in primary and secondary schools. Mincham outlines the stages in the development of procedures for assessing and reporting students' performance in producing different types of spoken and written texts. Her starting point is systemic-functional linguistic theory which offers a model for analysing the characteristics of spoken and written texts. Mincham demonstrates how descriptions of the discourse structure and key linguistic features of the different types of oral and written language encountered by the target group were used to devise proformas for assessing task performance, thus integrating assessment with the teaching/learning process. Because of their close link to the curriculum, Mincham concludes that the assessment procedures can be used both as a way of informing teaching and as a means of external reporting.

The chapters by Corbel and McIntyre focus not so much on the question of curriculum-related task performance but rather on assessment of 'curriculum-free' language proficiency. Both contributions concern the Australian Second Language Proficiency Rating Scale (ASLPR), a scale widely used in Australia to assess the general language proficiency of adult ESL learners. Corbel describes the development of Exrater, a computer program incorporating an 'expert system' aimed at assisting language assessors to apply the ASLPR. He outlines the utility of expert systems technology in education and demonstrates how it can be harnessed to systematise and improve the language proficiency rating process by allowing the rater access to different levels of detail on learners' task performance. Corbel outlines ways in which Exrater has improved reliability by forcing teachers to focus closely on the ASLPR descriptions, thus making them more aware of their decision-making processes. At the same time, he shows how trialling of the program has provided useful evidence on the effectiveness of analytic methods of scoring. Corbel goes on to discuss the potentially different uses of the profile produced by Exrater and considers some of the ethical dilemmas involved in using proficiency information in high-stakes contexts. Finally he notes a range of other applications for Exrater and draws on an evaluation of the program to suggest a number of research issues for further investigation.

McIntyre's chapter summarises a comprehensive review which he conducted of the ASLPR. He outlines the historical context in which the scale was developed and discusses its various uses in the Adult Migrant Education Service. He looks at the question of the reliability of ratings across teaching centres and draws attention to some of the problems which can arise when different assessors use different assessment tasks. McIntyre identifies a range of factors which can cause inconsistency in ratings and puts forward a number of suggestions for improving reliability, including the use of the Exrater program described in the previous chapter by Corbel. The author then summarises the outcomes of a study of the ASLPR interview procedures, accentuating the need for moderation of the procedures to ensure consistency in rating. He then describes a range of materials and training procedures designed to help teachers apply the scale reliably and documents various factors which affect rating patterns. Finally, in a consideration of future directions for the scale, McIntyre suggests various ways in which the content and construct validity of the ASLPR might be investigated, stressing the need for predictive studies to investigate learners' performance in real-life non-test situations. He concludes, following Bachman (1990), with a call for a synthesis between 'real-life' and ability-based approaches to scale development.

The chapter by Brindley reviews recent developments in competency-based (CB) ESL assessment in Australia. He discusses the key features of CB assessment approaches and proposes a set of criteria according to which their validity and reliability might be evaluated, in the process taking up many of the themes evoked by other contributors. In particular, he draws attention to the need for a clear definition of the language domains being assessed as a starting point for assessment task design and illustrates how differing interpretations of communicative ability can lead to quite different criteria for assessing language performance. Addressing the critical problem of the generalisability of assessment tasks (also identified by McIntyre in the previous chapter), he underlines the importance of sampling performance widely and systematically using multiple tasks and assessment formats. He then considers ways in which the problem of inherently variable subjective judgements of performance might be addressed. The author concludes by outlining some of the benefits of CB assessment and suggesting a number of avenues for further research into its validity and reliability.

The chapters by Clarkson and Jensen, Grierson and Gunn offer a variety of perspectives on classroom assessment practices in both secondary and adult ESL contexts.

Clarkson and Jensen relate their experience in developing a task-based instrument for assessing achievement of objectives in an English for Professional Employment (EPE) course for adult immigrants. They begin with an account of the methods used to derive the criteria for assessing different levels of success in the key tasks required by the course, drawing on both teacher and learner judgements. The authors then describe how they used the elements of language competence outlined by Bachman (1990) to identify the specific language abilities drawn on by each task. They note that this categorisation provided an explicit checklist of task components which served as a concrete starting point for setting goals with learners. Clarkson and Jensen then describe the development of the rating scales that were used to assess task performance and evaluate their reliability and validity. They note that low levels of rater agreement were obtained in the simulated job interview tasks and suggest a number of possible factors which may have contributed to differing interpretations of the scale. The authors then outline the results of a teacher survey aimed at establishing the applicability of the scale across EPE programs and the relevance of the task components. On the basis of responses indicating substantial agreement on the components of the three 'core' tasks, they conclude that the scale is an effective tool for providing information on achievement to teachers and learners.

Grierson's chapter reports on a study of language assessment practices in secondary Intensive English Centres (IECs). He begins with a discussion of criterion-referenced assessment in language learning and stresses the need to develop assessment criteria which are consistent with current theories of language learning and use. In this regard, in line with a number of the other contributors, he suggests that the Bachman (1990) framework of communicative language ability could serve as a basis for defining the abilities to be assessed and monitored in the classroom. He also notes the contribution of systemic-functional text analysis (described by Mincham in Chapter 3) to assessment. Grierson then outlines the results of a survey of teachers' attitudes and practices in the area of classroom assessment. The survey found that assessment was accorded an important role in the IECs as a source of ongoing diagnostic information which assisted teachers to make decisions on setting learning objectives and that informal assessment methods such as discussion and observation were most favoured. He also found that although teachers had a range of concerns about assessment (in particular the time it took) their attitude was generally positive. In follow-up interviews aimed at eliciting more in-depth information, however, Grierson found evidence to suggest that teacher-assessments were based on a restricted and somewhat 'traditional' view of communicative language ability which accentuated the role of grammatical competence and that there was limited use of systematic procedures for classroom observation. In order to address this gap, he concludes by recommending that domains of language use for IEC learners should be carefully spelled out and systematically drawn on to develop teaching curricula and assessment criteria.

Gunn's contribution focuses on the development of a set of criterion-based assessment procedures for a group of adult immigrant ESL learners. She begins with an overview of assessment issues in the Adult Migrant Education Program (AMEP) from the point of view of the classroom practitioner, highlighting the confusion that may be created with neither the purpose nor the audience for classroom assessment is clear. Gunn then outlines a project aimed at investigating the impact of the adoption of criterion-based assessment in the classroom. This involved the identification of a number of key language activity types and the development of assessment tools for assessing and reporting learner attainment in a variety of forms. An important aspect of the project was an investigation of the day-to-day consequences for the teacher of implementing systematic assessment and reporting procedures. Gunn's findings indicate that developing and maintaining such procedures can be both time-consuming and difficult for practitioners (though professionally very beneficial) and, like other contributors, she underlines the particular problems involved in identifying suitable criteria for assessing task performance. In evaluating the extent to which the assessment tools developed by the project yielded useful information to the various audiences involved in the program (teachers, learners, employers and funding authorities), Gunn notes that few learners expressed interest in knowing about their progress and stresses the importance of making course goals and assessment criteria available in an accessible (if necessary, translated) form in order to involve them more closely in their own learning. At the same time she highlights the difficulty of using the detailed diagnostic information on individual achievement collected by teachers to describe group outcomes to external audiences. She concludes by identifying the need to develop an assessment system which allows achievement to be reported in a way that conveys the complexity of individual learner achievement without oversimplifying the learning process.

The final two chapters by Cram and Wilkes address the issue of self-assessment (SA) in language programs and in so doing remind us of the crucial role that learners themselves can play in assessing their own progress and achievement. This role is, however, not always exploited to the full owing to various misgivings concerning the feasibility of SA. Cram begins by critically examining these misgivings and putting forward a case for systematic incorporation of SA into the language curriculum, citing evidence from a range of research studies which indicate that SA can significantly enhance learner's control of their own learning. She then describes the key components of a professional development resource for teachers in the form of a workshop guide aimed at assisting teachers to develop SA tools appropriate to their own circumstances. The guide provides activities which allow participants to explore a range of theoretical and practical issues which arise when introducing SA into language programs. These include the purposes and audiences for SA; learner characteristics and the use of SA; constraints on SA; learner training for SA; and the development and implementation of specific SA tools and techniques. In conclusion, Cram reiterates the key role that SA has been shown to play in developing autonomous learners and stresses the importance of introducing self-reflection and awareness-raising activities into the learner-training program at an early stage. She notes, however, that SA may not appear to yield immediate benefits in all teaching/ learning situations and that decisions to introduce it need to take into account both the needs of the learners involved and the constraints on the program.

Wilkes' chapter provides a useful counterpoint to the arguments for SA put forward by Cram. She describes a replication of a study carried out by Rolfe (1990) which set out to investigate the relationship between SA, peer-assessment (PA) and teacher-assessment (TA) of oral proficiency. Rolfe's study found that PA correlated more highly with TA than SA and concluded that PA was just as reliable if not more so, than TA. In her replication study Wilkes describes considerable variability in assessments given by learners to their peers and finds that SA ratings tend to be lower than both PA and TA ratings. She attributes this tendency of learners to underrate themselves to the possible influence of affective factors. Like Rolfe, she finds that SA does not appear to be a reliable indicator of oral proficiency in relation to TA. However, in contrast to Rolfe's study, which found a strong relationship between overall PA and TA ratings, she finds that both overall PA and SA ratings correlate weakly with TA ratings, though significantly with each other. She concludes that one possible reason for the lack of consistency in PA/TA agreement is that learners in the study were not trained in judging their own or their peers' proficiency level. Echoing the findings of McIntyre in Chapter 5, she also draws attention to teachers' differing interpretations of the ASLPR scale which was used for TA. In conclusion, Wilkes argues for greater attention to training teachers in the use of rating scales and stresses the importance of involving learners in the assessment process as a way of helping them formulate realistic standards and goals.

Although the eleven chapters in this volume deal with the development and implementation of assessment procedures in quite different conditions, it is nevertheless possible to identify a number of commonly recurring issues and concerns which consistently emerge in the contributions. Interestingly, many of these are also reflected in the recent literature in both language testing and general education (see, for example, Bachman 1990; Taylor 1994) and could be roughly summarised as follows:

- An increasing acceptance of the central importance of construct validity in test design and validation, evidenced by the growing number of test development projects which draw explicitly on current theoretical frameworks of communicative language ability, in particular those proposed by Bachman (1990) and Bachman and Palmer (forthcoming).

- A recognition of the potential conflict of purposes between external testing and classroom-based assessment which makes it difficult to design assessment systems which can simultaneously meet the information needs of different audiences.

- An acknowledgement of the ongoing tension between behaviourally-based approaches to test design based on 'real-life' tasks and theoretically-motivated approaches based on underlying models of ability.

- An ongoing concern with the apparent failure of expert judges to interpret and apply rating scales in a consistent manner.

- An increasing awareness of the heavy demands made on teachers by the introduction of more stringent assessment and reporting requirements.

- An 'in principle' acceptance of the desirability of self-assessment coupled with the recognition that learner training in the use of SA techniques is crucial if SA is to be effective.

Despite significant progress over the last few years, it is clear that a great deal of research remains to be done in order to address some of the major issues and problems outlined above. If these issues are to be approached in a systematic manner, however, one thing is clear — a collaborative effort will be needed. Assessment is not just the problem of teachers, of administrators or of language testers — it is everybody's problem. As we move towards the turn of the century, it is to be hoped that applied linguists, language testers, practitioners and other stakeholders in language programs will be able to harness their collective energies and resources to confront the many challenges in the field of language assessment that lie ahead.

References

Bachman, L.F. 1990. *Fundamental considerations in language testing.* Oxford: Oxford University Press.

Bachman, L.F. and A.S. Palmer. Forthcoming. *Language testing in practice.* Oxford: Oxford University Press.

Cohen, A. 1994. *Assessing language ability in the classroom.* Boston: Heinle and Heinle.

Heaton, J.B. 1988. *Writing English language tests.* London: Longman.

Hughes, A. 1989. *Testing for language teachers.* Cambridge: Cambridge University Press.

Rolfe, T. 1990. Self- and peer-assessment in the ESL curriculum. In G. Brindley (ed.) *The second language curriculum in action.* Sydney: National Centre for English Language Teaching and Research.

Taylor, C. 1994. Assessment for measurement or standards: the peril and promise of large-scale assessment reform. *American Educational Research Journal* 31, 2.

Weir, C.J. 1993. *Understanding and developing language tests.* London: Prentice Hall.

Shohamy, E. 1985. *A practical handbook in language testing for the second language teacher.* Tel Aviv: Tel Aviv University. Experimental Edition.

1 Assessing the language proficiency of overseas-qualified teachers: the English Language Skills Assessment (ELSA)[1]

Clare McDowell

Introduction

The NSW Department of School Education (DSE) policy document released in April 1991 on *Employment of teachers with overseas qualifications* stated that the best indication of competence in teaching was classroom performance. However, before a teacher would be given the opportunity to demonstrate his or her skills in the classroom, there were a number of basic conditions set down which prospective teachers had to fulfil.

Firstly, overseas qualified applicants for employment had to be competent in the use of English before they could teach in New South Wales. Secondly, overseas qualified applicants had to be recognised as qualified primary or secondary teachers in their country of training and have their personal suitability, attitudes and ideas on teaching assessed at interview by a delegated officer of the DSE. Thirdly, they should satisfactorily complete a five-week DSE Bridging Course including a two-week supervised practicum, during which their English was also to be assessed. If successful thus far, they would then have to serve an initial probationary period of at least one year from the date of appointment before being granted a full-time position. Some of these requirements have since been relaxed but this was the state of play when the ELSA test was commissioned.

The English requirement was more fully outlined in the April 1991 document under the section entitled *Competence in English* which stated that assessment of non-English speaking background (NESB) applicants' English language proficiency would involve the administration by designated regional officers or other personnel, of the Australian Second Language Proficiency Ratings (ASLPR) (Ingram and Wylie 1984) where a minimum rating of Level 4 would establish that the applicants' command of English was sufficiently high for the purposes of classroom teaching. Ensuring that this standard was being met by applicants coming from a non-English speaking background proved problematic in practice because of the lack of suitably qualified personnel within DSE to administer the ASLPR in accordance with the guidelines and indeed the broader question of the suitability of the ASLPR rating procedure for this purpose at all.[2] In real terms, before the introduction of the ELSA test, the English assessment of NESB teachers had taken place during the DSE suitability interview, an arrangement which was neither adequate, accountable nor equitable and thus in need of review.

In July 1991, the Adult Migrant English Service (AMES) commissioned the research and development of a test to assess the language, on behalf of the DSE, of NESB teachers qualified overseas. This test was to retain the concept of ASLPR Level 4 as a benchmark for full vocational proficiency but required the development of an instrument in its own right, to be known as the English Language Skills Assessment (ELSA). It was not intended to be specific to any one discipline as it was felt that all teachers within the DSE, regardless of their actual teaching methods and additional to their classroom duties, confronted similar daily language tasks, such as communicating with parents, writing school reports, disciplining students, working with clerical staff, negotiating with peers, to name but a few. In addition, having different subject modules in one test poses serious reliability problems as standardising the module versions adds yet another variable to the process. It was also felt to be the Department's job to assess subject competency which would emerge during the five-week bridging course after the initial English test.

This was, then, the background against which the ELSA test was commissioned and developed. This paper will set out to describe the way in which the test was conceptualised, piloted and put into practice.

Theoretical considerations in test development

Defining language ability in the school context

Teachers need to possess very specific linguistic skills in order to function effectively in and outside the classroom and are required to provide good models of spoken and written language to their students. The first task was therefore to ascertain precisely what these skills were and what was expected of teachers by colleagues, parents, students and the outside world in general to inform the development of a valid and at the same time reliable means of measuring these skills.

As a point of departure both for the initial research phase and for the design of the ELSA test itself, the test developers chose to use Bachman's framework of *Communicative Language Ability* (Bachman 1990:85) which underscores the importance of viewing language as a combination of knowledge or competences coupled with the ability to implement that knowledge in language appropriate to any given context. This view of language is not in itself unique to Bachman but his belief that language test design can benefit from this approach is useful. Bachman (1990:81) suggests that this framework provides a broad basis for both the development and use of language tests and it was felt to be particularly relevant for the design of a test for NESB teachers working in primary and secondary schools in New South Wales. Real-world knowledge would therefore play a significant role; the research phase would be school-based and input texts, tasks and even items would be drawn from authentic teaching situations.

It is important to emphasise that the decision to proceed in this way was not merely an exercise in achieving so-called face validity but rather an integral component of the test specifications and design. In addition, it should be remembered that ELSA was to be a test for already qualified teachers, most of whom had considerable work experience in their countries of origin. They were new to the Australian scene but not new to the context of the classroom, although attitudes towards teachers and teaching vary enormously from one culture to another, and this variance is bound to be reflected in pragmatic competence. The culture of the Australian school was thus certainly something that needed to be taken into account in the test design phase just as the 'baggage' teachers brought with them to the test was of significance.

In Bachman's terms (1990:85) language competence is part of what he calls communicative language ability and is composed of Organisational Competence and Pragmatic Competence (see Figure 1 below).

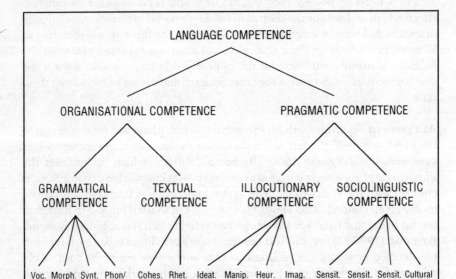

Figure 1 Components of Language Competence (Bachman 1990)

Under the heading of *Organisational competence* we find the 'nuts and bolts' of language: vocabulary, morphology, syntax, phonology, graphology (otherwise known as grammatical competence) and, regrettably, the stuff of most traditional language classrooms and language tests. Spliced to grammatical competence is textual competence which includes coherence and cohesion, reference, the conventions of ordering given and new information, the rules of conversation and the rules of written discourse to name but a few; areas that are far too often neglected in tests, primarily because they pose too much difficulty for the test designers.

Pragmatic competence involves an understanding of the social rules governing the use of language. The speaker/writer must know what is socio-linguistically acceptable or appropriate in a given context and be sensitive to varieties of language, to register, native-like naturalness and to cultural references. Clearly one cannot be familiar with every possible discourse domain, dialect or variety of a language but to be familiar with the jargon of one's profession and to be capable of choosing appropriately is a reasonable expectation of a speaker who is judged to possess full vocational proficiency. This pragmatic competence applies as much to the written form of language as to the spoken though the rules governing acceptable use will vary depending upon the users and the speech community or discourse domain within which they are operating. The contemporary French social theorist Bourdieu (1991:18) reinforces the point when he speaks of 'linguistic capital':

> *On a given linguistic market, some products are valued more highly than others and part of the practical competence of speakers is to know how, and to be able, to produce expressions which are highly valued on the markets concerned. This aspect of the practical competence of speakers is not uniformly distributed throughout a society in which the same language... is spoken. For different speakers possess different quantities of 'linguistic capital' — that is, the capacity to produce expressions* a propos, *for a particular market.*

or in Bachman's (1990:102) words:

> *... communication involves a dynamic interchange between context and discourse, so that communicative language use is not characterized simply by the production or interpretation of texts, but by the relationship that obtains between a text and the context in which it occurs.*

Research phase for ELSA

A brief literature review was carried out to ascertain what assessment procedures existed already for NESB teachers. A project being carried out at the University of Melbourne (Elder 1993) to assess the language of mathematics and science teachers in the classroom was of interest but here the focus had been on the classroom language of NESB teachers in training and, unlike ELSA, was discipline-specific with an emphasis on classroom performance indicators. A review of the literature on foreign teaching assistants at American universities revealed a number of studies focusing on communication difficulties. Bailey (1982) working in the US with Asian teaching assistants in the early 1980s comments that many communication problems stemmed from the non-linguistic difficulties experienced by NESB assistants, their manner and delivery of language. Jones (1979) describes how NESB teaching assistants who had sat for general English proficiency tests prior to coming to the States, often proved to be highly ineffective in the teaching context where they could neither make themselves nor be understood. He comments that the UCLA interview test designed for NESB teachers which stemmed from the American experience proved to lack the necessary specificity to assess language for real-life teaching situations.

The test developers then turned to the personal experiences of professionally-qualified immigrants with a number of contemporary public language tests; in particular the Occupational English Test for Health Professionals (McNamara 1988). While different in content, this test was an example of large scale, vocational testing within the Australian context and had already shown that it was both feasible and effective.

They also examined the International English Language Testing System (IELTS)[3] and a number of tests from the Cambridge suite of EFL examinations and were able to incorporate first-hand experience of how these tests, and in particular the oral component, are administered and marked. Knowledge of these practical issues was important since the test was to be administered during the pilot phase by the developers themselves before being handed over to AMES.

Developing test specifications

With the brief literature revue complete, draft specifications for ELSA were drawn up. Bearing in mind the key issues referred to above, a number of areas were proposed for classroom and ethnographic research though the limited time frame, human resources and budget imposed severe limitations. Two broad areas of investigation were established, however:

1. to identify the main domains of discourse which operate within a school community;

2. to establish the aspects of language competence that characterise an effective NESB overseas trained teacher.

The first step in the development of test specifications was to visit primary and secondary schools to gather samples of spoken and written discourse and to establish the types of speech acts teachers typically engage in. This investigation thus included the language of the classroom, the staffroom, the playground, parent/teacher interactions and meetings.

The second step was to collect documents relating to policy, curriculum and day-to-day running of a school. The aim of this exercise was to collect information on discourse types and to provide potential input material for test items.

The third step was to track down and interview teachers of English and non-English speaking backgrounds in order to obtain written and spoken texts which could be analysed to create a 'benchmark' against which to measure performance. In this way it would be possible to produce a picture which would function as a 'standard' of an NESB teacher who was seen to be effective in his/her workplace. In addition, standard ASLPR ratings were obtained for all of those interviewed.

The fourth step was to conduct interviews with DSE staff working with NESB teachers to focus on aspects of language competence which separated effective from non-effective NESB teachers working within the system.

The following is a summary list of language abilities that emerged from the interviews which characterise effective overseas trained teachers:

*   ability to process student input within real-time;
*   sufficient control over language to perform routine teaching tasks and demonstrate effective teaching behaviours;
*   intelligibility;
*   ability to use flexible discourse strategies;
*   command of register.

(Iles and McDowell 1992:9)

A list was also compiled of non-effective behaviours gathered from interviews with DSE executive staff, teachers and students who had worked with NESB teachers. These covered the following areas:

- student rapport;
- classroom management;
- knowledge about the culture of the school;
- lack of familiarity with new methodology;
- inability to follow instructions.[4]

(Iles and McDowell 1992:9)

Draft specifications were then drawn up for each of the four macro-skills: reading, writing, listening and speaking. These were based on the language recorded, activities observed and interviews conducted with staff and students during the visits to the schools. Here, the advice of Hughes (1989) proved useful. He points out that for any one version of the test, test developers need to sample 'widely and unpredictably' from the full range of possible content. From the performance on a given sample of tasks it is possible to make inferences with regard to performance generally. Because the skills being tested are those that the testee will need in the future, content validity and 'washback validity' (the effect of testing on teaching) are enhanced.

What follows is a broad summary of the micro-skills considered to be relevant for teaching and working within a school. More detail is available in the revised specifications.[5]

Reading: understand literal and implied meaning;
skim for gist;
scan to extract specific information;
read for overall comprehension;
decode meaning within reasonable time;
interpret text for attitude and style.

Writing: convey exact meaning accurately and clearly;
organise ideas in a clear logical structure;
use register appropriate for task/situation.

Listening: understand instructions;
understand main idea and purpose;
extract specific information;
understand tone;
understand inference;
select relevant from irrelevant;
process spoken text within real-time;
deduce meaning of works through context.

Oral: express oneself intelligibly;
convey intended meaning accurately with sufficient command of vocabulary;
use language appropriate to context;
interact with other speakers fluently.

Washback

Washback can be harmful or beneficial (Hughes 1989:1). Despite reservations expressed by Alderson and Wall (1993) about the widespread acceptance of the concept, it was felt that candidates for the ELSA would work towards establishing strategies for 'passing' the test by becoming test-wise and teachers would likewise seek ways to prepare their candidates to maximise their chances of success. This has already proved to be the case. It therefore seemed essential to ensure that item types, content and tasks were based on authentic tasks undertaken by teachers in their regular duties so as to minimise negative washback. Indeed, at the same time as the ELSA test was commissioned, DEET[6] gave permission to language teaching providers to run English courses for those teachers who had narrowly missed achieving the required standard. It therefore seemed clear that there would be a close relationship between the test and the program syllabus and it was important to ensure that this proved positive.

Development of the test

With the research phase completed, the initial task was to arrive at a format for the test which reflected the desired linguistic elements but which could be delivered within the existing administrative constraints. In line with the findings of our research into teachers' language use, it was decided to treat reading and writing as integrated rather than independent skills and to test them together in the one sub-test. We had found that writing in the school context usually occurred in response to written input (notes from colleagues, letters from parents, memos from the department); reading texts of different genres and script types (including original printed format, reformatted text and handwritten text) could therefore double as authentic input for the writing tasks.

A decision was made to test listening separately from speaking, however, since the feedback from the school interviews indicated that an ability to accurately process input in real-time was seen as a priority by teachers and DSE executive staff. Speaking, on the other hand, would be assessed by means of a paired interview as in this way interactive and pragmatic skills could be tested reasonably authentically. Listening, of course, forms part of spoken interaction, but is not assessed formally in the Oral test.

Assessing reading and writing in order to develop the reading part of the Reading and Writing section texts were selected from a wide variety of possible text types, ranging from formal to informal, official to journalistic. A number of items were drawn up and trialled on native speakers and non-native teachers. In the initial phase, item types included multiple choice comprehension items, short answer questions, matching meaning and error correction tasks. The texts were drawn from genuine school documents relating to classroom teaching and student management, newsletters to parents, newspaper articles on education and academic papers. Writing items ranged from short answer type to direct writing tasks based on input material for a variety of audiences. A transformational exercise was included requiring candidates to manipulate language in accordance with the rules of English syntax. This was designed to identify those candidates who, when constrained by given language, could maintain coherence and cohesion, display a knowledge of English morphology and an understanding of tense and aspect.[7] In order to ensure that the items used in the test displayed acceptable characteristics, a larger number of tasks and item types than would appear in the final version of the test were initially trialled.

Assessing listening

Scripts for the listening sub-test were created, using as a source the recordings and observations made during the research phase.[8] Having created several 'mini scenarios', tasks were developed to assess the micro-skills identified during the research phase and included in the specifications, such as receiving instructions, the focus of which might be to understand and reproduce accurately numbers, dates and times. These items were then trialled on native speakers and non-native teachers alike. Items which proved inappropriate for either the native speakers or the NESB teachers whose English had already been deemed to be of a sufficiently high level were discarded. After a lengthy process of trialling, the listening sub-test was reduced to five sections, with item types and tasks graded in difficulty.

Assessing speaking

The development of the speaking test was guided by Bachman's concept of Communicative Language Ability, focusing wherever possible on Pragmatic Competence. As stated above, organisational competence has in the past tended to be the focus of most language tests, above all because it is quantifiable.[9] It is not easy to assess pragmatic competence, that is, the ability to match utterances to contexts, more because it is difficult to elicit than because it is difficult to measure. With this in mind, we took the decision to assess the candidates in pairs to enable us to provide a forum for some kind of interactive communication and thus to judge a candidate's control of register, his or her sense of appropriacy and sensitivity to other speakers.

The ELSA interview is a four way interaction between two candidates and two examiners. The candidates are paired randomly and the examiners play the roles of interlocutor and assessor respectively. The interview has a number of phases; candidates interview one another building on the authentic information gap which exists and then move to a role-play with one of the assessors acting as interlocutor which culminates in the candidates discussing a joint problem arising from that role-play situation. The third phase is a discussion on a contemporary issue relating to education and involves all four participants.[10] By moving through a number of different interactive modes it is possible to sample language across a variety of speaker/listener patterns. These are:

Pattern 1 — Candidates interact with minimal input from assessors.

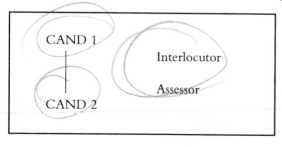

CAND 1

Interlocutor

Assessor

CAND 2

Pattern 2 — Role play: Candidates interact with interlocutor and then with each other.

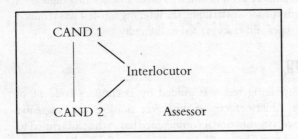

Pattern 3 — Four way conversation.

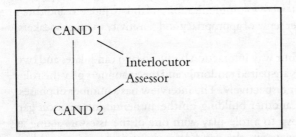

A number of interview formats were trialled in the early stages of the development of the test, and using taped interviews of these varying formats, the first assessment team was able to contribute to the process by providing valuable input and advice. Members of the DSE Human Resources section were also able to contribute providing valuable insights into what was deemed acceptable. After trialling, the two role-plays originally proposed were reduced to a single one, with greater emphasis being placed on the interactive skills of the candidates at the start of the interview. Suitable interview tasks emerged after a lengthy process of trialling and listening to the interviews.

Scoring the interview

ELSA is scored on a six-point scale which forms the upper level of a notional proficiency scale which would range from 'beginner' to 'expert user'. Since

ELSA was not intended to be used to assess candidates at the lower end of this notional scale, there is no provision to assess such candidates. An analytical, as opposed to global approach was adopted and candidates are rated in four areas:

Interactive communication	– fluency/effect on listener
Intelligibility	– pronunciation/prosodic features
Appropriacy	– pragmatic competence/register
Accuracy	– structure and vocabulary resource

A score is given in each of these areas on a six-point scale. The scale used does not, however, cover the full range of language proficiency but forms the upper level of a notional full proficiency scale. There are no descriptors as there is a tendency, as Davies (1992:14) says, for these to manifest themselves as discrete items in the eyes of the assessors.

> *The paradox is that through the attempt to refine proficiency scales by removing their defects… the precisioning of the descriptors tends more and more towards a list or bank of test items. Descriptors which are useable in an objective sense are test items.*

In other words, the assessors may be tempted to look for the points mentioned in the descriptors and to give lower scores if they do not find them, or if they go unnoticed. Having four broad areas on which to focus provides pointers for the assessors without over-burdening them with detail. The key to ensuring uniform interpretation of the rating criteria is training.[11]

Reliability

The issue of reliability in public tests is vital and featured throughout the development of ELSA. Item types and methods of scoring were considered in relation to one another to ensure a balance between the dichotomous 'selected response' items which could be scored with a high reliability coefficient and the more open ended 'constructed response' items requiring a score based on a human judgement. Although the latter type of item may sometimes produce a lower reliability coefficient, tests which do not allow the candidate an opportunity to produce original language are open to criticism on the grounds of validity. Wherever human judgment is required in the scoring of the ELSA test, marker training is provided and double marking has been adopted in all cases.

An analysis of the items using Rasch techniques was carried out on the Listening and Reading/Writing sub-tests, mapping the ability of individuals and the difficulty of items on the same scale (Brown et al. 1992). This item/ability map gives a picture of the extent to which the difficulty of the test matches the ability level of the candidature. At the same time Rasch analysis generates item fit statistics which indicate the extent to which the items fit the predictions of the underlying mathematical model of ability. This information can then be used when deciding to select or reject items for the final versions of the test. Items in both sub-tests appeared to be at an appropriate level for the candidature with reading proving to be a good predictor of writing ability. Reliability estimates for both tests were high (over .90).

Validity

Four main types of validity have conventionally been defined in testing: *content, construct, concurrent* and *face* validity, though some dispute surrounds the status of the latter. While the critics of the term may have a point, face validity is similar to washback in that it relates to the way in which the outside world perceives the test. In the case of ELSA this was an extremely important consideration. Content validity was addressed from the outset by ensuring that only authentic documents and language tasks based on the language observed in the schools visited during the research phase were included. Similarly, we aimed to achieve construct validity by ensuring that specifications drawn up during the initial stages which were based on a careful definition of the candidates' future language use were closely adhered to. As part of the validation process, the test was trialled on students and mock candidates who had recently sat for other public tests or who had been assessed by ourselves using other previously validated tests.

Feedback both from candidates and DSE personnel indicated that the ELSA test was publicly perceived as a valid test for its population and purpose. While some candidates would like the emphasis to be more on their classroom skills, because they feel more secure with the language, say, of the maths classroom, many admitted in interviews after sitting the test, that their areas of weakness were precisely the areas targeted by ELSA. Successful candidates — although it might be argued that they had a vested interest in supporting the format — felt that the content of the test was relevant to their needs and welcomed the non-subject specificity of the test.

Training

As noted above, training is a vital component of any test which involves subjective marking of any kind and is essential in order to achieve reliability. Training for ELSA took place within weeks of the commencement of the development stage. This was because once the prototype interview had been designed and trialled to obtain early raw data on which to work, it was necessary to train a number of experienced AMES teachers in the procedure so that they too could trial the format. Training takes place on a regular basis at AMES and refresher sessions are held every six months for assessors of the writing as well as the speaking sub-tests.

Operation

The test is now fully operational and has been adopted as part of the employment policy for NESB teachers seeking work with the DSE. It is administered by AMES NSW and to date there have been some 350 candidates. Since the initial version was developed in 1991, further parallel versions of the test have been developed and are now used on a rotational basis. The first version has been withdrawn and the number of administrations has been restricted to four each year. A sample test was also developed in the early stages of the test and this has been updated to reflect the final format of the test.[12]

Ongoing test activity will include monitoring and training of raters which is necessary to ensure that reliability is maintained. At the same time it would be useful to undertake a tracer study of successful candidates who have been employed as part of the validation process, though such a study would be difficult since relatively few successful candidates have found employment due to the shortage of teaching positions. However, in terms of the requirements of the Department, the test has fulfilled its brief and represents a milestone in the field of occupationally oriented English language testing.

Notes

1   The ELSA test was jointly researched, designed and developed by Diana Iles of the Language Centre at the University of Sydney and Clare McDowell of *LTC*

Language Training Consultants. The test was commissioned by the Director of AMES NSW and remains as at the date of this paper the property of that body.

2   Regardless of the position one takes on the validity of general proficiency rating scales, (see Davies 1992), it must be agreed that the ASLPR is not an instrument designed to assess the language of specific vocations and full vocational proficiency with regard to language competence must surely differ from one profession to another.

3   English test to assess the language of NESB students seeking access to universities in UK and Australia. Jointly owned by University of Cambridge Local Examinations Syndicate (UCLES), British Council, International Development Program of Australian Universities and Colleges (IDP) 1989.

4   It must be said that not all NESB teachers display all or any of these non-effective behaviours and indeed many could be attributed to native speaker teachers. Nevertheless, the need for ELSA had arisen as a result of these behaviours being observed within the Department and they cannot therefore be ignored.

5   Iles, D. and C. McDowell. 1994. *Revised specifications for ELSA*. Available from AMES NSW.

6   DEET (the Commonwealth Department of Employment Education and Training) funds English programs designed for NESB migrants who are professionally qualified and whose English is approximately ASLPR 3 or above. TAFE also runs similar programs often referred to as 'ELSA preparation programs'.

7   The order in which the sections of the test appear has been altered since the development of Form 1 of the test, to ensure that all candidates attempt the writing component. Some minor changes have also been made to the layout since the earlier version was written.

8   While obtaining truly authentic listening material would seem to be the appropriate way to proceed, it is often difficult to obtain high quality authentic recorded discourse. 'Poor recording introduces difficulties additional to the ones that we want to set and so reduces the validity of the test' (Hughes 1989:135). In addition, there are problems related to ethics which need to be addressed coupled with the question of 'how authentic is authentic?' once subjects know they are being recorded. The test developer is faced with two choices: (i) to record authentic discourse and re-record it, or (ii) to create the discourse from scratch based on informed data and then

to make high quality recordings of the discourse. The advantage to this second approach is that the text becomes item-driven and can be created with the test specifications and even actual tasks in mind.

9 Some tests claim to equate structural accuracy with language competence and even claim to be able to measure that competence by counting the number of errors.

10 Critics of the paired interview have argued that unless candidates are similar in level, interaction cannot work. Since information is now available on ELSA, including an exemplar which gives an idea of the standard expected, weaker candidates are self selecting out with the result that a greater degree of homogeneity exists among candidates. Facilitating conversation with a weaker speaker may highlight a candidate's pragmatic competence.

11 Since the initial form of the test was developed, a decision was made to include a criterial statement of satisfactory performance to which the assessors could refer as a guide. This has now been included in the Guide to Assessors.

12 It is worth noting that the development of this exemplar test has been very much in response to popular demand both from candidates and language teachers as well as from the DSE. It is not the author's opinion that complete sample tests are necessarily useful since they can erode the integrity of the live test by inviting public discussion on issues relating to content. A more appropriate approach and one which is adopted by many test developers today, is to provide sample texts and item types rather than whole tests, as this allows for changes in different versions to be made. It must be remembered that when drawing up test specifications, it is necessary to include all possible text and item types, but not all will be included in every version of the live test nor in a sample test. This is particularly relevant as test development moves away from the 'whole test' approach to a process based on the development and banking of items which are then selected to produce a number of different tests.

References

Alderson, J.C. and D. Wall. 1992. Examining washback. Paper delivered at *26th TESOL Convention*, Vancouver.

Alderson, J.C. and D. Wall. 1993. Does washback exist? *Applied Linguistics* 14, 2.

Bachman, L.F. 1990. *Fundamental considerations in language testing*. Oxford: Oxford University Press.

Bailey, K. 1982. The classroom communication problems of Asian teaching assistants. In L. van Lier (ed.) *Selected papers in TESOL*. Monterey: Institute of International Studies, Monterey.

Brown, A. et al. 1992. Mapping abilities and skill levels using Rasch techniques in A. Brown (ed.) *Melbourne papers in language testing* 1, 1:37–67.

Bourdieu, P. 1991. *Language and symbolic power*. Cambridge: Polity Press.

Davies, A. 1992. Is proficiency always achievement? In A. Brown (ed.) *Melbourne papers in language testing* 1, 1:1–16.

Elder. 1993. How do subject specialists construe classroom language proficiency? *Language Testing* 10, 3.

Hughes, A. 1989. *Testing for language teachers*. Cambridge: Cambridge University Press.

Iles, D. and C. McDowell. 1992. *Interim Report on ELSA test*. Submitted to the Adult Migrant English Service NSW. Sydney: Unpublished.

Iles, D. and C. McDowell. 1994. *Revised specifications for ELSA*. Sydney: Unpublished.

Ingram, D.E. 1982. *Report on the formal trialling of the Australian second language proficiency ratings (ASLPR)*. Canberra: Australian Government Publishing Services.

Ingram, D.E. and E. Wylie. 1984. *Australian second language proficiency ratings (ASLPR)*. Canberra: Australian Government Publishing Services.

Jones, R. 1979. Performance testing of second language proficiency in E.J. Briere and F.B. Hinofotis (eds) *Concepts in language testing: some recent studies*. Washington DC.

Lenzuen, R. 1989. *Interview type tests of oral proficiency as unequal encounters.* Unpublished MA dissertation. University of Reading.

McNamara, T.F. 1987. *Assessing the language proficiency of health professionals. Recommendations for reform of the occupational English test.* Report submitted to the Council on Overseas Professional Qualifications.

New South Wales Department of School Education. 1991. *Policy on the employment of teachers with overseas qualifications.* Sydney: Department of School Education.

2 Developing ESL proficiency descriptions for the school context: The NLLIA[1] ESL Bandscales

Penny McKay

Introduction

The current move in the education world towards the monitoring of learner progress through sets of progressing descriptions of ability, called profiles (e.g. by the Australian Education Council), levels of attainment (e.g. by the South Australian Education Department 1991), and learning outcomes (e.g. by the Northern Territory Department of Education 1992), together with a call from several quarters (e.g. Campbell et al. 1984; Centre for English as a Second Language, University of Western Australia 1991) for proficiency scales in ESL in schools, provided the impetus in 1991 for funding for the NLLIA ESL Development: Language and Literacy in Schools Project[2]. The ESL Development Project's brief was the development of an assessment and reporting package for ESL language development in schools; a major component of this assessment and reporting package was to be a profile, or a set of proficiency descriptions for ESL learning in schools.

The aim of this paper is to describe some of the key issues behind the development of the the ESL Bandscales[3], the profile component of the NLLIA ESL Project. The ESL Bandscales are an integral part of the wider ESL Development Project and for this reason, a brief outline of the full assessment and reporting package developed by the ESL Project is provided.

The NLLIA ESL Development Project: an integrated ESL assessment package

Purpose of the project

The NLLIA ESL Development Project's brief was stated in broad terms, namely, to work towards providing:

- an increased capacity to measure proficiency development among school students;

- a better understanding of the interrelationship between mother tongue/English as a second language/English language development issues and improved advice to schools about these matters and their impact on English theory;

- an improved capacity to develop an information base to establish needs and policy determination;

- assistance to teachers in maximising effectiveness of instruction for students of non-English speaking background;

- more accurate targeting of resources to ESL and mother tongue teaching and English literacy;

- a basis established for ongoing professional development.

(Extract from NLLIA Project document)

The ESL Development Project materials became a major focus of attention for the ESL field in Australia over almost two years; many educators contributed significantly to the outcomes of the project. Contributors included professional associations, ESL education personnel from each state/territory in Australia who served on a national reference group, a large number of practising ESL specialists and teachers around Australia and consultants in universities in Australia and overseas.

The political and educational influences on the ESL Development Project were strong, with the result that a set of principles was developed out of consultations to establish understandings and agreements about the direction of the project (see Figure 1). These principles became a vital reference point for the developmental work of the project, since it was recognised from the outset that the project must operate within the current political and philosophical context of Australian education. The principles are reflected strongly within the materials developed within the ESL Project.

PRINCIPLES INFORMING THE ESL DEVELOPMENT PROJECT

1. **The ESL Development Project should address the requirements of the political context.** To do this the ESL Development Project should:

   - undertake wide consultation;
   - work as far as possible towards state and national (AEC CURASS) requirements.

2. **The ESL Development Project should draw on a broad philosophical and research base.** To do this the ESL Development Project should:

   - incorporate theoretical perspectives according to the focus of the materials being developed, that is
   - use the Bachman (1990, forthcoming) model as an informing model for the ESL Bandscales and the assessment exemplars; draw on other models as needed; focus on Second Language Acquisition theory in research into acquisitional sequences;
   - consult the literature, and colleagues widely;
   - hold a colloquium to draw on school ESL research and ESL expertise in Australia.

3. **The ESL Development Project should represent all ESL learners as far as possible, and do so positively and equitably.** To do this the Project should:

   - aim to broadly include, as far as possible, all ESL learner groups;
   - recognise positive starting points for ESL;
   - provide positive descriptions of growth;
   - stress the key role of the L1 in the learning of English;
   - stress individual differences as commonalities are explored.

Figure 1 Principles informing the NLLIA ESL Development Project

Continued over page

4. **The ESL Development Project should accommodate the realities of and the shared perspectives about ESL teaching and learning in the school ESL field:**

   - recognise and accommodate as far as possible the range of approaches to ESL delivery in the school context;
   - accommodate developmental and contextual changes, together with multiple entry points, K - 12;
   - describe and assist teachers to assess and report on "ESL-ness" in the school context;
   - recognise and cater for the integrated nature of ESL teaching and learning (ESL across the curriculum; language and content; interrelationship of four skills; interrelationship of the curriculum and assessment process) in the school context;
   - aim the materials towards both ESL specialists and mainstream teachers.

5. **The ESL Development Project should recognise the practical constraints of ESL teaching and support in schools.** To do this, the ESL Development Project should:

   - take account of the constraints in the use of the materials (e.g., time, numbers of students, a range of expertise) in the school context;
   - emphasise the need for professional development.

6. **The ESL Development Project should emphasise the need for further research and development in school ESL.** To do this, the ESL Development Project should:

   - promote the Project materials as a contribution to ongoing research and developement in school ESL;
   - encourage further research and development work on the Project materials and in the area of school ESL proficiency assessment and reporting;
   - emphasise the need for professional development activities around the Project materials.

Figure 1 Cont. Principles informing the NLLIA ESL Development Project

Project materials

The final materials developed through the project and published in the NLLIA ESL Development: Language and Literacy Project Report (NLLIA 1993) were as follows:

- Three sets of ESL Bandscales covering junior primary, middle/upper primary and secondary learners in the school context (Volume I of the Report).

- Exemplar assessment activities and observation guides providing tools to teachers (ESL and mainstream teachers) for in-class and within-curriculum observation of language proficiency of ESL learners as they interact and learn in the school context (Volume I of the Report).

- Reporting formats and guidelines for both ongoing recording and for profile reporting of ESL learners' language development, again as they interact and learn in the school context (Volume I of the Report).

- A research report 'An empirical study of children's ESL Development and Rapid Profile' and papers relating to the project work (Volume II of the report).

Together, the components of the project provided an integrated approach to assessment of ESL learners' language in the context of the school. The relationship of the components of the ESL Development Project is set out in Figure 2.

The role of assessment

The central place in the ESL Development Project's assessment and reporting picture belongs to teaching and learning where ESL is taught and learned within the context of, and integrated, with the school curriculum. This positioning restates the well established perspective within school education that the role of assessment is to provide support for, rather than to become the driving force for teaching and learning.

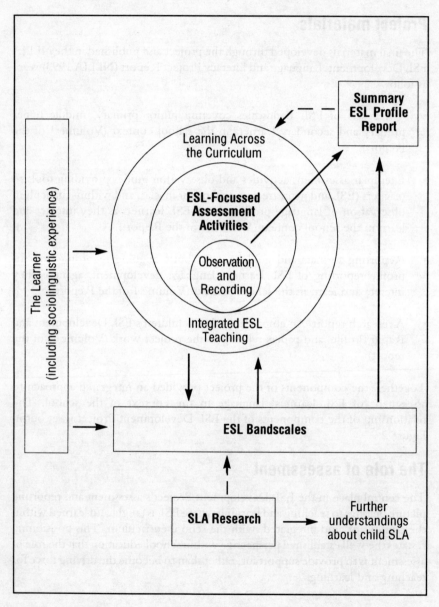

Figure 2 Relationship of components of ESL Development Project

Assessment activities

ESL-focused assessment activities, which are derived out of the planned curriculum but which are also informed by understandings of ESL proficiency development, guide teachers to focus on the various aspects of the language development of their ESL learners within the context of the specific teaching program. The assessment activities, with accompanying observation guides, have been developed in close consultation with teachers, as exemplars to assist teachers to select appropriate assessment activities for their teaching program and their particular learner group. Ongoing recording is central to effective assessment and reporting.

Reporting profile

Guidelines and suggested formats for ongoing recording are provided in the ESL Project Report. A final Summary ESL Report is needed to report to others (other teachers, parents, education bodies) on the progress of the learner. A suggested format for a Summary ESL Profile report, with guidelines for teachers on ways to incorporate the learner's estimated ESL Bandscale levels accompanied by profiled information about the learner's background and performance, are also provided in the Project Report.[4]

The ESL Bandscales

The ESL Bandscales play important roles within this coordinated picture of ESL assessment. The ESL Bandscales will:

* assist teachers of ESL learners to make more informed decisions about their selection of learning activities for ESL learners, and about the kind of language-focused teaching and support individual ESL learners will need, in mainstream and intensive-ESL learning activities;

* provide teachers of ESL learners with a shared reference document as they assess and record ongoing progress of ESL learners, and as they report on learner progress in ESL through the Summary ESL Profile report;

* provide teachers with a common reference point for long-term monitoring of ESL learners' progress from K/entry–12.

Development of the ESL Bandscales

Processes of development

Initially, the processes of development of the ESL Bandscales relied on empirical, psychometric methods (employing Rasch analysis) to determine the nature and relative placement of indicators on a continuum (Griffin and McKay 1992). The initial process was described as bottom-up consultative (Griffin and McKay 1992): practitioners were asked to provide descriptions of tasks and indicators, and then students were to be observed and rated on each of the indicators in order to obtain calibration data (Griffin 1990). There was concern amongst many teachers that the outcomes of these processes lacked validity, in part because learner characteristics (age, maturity, background knowledge etc.) and context (the nature of the task, degree of interlocutor support etc.) were not being adequately addressed when individual indicators were calibrated and grouped through such a statistical process. The project subsequently moved towards developing more integrated and context-related descriptions, following a top-down consultative process: that is, the indicators were written into integrated proficiency level descriptions, with reference to current second language learning and assessment theory; a small group of specialists who were themselves experienced teachers provided initial, draft and final descriptions of language progress, engaging practitioners in an iterative process of dialogue and response as they did so.

Existing proficiency scales

A number of proficiency scales have been developed for adults learning English as a second language (e.g. the FSI Scales 1968; Ingram and Wylie 1984; Interagency Language Roundtable 1985). A short but valuable five-level scale for primary ESL learners is available from Britain (Hester in Barrs et al. 1988). A wide search found two short and unpublished Australian ESL scales in the school context (e.g. Grierson 1991; Metropolitan North Intensive Language Centre, Chatswood, n.d.), with no significant school-based ESL proficiency descriptions from overseas (see McKay 1992). The ESL Framework of Stages (McKay and Scarino 1991) provided a framework for the structure of the Bandscales.

The school context

Without doubt the major concern in the development of the ESL Bandscales was that the Bandscales address the development of ESL proficiency specifically within the school context. Although the available ESL scales for adults provided vital initial guidance, the writers were essentially starting from scratch as they tackled the issues around school-based ESL development.

What are the key implications of the school context for an ESL proficiency scale? In summary, a ESL scale should be able to take account of the following:

*   That ESL learners in Australian schools range from around five years old to seventeen years old and over, and are at markedly different levels of social, emotional and cognitive development with markedly different experiences of the world.

*   That ESL learners enter Australian schools at any phase of schooling and at any age, with a full range of experience in English (none or a little to advanced).

*   That ESL learners bring with them a wide range of experiences in their first language and a range of educational experiences (in their first language and/or in English).

*   That once in school, there are expectations for ESL learners to become increasingly and quickly competent, through English, in a broad range of knowledge, understandings, skills and attitudes related to everyday living in Australian society and to the school curriculum (the expectations varying and increasing as learners move from K–12).

*   That ESL learners need to be able to become increasingly competent in academic language use of English in a range of subject areas (the characteristics of these expectations varying and increasing from K–12).

*   That there are expectations and opportunities for ESL learners to enter into learning through mainstream subject areas often whilst they are still at early levels of English proficiency.

The school context is probably best described as a dynamic interrelationship of growth (maturation, language learning and mainstream learning) and pressures to grow, all in a new or second language, English.

Three strategies

The writers of the ESL Bandscales adopted three major strategies in order to construct the ESL Bandscales in a way which would take this context into account. These integrated strategies were:

- Adoption of a model of language ability able to account for the complexity of variables in the school context.

- Adoption of a three-tiered framework to account for the influence of age, experience and context on school learner second language development.

- The incorporation of descriptions of second language ability in academic contexts.

These strategies will be outlined in turn.

Strategy 1: Adoption of a model of language ability able to account for the complexity of variables in the school context

After careful consideration, the ESL Development Project chose to adopt as a theoretical base for the development of the ESL Bandscales (and the assessment and reporting materials) the Bachman (1990; 1991) and Bachman and Palmer (forthcoming) framework of communicative language ability. Whilst the project drew on other theories, it was felt that the Bachman/Palmer framework would be suitable as the theoretical basis for the project, since it was rich enough to conceptualise the issues involved in second language performance situations.

As part of their approach to language test development and use, Bachman and Palmer have developed a comprehensive and evolving framework of second language ability which provides a map rather than a prescription of language ability, setting out those areas of ability that need to be taken into account in second language assessment. It is a rich view of language which allows for a focus on both language use and the language user. Both sociolinguistic and psycholinguistic issues are addressed. The relationship between language use and language test performance is shown in Figure 3a. The components of communicative language ability in the framework are set out in Figure 3b.

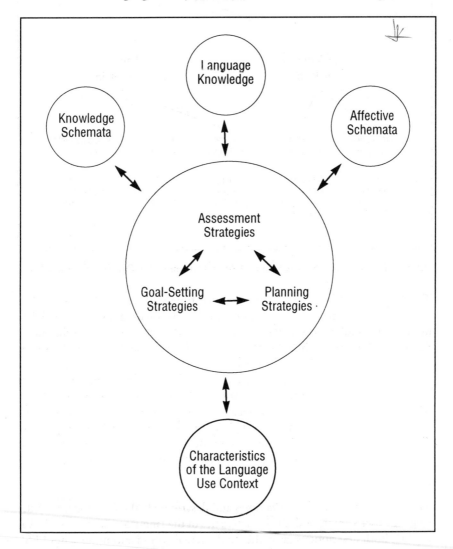

Figure 3a A model of language use (Bachman and Palmer, forthcoming)

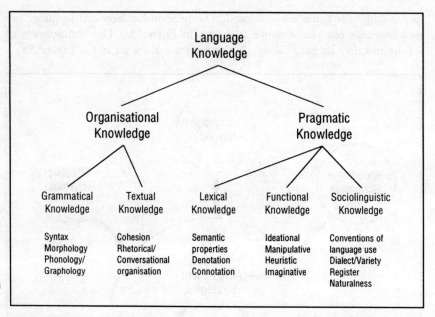

Figure 3b Areas of language knowledge (Bachman and Palmer, forthcoming)

The Bachman/Palmer framework is compatible with and draws on theories which provide information on more specifically-focused aspects and richer models of sociolinguistics (Bachman draws explicitly on the sociolinguistic theory of Halliday) and theories of second language acquisition and development. The writers of the ESL Bandscales needed to build the band descriptions on existing work in these areas, and on a current theory of language ability which enables the identification and classification of the many components of language which are considered relevant in language use. The Bachman/Palmer framework builds on the Canale and Swain (1980) framework and has widened considerably the construct that testers use for communicative competence. According to Skehan (1989:8), it is 'likely to have a considerable influence on language testing for some time to come'.

The framework as a whole examines and describes (1) the components of the language user's ability and (2) characteristics of the language use context. It was felt that both descriptions grasp the fundamental considerations of school ESL teaching and learning and provide a comprehensive basis for the development of ESL Bandscales.

The value of the framework to the ESL Bandscales (as well as to other components of the project) is in its recognition and integration of the many facets of language performance (as well as language knowledge), including knowledge structures, the learner's sociocultural knowledge and 'real world' knowledge ('knowledge structures' incorporate school content knowledge), strategic knowledge which Bachman (1991:84) describes as the mental capacity for implementing the components of language competence in contextualised communicative language use, ('strategic knowledge' can also incorporate literacy strategies involved in reading and writing), affective factors (affective factors are recognised as being of vital importance in school ESL learning), psychophysiological mechanisms, and the context of situation. Bachman (1991:119) provides a detailed model of the context of situation through an analysis of testing conditions described in a most relevant way for school ESL, incorporating:

- facets of the testing environment (familiarity of the place and equipment, personnel, time of testing, physical conditions);

- facets of the test rubric (test organisation, time allocation, instructions);

- facets of the input (format; nature of language);

- facets of the expected response (format, nature of language, restrictions on response) and

- relationship between input and response (reciprocal, non-reciprocal, adaptive).

The Bachman and Palmer model was thus able to name, organise and account for in a comprehensive framework, the complex influences and considerations for the descriptions which were to be written for the ESL Bandscales.

Operationalising the constructs of language ability

The issues in operationalising constructs of language ability in proficiency scales are complex. A case has been put forward by Bachman (e.g. Bachman and

Savignon 1986; Bachman 1990) that a scale should be devoid of test method factors (that is, of factors in the context of situation), that a number of separate scales should be developed for each components of communicative language ability, and that the scale should be couched in terms of relative absence or presence of the component. A key underlying aim in this approach is to make the construct, the underlying ability of second language ability testable. However there are difficulties in this approach, just as in the scales Bachman criticises, not the least of which is rater understanding of and agreement on the descriptions (Brindley 1991:148). Such an approach was problematic for the writers, and for the purpose for which the Bandscales were to be used. Firstly, the Bachman model, together with the insights provided by Cummins (1991) on the differences between conversational and academic proficiency, were attractive to the school ESL experience not least because of the sociolinguistic emphasis, with the recognition of the role of content and context in language performance. Secondly, ratings of language ability were to be done through observations across a range of tasks (with assistance in selection and observation through focused tasks). Whilst the inclusion of context in the band descriptions may cause some difficulties with regard to the the the testing of the constructs (Bachman 1990) (which can be addressed by using confirmatory factor analysis), decisions in the development of the ESL Bandscales were guided in the main by the assessor-oriented purposes of the Bandscales as opposed to the constructor-oriented purpose; that is by the fact that the Bandscales were developed in order to guide the rating process, rather than to guide the construction of tests at appropriate levels (Alderson 1991:73–4). A further influence on decisions was the underlying purpose of teacher professional development (awareness raising about the nature of second language development) which might occur in the reading and use of the Bandscales.

In effect, the NLLIA ESL Development Project has taken a 'weak' interpretation of the Bachman/Palmer framework, rather than the alternative interpretation of it as a 'God's truth' model of proficiency (Skehan 1991:15). The framework is used as a general guide, which is 'consistent with a wide range of theoretical insights, on the one hand, and which can be a systematising framework for research activity, on the other' (Skehan 1991:16). The literature on conversational/academic proficiency continuum, second language acquisition (SLA) theory and research, and genre theory, provided further information from within this framework.

In the band descriptions, knowledge schemata, the 'process dimension', areas of language knowledge, characteristics of the language use context, together with affective factors, are included where they are considered salient, that is where they are of value to the teachers in their rating of the student's proficiency level. Figure 4 shows the framework for the ordering of the descriptors used in the writing of each level of the ESL Bandscales. The various aspects of the Bachman/ Palmer framework are summarised to guide the process of writing, and subsequently, the reading and use of the Bandscales.

GENERAL STATEMENT
(designed to provide an overview of the level and to describe global aspects of language use).
e.g., range of activities/texts, nature of the context e.g., nature of interlocutor support, whether face to-face/group/class, learner's familiariaty with content.

SKILLS/STRATEGIES AND FEATURES OF SECOND LANGUAGE ACQUISITION ('THE PROCESS DIMENSION') REFERRED TO IN THE BACHMAN MODEL
e.g. specific skill development in Reading, Writing, Speaking, Listening; descriptions of second language acquisition strategies, including role of L1.

FEATURES OF LANGUAGE PERFORMANCE
e.g., salient details of discourse features, vocabulary, syntax, pronunciation.

HIGHER LEVEL FEATURES OF PERFORMANCE
e.g., ways in which learners are dealing with cultural aspects within the language such as idiom.
e.g., level of precision.

NOTES ON THE LEVEL
e.g. notes on specific learner groups, implications for placement, appropriateness to purpose and context.

Figure 4 Framework for Ordering of Descriptors in ESL Bandscales (NLLIA
        ESL Development: Language and Literacy in Schools Volume I:
        Teachers' Manual, 1994: A19)

Figure 5 An example of an exemplar assessment activity

Curriculum Area: Mathematics

Topic/Theme: Lego, Constructions

Target group: Junior Primary   Middle Primary

Proficiency Level: Lower

Assessment types (columns): informal observation | planned observation | discussion | analysis of samples | peer-/self-assessment

Description of the teaching cycle

Small group with teacher:

1 Decide on an object (e.g. truck) to be constructed with Lego blocks (from illustrations of Lego Information Leaflet — Grade 3/4 kit).

2 Select main Lego pieces needed — introduce/reinforce names of pieces. Label illustration.

3 Pair students — pairs and teacher construct object together. Teacher introduces relevant action verbs — put/press/find/make.

4 Re-count what was done — teacher/teacher and student.

5 Teacher writes simple recount/cup up sentences.

6 As a class/in pairs/students sequence sentences.

7 Repeat above procedure with another object.

8 **Planned assessment activity: Constructing and activity sharing.**

9 Students write (1 sentence) telling what they did.

10 Multi-age grouping: new arrivals students work with 1/2 students to help them construct some of the objects.

Assumed background knowledge/familiarity with task type*

1 Familiarity with Lego blocks

2 Some experience with the 'language' of building with Lego blocks

3 Experience working in pairs/small groups

* If this knowledge and experience cannot be assumed for a particular student then this activity should probably **not** be used for assessing his/her ESL development.

Possible resources

In-built peer-/self-assessment

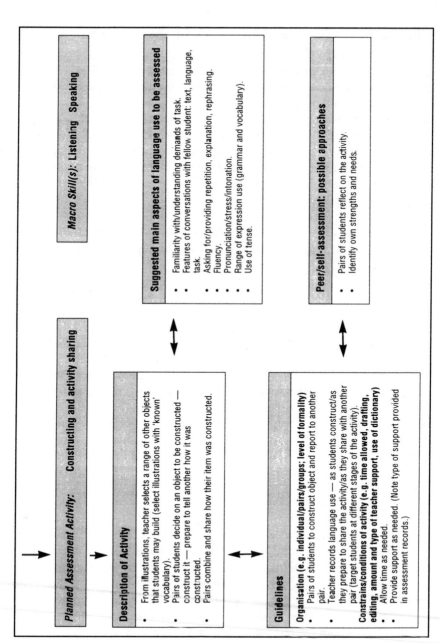

Planned Assessment Activity: Constructing and activity sharing

Macro Skill(s): Listening Speaking

Description of Activity

- From illustrations, teacher selects a range of other objects that students may build (select illustrations with 'known' vocabulary).
- Pairs of students decide on an object to be constructed — construct it — prepare to tell another how it was constructed.
- Pairs combine and share how their item was constructed.

Suggested main aspects of language use to be assessed

- Familiarity with/understanding demands of task.
- Features of conversations with fellow student: text, language, task.
- Asking for/providing repetition, explanation, rephrasing.
- Fluency.
- Pronunciation/stress/intonation.
- Range of expression use (grammar and vocabulary).
- Use of tense.

Guidelines

Organisation (e.g. individual/pairs/groups; level of formality)
- Pairs of students to construct object and report to another pair.
- Teacher records language use — as students construct/as they prepare to share the activity/as they share with another pair (target students at different stages of the activity).

Constrains/conditions of activity (e.g. time allowed, drafting, editing, amount and type of teacher support, use of dictionary)
- Allow time as needed.
- Provide support as needed. (Note type of support provided in assessment records.)

Peer/self-assessment: possible approaches

- Pairs of students reflect on the activity.
- Identify own strengths and needs.

Figure 5 Cont. An example of an exemplar assessment activity

The Bachman/Palmer framework in the exemplar assessment activities

The Bachman/Palmer framework provides a basis for the development of the assessment instruments within the project, and thus a unifying link between the ESL Bandscales and the assessment instruments. Figure 5 shows an example of an exemplar assessment activity[5]. The assessment activity is set within the context of a teaching cycle; teachers are alerted to the need to consider contextual factors such as assumed background knowledge, familiarity of the learner with the task type, and aspects of the text. Main aspects of language use to be assessed are noted, and observation is further supplemented by observation guides provided in the Teacher's Manual.

Strategy 2: Adoption of a three-tiered framework to account for the influence of age, experience and context on school learner second language development

In order to account for the influence of age, experience and changing context on the school learner's second language development, three ESL Bandscales were developed at three broad age groups or phases of schooling, as set out in Figure 6 below. This structure follows the conceptualisation of ESL learner development in the school context initially formulated in the ESL Framework of Stages (McKay and Scarino 1991). Separate ESL Bandscales (each with four scales covering each of the macro–skills) were developed, at the junior primary phase of schooling, at the middle/upper primary phase and at the secondary phase. Each of the Bandscales is embedded within the context of the school for that age group, and describes language ability in levels gradually moving towards a high proficiency level defined by the characteristics of personal, social and general school use for that age group, and by the demands of the school context for that phase of schooling.

This strategy was successful in that it allowed the characteristics of the language users and their context to be highlighted in the descriptions. In particular, differences between features of early second language acquisition of young children compared with that of older learners could be described. The descriptions will assist teachers to recognise and rate the features of literacy and language development of the relevant group, taking into account the features and influences of literacy development and second language ability, and the nature of the school context for the age group in question. Extracts from the

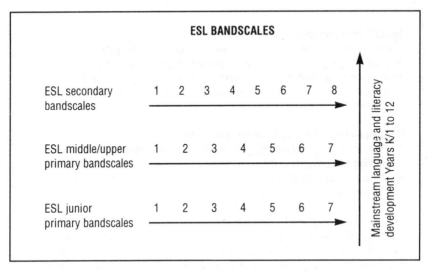

Figure 6 The three ESL Bandscales and their relationship to mainstream language and literacy development, K–12

three Bandscales in Figure 7 give an indication of how the influence of developing literacy (in younger children), and second language literacy, and differences in the language and learning context are incorporated into the descriptions.

A disadvantage of adopting the three-tiered structure for the Bandscales is that there are many levels for teachers (and particularly administrators) to become acquainted with. The developers decided that in these initial descriptions, which were breaking new ground for others to follow it was better to err on the side of detail rather than to fall for a reductionist approach. The level of detail provided, in other words, was commensurate with the information needs of the audience. Alderson's (1991) distinction between assessor-oriented (where the purpose is to guide teacher observations and ratings) and user-oriented orientation (where the purpose is primarily a reporting one from the perspective of employers and others) is relevant here. As Alderson points out, problems arise when the functions of scales are confused. It was important to avoid this. Subsequent scales designed, for example, for administrative purposes, that is, with a user orientation, might simplify, using the NLLIA ESL Bandscale descriptions as a base reference.

Junior Primary Reading Level 2 (extract only)
Can recognise words and short word clusters in English if these have been recycled often in a variety of language activities. Are showing signs of becoming active readers, showing response to text (e.g. responding appropriately in the right places through laughter, surprise, disappointment). Are unable to fully comprehend and to predict meaning in text, even if they are able to decode.

Middle and Upper Primary Reading Level 2 (extract only)
Are showing signs of becoming active readers, showing response to text (e.g. responding appropriately in the right places…). Will join in with key words and repetitive phrases in familiar texts (e.g. picture stories, written chants and rhymes) in shared reading sessions…

Secondary Reading Level 2 (extracts only)
Language ability across a range of personal, social and general school contexts
Can comprehend short, high frequency written cues (e.g. written school signs such as directions and labels — *Return Books Here*; *Exit*; *Ticket Office*; *Library*; *Office*). Are able to read simple factual descriptions and informational texts which are contextually-enhanced (e.g. with pictures) and on familiar topics.

Application and extension to academic contexts
Can comprehend short recounds written by peers based on personal experiences… Can read a teacher-written simple procedure (e.g. simple written teacher instructions to follow to carry out a listening task such as using a tape recorder).

Figure 7 Extracts from Junior Primary, Middle and Upper Primary and Secondary Bandscales at Reading Level 2

Strategy 3: The incorporation of descriptions of language ability in academic contexts

Cummins' work on what he originally termed basic interpersonal communication skills (BICS) and cognitive academic language proficiency (CALP) with its later revisions (Cummins 1981, 1983, 1991) in which he referred to continua of context-dependent/context-independent and cognitively less demanding/ cognitively-demanding language use was influential in the writers' approach to descriptions of language proficiency in the ESL Bandscales. Descriptions of learners' abilities to extend their language proficiency to academic contexts are integrated in the junior primary and middle/upper primary Bandscales, and are separate in the secondary Bandscales, where the language demands of academic contexts become more distant from social language contexts and are in even more need of close observation by teachers. Speaking Level 4 from the Middle/ Upper Primary Bandscale Level 4 (Figure 8) shows how the primary Bandscale descriptions distinguish between social and academic contexts of language use, and how contextual support (e.g. modelling, scaffolding, recycling of language by the teacher, and reliance on written text for support), and low-level cognitive demands are features of learners' early proficiency in academic contexts.

Middle & Upper Primary ESL S4
Speaking: Level 4

Extending the range of language beyond own immediate social environment and experimenting with learning through English: drawing on knowledge of the world in L1 and English, and on L1 and English language and literacy (to varying degrees).

Are able to interact socially with peers and familiar adults in most informal school contexts (e.g. teacher on playground duty; with peers in playground games; with peers in the classroom in informal learning contexts [e.g. art and craft, games, organisational language in group work]). Can give personal information, and describe past and present events without great difficulty; able to use words and phrases in strings to participate in longer speaking turns.

Are able to recount an event or a series of events orally (e.g. in individual presentations such as morning news [for middle primary learners]).

Can participate in academic learning activities on familiar topics if teacher and contextual support (modelling, scaffolding, recycling of language etc.) and time are provided (e.g. can describe processes such as The Water Cycle in simple terms). ESL features still occur (see below) but will not generally impede overall meaning. Can give a short prepared formal spoken report with heavy word-for-word reliance on their written text and with little ability to respond to questions beyond giving yes/no answers.

Are attempting to express more complex ideas and more precision of meaning as their English resource grows. Attempts at explaining more complex ideas in English

---

Figure 8   Sample of a level description (Speaking Level 4) in the Middle/
Upper Primary ESL Bandscales   *Continued over page*

(e.g. explaining a problem they have in specific subject areas) may cause errors in syntax, with breakdown in meaning sometimes occurring.

May experience frustration as they realise the mismatch between English they can understand and the English they can speak. May wish to use L1 for emotional support and as a break from continual use of English.

Are producing more complex language (e.g. using subordinating conjunctions such as *because, when, that*). Are able to apply syntactic rules correctly (e.g. subject verb agreement, appropriate tense) but not consistently as they continue to make hypotheses and place more emphasis on getting their meaning across. Are showing signs of early modality (if…; could; might; will; must; perhaps) (e.g. *if I let it go they'll score me I'll go.* [Alfonso]).

SAMPLE
no my brother he told me he dream about when he gave me lots of cars and lots of things for boys like aeroplanes and robots and they say I was magic and I um take little ropes and I (packed/tacked?) everything with that rope and there came um little um cats was hairy and hair is to play with books and other things like this… (Aga).

Figure 8 Cont. Sample of a level description (Speaking Level 4) in the Middle/Upper Primary ESL Bandscales

In the secondary ESL Bandscales, two headings are provided in each level description, namely (1) Language ability in personal, social and general school contexts ('social contexts') and (2) Extension to academic contexts. The first heading introduces a description of language use outside specific academic contexts; the second extends this ability into academic contexts (see Figure 9). It is important to note that the second is intended as an extension of the first and not a separate description. However as the Bandscales levels took shape it was discovered (and confirmed through teacher consultation) that the language proficiency in academic contexts might sometimes be a 'maverick' extension from earlier levels (where the learner has been able to draw on his depth of specific subject knowledge, and his strategic competence — including study skills — to reach a higher level of academic language ability in a chosen subject area). The academic extension may also be a 'fallback' from more advanced levels of language ability in social contexts. Because of differential development in social and academic contexts such as this, the reporting formats allow for ratings (with accompanying comments) in (1) personal/social and general school contexts and (2) academic contexts, at the secondary level. A sample of a secondary ESL Bandscale description is provided in Figure 9.

In the junior and middle/upper primary ESL Bandscales, headings defining language ability in social and academic contexts were not used, though the continuum provided an underlying framework for level descriptions, particularly in the middle/upper primary Bandscales, and particularly in upper levels of proficiency.

Understandings about language ability in specific academic contexts are still developing in the school ESL field. Further research is needed and hopefully will come out of these first descriptions. In particular, little is known about the characteristics of the development of the academic language proficiency of low literacy-background learners. Within the ESL Bandscales specific characteristics of the proficiency of learners with a low-literacy background were provided in note-form within the level descriptions, otherwise low literacy background learners were presumed to be included through the existing descriptions (that is, most likely being rated at lower levels because of the effects of their low-literacy background). However, it is known that the picture is more complex than this. The writers recommend that research into this aspect of school ESL be conducted urgently.

Validation of the NLLIA ESL Bandscales

Although further validation is needed (and this is, it is hoped, to be addressed through further funding from the Commonwealth Department of Employment, Education and Training), the ESL Bandscales derive their initial validity from a range of sources.

A number of studies (e.g. Ingram 1985; Dandonoli and Henning 1990) have investigated the construct validity (the establishment of the theoretical and psychological reality of the constructs) of 'real-life' (Bachman 1990) proficiency scales. It is generally recognised that there are a number of issues involved in the construct validity of proficiency scales in this tradition (e.g. Bachman and Savignon 1986; Brindley and Nunan 1992:24–7). Brindley and Nunan (1992:24)

Secondary ESL R5
Reading: Level 5

Transition towards successful learning through English. Beginning consolidation of understanding of the demands of the educational context: drawing on L2 and L2 literacy (to varying degrees) and knowledge of the world in L1 and L2.

LANGUAGE ABILITY ACROSS A RANGE OF PERSONAL, SOCIAL AND GENERAL SCHOOL CONTEXTS

Can comprehend a wide range of authentic non-technical factual texts that are not culturally overladen (e.g. school newsletter, popular newspaper articles, information on careers). Are markedly more able to comprehend above texts when topic is familiar. Can get the gist of more complex and abstract texts (within the range of ability expected at their phase of schooling) such as technical/analytical texts on unfamiliar topics (e.g. articles in *Bulletin*, *Time*, *Australian Geographic* magazines).

Will have difficulty with very lengthy texts (unable to follow and hold meaning throughout) and will tend to avoid them (e.g. long novels, long feature articles in magazines).

Will need to read at own pace and may need time to re-read.

Will make wide use of a bilingual dictionary or an English/English dictionary as a strategy to check guesses in comprehension of meaning from the above texts.

Are developing a wide general reading vocabulary, which gives a base for reading of general authentic reading texts.

Even in straight-forward texts will have difficulty drawing inferences directly from specific linguistic features of the text to discern author's point of view and intent (e.g. foregrounding of information to signify writer's emphasis, ordering and use of selected phrases which signify the writer's position [e.g. *after all, she was only…*], word choice [e.g. *hostility* rather than *dislike*]).

Can read many types of handwriting, such as those by peers and teachers.

APPLICATION AND EXTENSION TO ACADEMIC CONTEXTS

Are able to comprehend some textbook materials on context-enhanced (e.g. supporting pictures) and not highly abstract topics in subject areas. Are usually able to locate main ideas and details and predict meaning in these texts based on linguistic context and background knowledge. Are able to get the gist and main subsidiary ideas in specialist texts (at the level of, and within the range of ability of, their phase of schooling) in those subject areas in which they have strong background in their L1 and/or L2 studies (e.g. Maths, Physics).

May be able to comprehend technical words more easily than sub-technical words (e.g. words like *work, plant, feed, force* which have a range of meaning and are often used idiomatically, or words like *extends, negligible* associated with scientific phraseology). Will have a broad technical vocabulary which has not yet been consolidated and lacks depth due to swift change of topics across subject areas.

With additional ESL-informed support:

With support (accessing the text, use of bilingual dictionary, with additional time etc.) can skim, scan, get the gist, and repeat the content of extended informational, persuasive school texts, and short stories (which are not too reliant on cultural content). With support can cope with changes in genres within a text (e.g. historical recount to narrative in an Australian history textbook).

Figure 9 Sample of a level description (Reading Level 5) in the Secondary ESL Bandscales

Need a great deal of support with higher levels of reading (e.g. to infer the intentions and point of view of the author; to follow the chain of logical conjunctions in a text; to recognise the relevance and appropriateness of evidence and supporting details).

Even with simple task instructions/assignment questions, need support to determine appropriate response (e.g. choice of text-types) and to recognise and interpret key words which require detailed response (e.g. compare/contrast texts; *from your observations and your reading* requires a response to **both** key words).

Learners may take a long time to move from Level 4 to Level 5; they may appear to regress because of the increased demands of more complex and lengthy texts, to the sheer quantity from various subjects, and lack of time to read these in depth and assimilate new language due to swift change of topics which do not systematically build on each other in terms of language. A change in the level of support available of an ESL specialist may also be a factor.

Note: Level 5 — A 'plateau' level for some. Level 5 language, particularly in academic contexts, presents difficulties for many ESL learners. It becomes a 'plateau' level for a number of ESL learners ('plateau learners'), especially those without a solid grounding of content knowledge, or with interruptions in their L1 language and literacy development. Many learners (often from Group B [*low literacy background learners*] and Group C learners [*learners transferring from primary school*], who may be unnoticed because of their apparent ease in personal, social and general school contexts, find it hard to move beyond Level 5; yet further progress is essential for more sophisticated 'general' language use and for success in senior secondary study.

Note: Senior Secondary Group A (L1 school literacy background learners) (including Year 10). Some learners ('academically-focused' learners) are able to operate with more success in academic contexts than in personal, social and general school contexts because of their informed decision to focus on specific subjects for success (e.g. maths, science), their learning-how-to-learn skills and L1 educational background which is sometimes above that of native speaker peers in chosen subject areas. These learners will concentrate on becoming proficient readers of subject-specific registers and/or teacher–pupil language. These learners are highly motivated and are using a high level of strategic competence in L2.

Note: The extension of the *With Support* description at Level 5 reflects an inevitable increase in complex task demands on most ESL learners as they participate in mainstream learning contexts and in which ESL teachers are no longer able to select and filter activities and written texts to suit the reading level in English. Although ESL learners benefit from learning in more complex environments, learners are increasingly attempting reading tasks which they are unable to carry out independently due to their level of reading.

SUGGESTED IMPLICATIONS FOR PLACEMENT

Learners at this level will have some chance to succeed in the mainstream context (particularly junior secondary) if they are provided with ESL support and have the necessary background knowledge.

Initial teacher reaction would indicate that there are many learners who are still at Level 5 Reading in senior secondary school; such learners would have great difficulty dealing with the demands of senior secondary school level, even with support. Learners at this level are tending to develop 'horizontally' i.e. increasing their experience of English across a wider range of purposed, audiences and contexts. Learners may stay at Level 5 for an extended length of time as they develop in this way.

Figure 9 Cont.   Sample of a level description (Reading Level 5) in the Secondary ESL Bandscales

comment, for example, that there has been no real empirical support or established sets of principles for the construction of existing proficiency scales, nor for the multi-level bandscales which imply linear sequence. With regard to the development of the IELTS Draft listening scale, Brindley and Nunan (1992:24) write:

> *It is more likely, given what is known about the organic nature of language learning, that development… happens slowly and gradually such that a learner at any one point in time may well display evidence of behaviours which are characteristic of more than one ability level. While the concept of 'band' rather than possible 'levels' or 'point' addresses this problem to a certain extent since it covers 'ranges of possible scores, rather than precisely defined, invariable performances' (Alderson 1991:73), the measurement aspect of listening assessment can only be vitiated by the inevitable lack of precision of scale points.*

The use of vague and impressionistic terms ('frequent', 'many', 'some', 'a few') used to distinguish between the number of bands describing ability levels leads to subjective interpretation which is problematic (Brindley and Nunan 1992:24).

Construct validity in the ESL Bandscales is being addressed, though currently on a small scale because of funding constraints, through the analysis of teacher ratings of groups of students in primary and secondary schools. An initial investigation of how the secondary scale is operating has been undertaken, using Rasch modelling (Lee et al., in preparation). Four teachers[6] rated twenty-two students on each of the four skills, with each student rated by two teachers. An initial analysis has shown that the secondary ESL Bandscales operate in a true partial credit fashion in the teacher ratings. The spacing of the lower steps appeared to be comparatively closer than the higher levels, which bears out the conception of the scales by the writers. These results have been obtained without teacher (rater) training, and with three of the participating teachers being mainstream subject teachers. This result is encouraging. Further analysis is being undertaken, and ratings are currently being collected from junior primary and primary teachers using the relevant ESL Bandscales. Partial credit analysis (Wright and Masters 1982) provides a means for the empirical validation of rating scales. The Partial Credit Model can also be used to investigate the validity of the rating categories themselves and their relationship of the categories to the construct being measured, for example, whether some indicators (e.g. those related to accuracy) might have a disproportionate role in the ratings of performance (McNamara and Adams 1991).

Content and face validity in the ESL Bandscales have been established as far as possible through the fact that the ESL Bandscales are constructed by experienced and expert writers, in consultation with many experienced teachers who reacted according to their experience and their observations of learners' language performance in schools. The limitations of reliance on teacher observations, in that teachers' observations may be limited by a lack of knowledge of theoretical models, by inadequate observations skills and/or an inability to articulate descriptions of independent student language behaviour (Griffin and McKay 1992) are, however, recognised. The strong input from the specialist writing team, the coordination of teacher input, the close and ongoing contact between teachers and the team, was designed to counteract this effect as far as possible.

To ascertain content and face validity, a classroom-based survey of draft versions of the ESL Bandscales was carried out during the development of the Bandscales. The structure and content of the drafts were by this time close to the final ESL Bandscales, though feedback from teachers gave direction to a final refinement process before publication. Responses from teachers were extremely positive. Ninety per cent of teachers, many of whom had observed and rated learners with the draft Bandscales, rated the scales as either 'sufficiently representative' or 'highly representative' of ESL learner language development in school.

Ultimately, the content and face validity of the ESL Bandscales were considered to be high because of the nature of the developmental process, which was an iterative and wide process of consultation involving extensive input from practitioners and other specialists. Davies (1988:47–8) argues for content validity over statistical analyses of validity, because of the 'elusiveness of precision in language testing'.

> *Language testing needs to be about integrated pragmatic systems: the major skills we bring as testers must be linguistic-descriptive, the statistical analyses must always be ancillary and secondary.*

This view has been relevant to the development of the ESL Bandscales, and also supports the view held by the writing team that content validity plays a major role in the validation of the Bandscales.

Issues of implementation

The NLLIA ESL Bandscales are part of an integrated package of ESL assessment which, because of the wide consultation and involvement of teachers of ESL learners in schools which occurred during its development, has already had a major impact in the school ESL field in Australia. Professional development (rater training) will accompany trialling, and should certainly accompany further use of the materials. Some professional development activities have already taken place since the completion of the project. Further research arising from the ESL Bandscales and the ESL Project is inevitable, since many new questions have arisen out of the first major steps taken by the project team.

Two key areas for research relate to the proficiency development of low-literacy background learners, and of Aboriginal learners learning English as a 'foreign language' (e.g. in bush settings) or as a second dialect. It was not clear, for example, whether low-literacy background learners follow the same pathway of second language development as learners who have developed literacy in their first language but at a slower rate, or whether they 'hop across' the bands, taking with them large gaps in their language and conceptual development due to missed or partly-developed concepts and language skills in their earlier education. There is also a need to undertake research into the English language development of Aboriginal learners, whether as a second language or second dialect, taking into account particular features of language development due to particular cultural and contextual differences. Since the writers were careful to include the context as a major characteristic of the ESL Bandscale descriptions, it was inappropriate not to acknowledge that cultural and contextual differences would be evident in the case of Aboriginal learners. The ESL Bandscales can provide a base for further research and development in the field of Aboriginal education, which clearly needs to occur in close consultation with specialists and practitioners.

Ultimately, educational politics tied to the continuing development of state and national profiles, will determine the extent to which the ESL Bandscales and ESL Project materials will be adopted system-wide in Australian schools. Meanwhile, teacher-initiated use is occurring across Australia. In terms of research and development, the creative first step in the development of comprehensive, theory- and research-driven second language proficiency descriptions for school age learners has been taken. The ESL Bandscales will hopefully, as part of the total assessment and reporting package developed through the project, provide an impetus for more research into informed assessment and reporting of the language progress of ESL learners in school, and make a key contribution to the education of ESL learners in Australian schools.

Notes

1   The National Languages and Literacy Institute of Australia.

2   The Project was funded from the national element of the Australian Second Language Learning Program of the National Policy on Languages; the Australian Language and Literacy Policy, the NLLIA and the Department of Employment, Education and Training (DEET). The Project was carried out through the NLLIA Language Testing and Curriculum Centre at Griffith University, the NLLIA Language Testing Centre, Melbourne University and the NLLIA Language Acquisition Research Centre at Sydney University. The publications of the NLLIA ESL Development: Language and Literacy in Schools project (Volumes I and II) are available through the NLLIA, 6 Campion Street, Deakin, ACT 2600.

3   The writer wishes to fully acknowledge the contribution of Catherine Hudson and Marilyn Sapuppo for their major contribution to the development of the NLLIA ESL Bandscales.

4   The Catholic Education Office of Victoria are thanked for their contribution to the development of the ongoing reporting and Summary ESL Profile Report formats and guidelines within the Project.

5   A full introduction to and rationale for the exemplar assessment activities can be found in the NLLIA ESL Development: Language and Literacy in Schools Teacher's Manual (Volume I).

6   Dr. Rosanna McEvedy, Rachel Robson, William Parlet and Wendy McCallum at Wesley College, Western Australia are thanked for undertaking the ratings.

References

Alderson, J.C. 1991. Bands and scores. In J.C. Alderson and B. North (eds) *Language testing in the 1990s*. London: Modern English Publications and the British Council.

Australian Education Council/Curriculum and Assessment Committee. 1992. *The national English profile trialling and formal consultation*. Draft.

Bachman, L.F. 1990. *Fundamental considerations in language testing*. Oxford: Oxford University Press.

Bachman, L.F. 1991. What does language testing have to offer? *TESOL Quarterly* 25:671–704.

Bachman, L.F. and A.S. Palmer Forthcoming. *Language testing in practice*. Oxford: Oxford University Press.

Bachman, L.F. and S. Savignon. 1986. The evaluation of communicative language proficiency: a critique of the ACTFL oral interview. *Modern Language Journal* 70:4.

Barrs, M., S. Ellis, H. Hester and A. Thomas. 1988. *The primary language record*. London: Inner London Education Authority/Centre for Language in Primary Education.

Brindley, G. 1991. Defining language ability: the criteria for criteria. In S. Anivan (ed.) *Current developments in language testing*. Singapore: Regional English Language Centre.

Brindley, G. and D. Nunan. 1992. *Draft bandscales for listening. IELTS Research Project No. 1*. Sydney: National Centre for English Language Teaching and Research.

Campbell, W.J., J. Barnett, B. Joy and M. McMeniman. 1984. *A review of the commonwealth English as a second language (ESL) program*. Canberra: Commonwealth Schools Commission.

Canale, M. and M. Swain. 1980. Theoretical bases of communicative approaches to second language teaching and testing. *Applied Linguistics* 1, 1:1–47.

Centre for English as a Second Language, University of Western Australia. 1991. *An evaluative study of the commonwealth ESL program. (Herriman Report)*

Cummins, J. 1981. *The role of primary language development in promoting educational success for minority children in schooling and language minority students: a theoretical framework.* Los Angeles: California State University.

Cummins, J. 1983. Language proficiency and academic achievement. In J. Oller (ed.) *Issues in language testing research.* Rowley, MA: Newbury House.

Cummins, J. 1991. Conversational and academic language proficiency in bilingual contexts. *AILA Review* 8.

Dandonoli, P. and G. Henning. 1990. An investigation of the construct validity of the ACTFL proficiency guidelines and oral interview procedure. *Foreign Language Annals* 23, 1:11–22.

Davies, A. 1988. Operationalising uncertainty in language testing: an argument in favour of content validity. *Language Testing* 5:2–48.

Davison, F. 1991. Statistical support for training in ESL composition rating. In L. Hamp-Lyons (ed.) *Assessing second language writing.* Norwood, NJ: Ablex.

Foreign Service Institute School of Language Studies. 1968. Absolute language proficiency ratings. In J.L.D. Clark *Foreign language testing: theory and practice.* Philadelphia, Pa.: Center for Curriculum Development.

Grierson, J. 1991. *Oral communication rating scale* (draft). Metropolitan South West Region: NSW Department of School Education.

Griffin, P. 1990. Profiling literacy development: monitoring the accumulation of reading skills. *Australian Journal of Education* 34, 3:290–311.

Griffin, P. and P. McKay. 1992. Assessment and reporting in ESL language and literacy in schools project. In *NLLIA ESL development: language and literacy in schools project report. Volume II.* Canberra: NLLIA.

Ingram, D.E. 1985. Assessing proficiency: an overview on some aspects of testing. In K. Hyltenstam and M. Pienemann (eds) *Modelling and assessing second language acquisition*. Clevedon, Avon: Multilingual Matters.

Ingram, D.E. and E. Wylie. 1984. *Australian second language proficiency ratings (ASLPR)*. Canberra: Australian Government Publishing Service.

Interagency Language Roundtable. 1985. *Language skill level descriptions*. Washington, DC: Author. (Also available as Appendix E in R.P. Duran, M. Canale, M. Penfield, C.W. Stansfield, J.E. Liskin-Gasparro. 1985. *TOEFL from a communicative viewpoint on language proficiency*. A writing paper. [TOEFL Research Report 17] Princeton, NJ: Education Testing Service.)

Lee, T., E. Wylie, P. McKay and D.E. Ingram (in preparation). *Process-oriented language assessment*. NLLIA Language Testing and Curriculum Centre, Griffith University.

McKay, P. 1992. Long-term mapping and measurement in school ESL — some perspectives. In *NLLIA ESL development: language and literacy in schools project report. Volume II*. Canberra: National Languages and Literacy Institute of Australia.

McKay, P. and A. Scarino. 1991. *The ESL framework of stages: an approach to ESL learning in schools, K–12*. Melbourne: Curriculum Corporation.

McNamara, T.F. and R.J. Adams. 1991. Exploring rater behaviour with Rasch techniques. Paper presented at *13th Annual Language Testing Research Colloquium*, Princeton, NJ, 21–23 March.

Metropolitan North Intensive English Language Centre, Chatswood, N.S.W. n.d. *Suggested language rating levels for intensive English language centre students placement in high schools*. Unpublished report.

NLLIA ESL development: language and literacy in schools project. Volumes I and II. 1992 (First edition), 1994 (Second edition). Canberra: National Languages and Literacy Institute of Australia.

Northern Territory Department of Education. 1992. *The field of English, work requirements and learning outcomes.* Darwin: Northern Territory Department of Education.

Skehan, P. 1989. Language testing part II. State of the art article. *Language Teaching* 22, 1:1–13.

Skehan, P. 1991. Progress in language testing: the 1990s. In J.C. Alderson and B. North (eds) *Language testing in the 1990s: the communicative legacy.* London: Modern English Publications and The British Council.

South Australian Education Department. 1991. The attainment levels. *Teachers' Newsletter.*

Wright, B.D. and G.N. Masters. 1982. *Rating scale analysis: Rasch measurement.* Chicago: Mesa Press.

3 ESL student needs procedures: an approach to language assessment in primary and secondary school contexts

Lexie Mincham

Introduction

The past decade has seen considerable change in approaches to both language teaching and assessment practices in the context of Australian primary and secondary school education. Theories of language competence have been broadened, as Bachman (1990:83) and others have noted, to include:

> *in addition to the knowledge of grammatical rules, the knowledge of how language is used to achieve particular communicative goals, and the recognition of language use as a dynamic process.*

The teaching of languages, including English as a second language, has consequently moved beyond a narrow focus on the structure of language at the level of sentence, with an accompanying emphasis on correctness of form, to a much broader approach which recognises the importance of being able to use language in socially and culturally appropriate ways. In communicative language classrooms ESL students are engaged in authentic, interactive tasks and activities which provide them with opportunities to develop their ability to use language for a range of interpersonal, informational and aesthetic purposes· with a particular focus on the use of English as a tool for learning across the curriculum.

While this change in emphasis has led to the development of more innovative programs and a richer language learning environment, it has not in itself contributed significantly to our understanding of how choices can be made from the language system in order to achieve particular communicative goals. Relying on descriptions of language derived from traditional approaches to grammar, teachers have often been unable to make sufficiently explicit the linguistic demands of different language tasks. This becomes a critical issue in the context of mainstream education when we consider that teachers need to be able to help students understand the ways in which different subject disciplines use language in order to construct the knowledge and concepts of their particular field. Likewise, essential differences between spoken and written texts have remained largely unexplored so that the role of oral language as a powerful tool for learning has not been well exploited in the majority of classrooms.

In the context of assessment, the lack of a systematic framework for describing language in use, has meant that teachers have not had the necessary tools to undertake an explicit linguistic analysis of students' oral and written texts. This is often reflected in the comments that are made about students' performance on different tasks. How often do we find statements such as 'A great story — beautifully described', or 'This doesn't hang together — 6/10'? Such comments do not provide students with meaningful feedback about their achievements and about the ways in which they can improve their work. The criteria for successful performance remain largely undefined and a source of mystery and frustration for students who are unable to decipher the requirements of the academic classroom — the so-called 'secret English' — the English of social power.

Assessment issues in general have become a much greater focus for debate in the schools sector over the past five years as educational authorities work towards the development of national goals for schooling and the establishment of common curriculum and assessment frameworks. A need for increased accountability has also arisen out of the competing demands being made on the limited resources available for education. Demands for formal testing to satisfy public concerns about standards are counter-balanced by arguments for alternative forms of assessment which many consider to be not only more informative but also better able to take account of new approaches to teaching and learning in language and literacy development.

As a consequence, teachers at all levels are now being asked to assess and report on students' performance more than at any other time. As part of their program planning, teachers need to make initial and on-going assessments of individual students in order to decide how learning should be taken forward within the classroom. They also need to undertake summative assessments of students' achievements in relation to a particular unit of work or study in order to report on the outcomes of learning to parents, caregivers and others concerned with the education process. Such reporting is frequently done in a descriptive way, but as education systems demand more information for planning and review purposes, assessment and reporting procedures are required which can provide such information in more readily accessible ways

As Brindley (1989:19) notes:

> *in most educational contexts, the demands that are imposed by funding authorities and programme administrators for accountability require the presentation of some form of aggregated, quantitative information on achievement.*

In the current economic climate, this trend is likely to be an on-going one. Brindley (1989:19–20) concludes:

> *It would be quite unrealistic to imagine that these demands will not continue, particularly in view of the emphasis which is currently being placed by education ministries in many Western democracies on business concepts such as 'efficiency' and 'cost-effectiveness'. In short, people from inside and outside language programmes will continue to want different kinds of information concerning learners' achievement for a variety of purposes. The crucial issues are how to determine these purposes, and then, how to find ways in which the information can be gathered and presented in a form which meets the requirements of multiple audiences.*

This chapter outlines an approach to language assessment which has the potential to serve a range of different purposes at the classroom, school and system level (Mincham 1992). The ESL Student Needs Assessment Procedures described below have drawn on systemic functional linguistics in order to provide ESL and mainstream teachers with a mechanism for assessing and reporting on the English language development of students from non-English speaking backgrounds in mainstream school contexts from junior primary to senior secondary level. The procedures go some way towards addressing the need that has existed for an assessment tool which is able to assist teachers in analysing students' English language performance in a range of common oral and written activities across the curriculum. As Mincham (1990, 1992) notes, in contrast to conventional assessment methods such as standardised testing, the approach taken is integrally linked to and supportive of the teaching and learning process and information obtained through the procedures is able to be used in a number of ways.

At the classroom level, the procedures can be used to provide diagnostic information about students' on-going learning needs. This type of information is essential if teachers are to make appropriate decisions not only about modes of support, but also about the types of learning activities that they will provide. The information also serves as a basis for giving students clear and understandable targets for language learning, together with explicit feedback about their progress and, particularly, about the ways in which they can improve their performance. Students can be encouraged to become directly involved in the assessment process through adaptation of the procedures for use in self and peer group learning activities. In this way greater responsibility can be given to students in managing and evaluating their own learning.

At the school level, the procedures provide a consistent framework for reporting on students' English language development across the curriculum. In using the procedures, opportunities also exist for ESL and mainstream teachers to collaborate in the assessment process, thus developing shared understandings of the language demands of different learning tasks across the curriculum.

At the system level, the procedures allow for the aggregation of assessment information, thus having the potential to be used for a range of purposes, including program evaluation and decision-making related to resource allocation.

Rationale for the development of the ESL Student Needs Assessment Procedures (SNAP)

The impetus for the development of the Student Needs Assessment Procedures came from a review of the ESL Program conducted by the South Australian Education Department in 1987. One of the review findings, which related to the provision of resourcing for ESL students within the General Support element of the Program, indicated that the needs of many students were not being met under the existing criteria used to allocate specialist ESL staff to mainstream primary and secondary schools. In the South Australian context, ESL staffing provision is made on the basis of length of residency of all students from non-English speaking backgrounds.

According to the criteria, students who have been in Australia for less than one year are staffed at a ratio of one full-time equivalent teacher (FTE) to twenty students; students who have been in Australia between one and five years are staffed at a ratio of one FTE teacher to thirty-six students and those who have been in Australia for more than five years, including those who were born here but have either or both parents from non-English speaking backgrounds, are staffed at a ratio of one FTE teacher to 200 students. Schools which have a high percentage of government assisted students receive a small additional weighting to these figures as part of the Education Department's Social Justice strategy. The majority of students in the first category are eligible for and attend intensive English Language Centres across the Adelaide metropolitan area for periods of up to twelve months. These centres cater for primary and secondary students and adults wishing to re-enter the schooling system. Secondary-aged students who have experienced severely disrupted schooling and who, as a consequence, have low levels of literacy in their first language are given the option of spending an additional twelve months in an intensive program. Recently-arrived students who are unable to attend such programs are supported in their local school by mainstream staff or by ESL staff if they are available. Some bilingual school assistant support may be provided in such cases.

The needs of recently-arrived ESL students are quite well served within this system, however, the needs of those who are longer term residents, most particularly those who were born in Australia, but who come to school speaking little or no English, are a cause for some concern under such arrangements. Clearly, the language and learning needs of such students cannot easily be equated with length of residency. Systems should acknowledge the fact that ESL students bring to the learning situation, a range of needs which operate together in complex ways to affect the language learning process. Factors identified by Campbell and McMeniman (1985) which are likely to influence schooling outcomes include:

- students' previous language learning experiences i.e. language and literacy development in the first language, and in English as well as in other languages;

- educational background, including disruptions to schooling;

- personal, social and economic factors such as motivation, physical and emotional well-being and socio-economic circumstances.

As Mincham (1992:42) notes, the inadequacy of residency-based criteria for determining specialist support becomes most obvious when we consider the case of students who were born in Australia but who enter the schooling system with similar English language learning needs to those who are recently-arrived and yet who are eligible for support at a ratio which is only one tenth of that provided for students in the New Arrivals Program. Similarly at risk are secondary-aged students who enter the schooling system with limited English **and** with minimal literacy in their first language.

Research findings

Longitudinal studies conducted by Virginia Collier in the United States of America (1987) provided empirical evidence which supported the South Australian ESL Program's Review findings. Collier's research followed-up earlier work by Skutnabb-Kangas and Toukomaa (1976) in Sweden and by Cummins (1981, 1984) in Canada which indicated that immigrant children appeared to attain reasonable fluency in English for everyday, communicative purposes within one or two years but remained significantly below their peers in academic performance for a much longer period. This research led Cummins (1979) to distinguish between ESL students' English language performance in terms of conversational fluency and academic proficiency; the distinction being commonly referred to as BICS (Basic Interpersonal Communication Skills) and CALP (Cognitive Academic Language Proficiency). Collier's research compared the achievement of upper-middle class immigrant students in mainstream programs compared with their English-speaking counterparts. Results on standard performance tests in key curriculum areas revealed significant differences between the two groups, with the majority of ESL students needing between four and eight years to reach the fiftieth percentile. While acknowledging the limitations of such standardised tests (e.g. among other things, they measure only limited aspects of language proficiency and impose potentially difficult time constraints on students), Collier nevertheless felt that they were able to provide useful information about students' English language performance in mainstream contexts. She further investigated the relative disadvantage of particular groups of ESL students, and found that the five to seven year old and twelve to fifteen year old age groups appeared to be most at risk.

This research bears out what teachers in the Australian context have been able to identify from their own experience; viz., that while many students from non-English speaking backgrounds appear reasonably confident and fluent in the informal, face-to-face interactions of the classroom and playground, without support, they are often unable to successfully negotiate the types of language tasks required for learning in subject areas such as the physical and social sciences, particularly in relation to tasks which involve the production of written texts. The difficulties students face in these areas can be in some way explained when we come to understand something of the differences between the ways in which subject disciplines construct and represent knowledge as well as the similarities and differences which exist between spoken and written language.

It has been largely due to the work of theorists and applied linguists in the area of systemic functional linguistics (Halliday, Hasan, Martin, Painter and others) that we have recently begun to understand how these differences are realised in practice. In addition, the work of researchers such as Biber (1986), who analysed a large corpus of spoken and written textual material in order to uncover the basic dimensions underlying textual variation, has been important in contributing further to our understanding of the linguistic characteristics of different classroom tasks. The significance of this recent work, in relation to Collier's findings is that it highlights the need for assessment processes which are able to adequately describe ESL students' performance in the types of cognitively and linguistically demanding tasks that are required in the subject classroom at all levels of schooling.

Description and analysis of the development process: stages in the development of SNAP

Initial planning phase

Examining the research of Collier and Cummins in relation to ESL students' achievement in mainstream classrooms constituted one aspect of the preliminary work of the project. As Mincham (1990:11) reports, further literature-based research was carried out in order to clarify issues in relation to second language acquisition, the assessment of language proficiency, and the role of assessment in the curriculum process. An evaluation was undertaken of existing needs-based identification procedures used in other systems nationally. The evaluation report concluded that the adoption of the procedures investigated would be inappropriate for the South Australian context, principally because of practical issues concerning the much larger cohort of students involved. A survey of existing assessment and reporting practices in the South Australian ESL Program R–12 was also carried out. This revealed a diversity of understanding about assessment issues on the part of ESL teachers generally. At primary level, approaches to assessment practice involved mainly informal methods directed towards the assessment of what Brindley (1989:17) calls 'Level 3' achievement, emphasising 'structural' proficiency or 'the ability to manipulate the sub-systems of the second language'. At secondary level, assessment methods tended to be more formalised and performance-oriented, influenced no doubt by the type of assessment practices required in ESL and other publicly-examined and school-assessed subjects accredited by the Senior Secondary Assessment Board of South Australia. It is fair to say that, in the initial stages of the project, debate about assessment issues was only just beginning to have an impact at the school level since teachers were generally not as well informed about assessment as they are today. Recent changes in attitudes towards assessment as well as in approaches to assessment practice have largely been the result of major systemic initiatives at both state and national level. These include, at state level, the AWRITE Program, the Attainment Levels Project, the Writing and Reading Assessment Program survey at Years Six and Ten, and the compulsory Writing-based Literacy Assessment at Year 11 as part of the South Australian Certificate of Education. At national level, the development and trialling of national subject profiles is also now beginning to have a significant impact, as are initiatives outside of the school sector including proposals for competency-based assessment in the post-compulsory years.

The final part of the initial planning stage of the project was to establish mechanisms for the development of the procedures and the trialling processes to follow. The importance of an interactive approach to development was highlighted in recognition of current understandings about the nature of curriculum change. Issues affecting the implementation of curriculum initiatives at the broad systemic level are discussed in detail by Brindley and Hood

(1990:241–245) who suggest that the following guiding principles for curriculum change taken from Fullan (1982) could be applied in any language program context.

- *For a change to get underway, there has to be an educational need on a political agenda.*

- *Rational argument alone will not bring about change.*

- *Individuals need to experience the change personally.*

- *The intentions of proponents of curriculum change will frequently be misunderstood.*

- *The social and political climate in which change takes place will significantly affect the extent of the implementation.*

- *Curriculum implementation requires adequate support and coordination.*

- *Successful change requires on-going professional development.*

- *Innovations need local advocates.*

At the systemic level, the ESL Review findings had set a very clear agenda for change in the way assessment issues were being addressed within the ESL Program, particularly in regard to the collection of data for potential resourcing purposes. While ESL teachers were generally supportive of a move to needs-based resourcing, the implications of this for assessment practice at the classroom level were not well understood. Several major conferences were held in metropolitan and country areas to raise ESL teachers' awareness of assessment issues generally and to provide a forum for consideration of the Review's proposals and their implications. Issues discussed related to the nature of the assessment process including: the range of purposes and methods for assessment; issues of standard-setting and the likely practical implications for classroom teachers, including future training and development needs and the role of the ESL teacher in the future assessment process. To provide system level support, a reference group was established consisting of representatives of school-based personnel, including principals and teachers, and Departmental representatives, including ESL Program administrators.

For the major development stage of the project, an interactive process was proposed which would involve the Curriculum Officer responsible for the management of the project working collaboratively with mainstream and ESL teachers from a range of different situations, including the independent schools sector. In the final analysis, more than ninety ESL and mainstream teachers have been involved in the development and trialling processes in some way, operating where possible in a partnership model so that the understandings that teachers have gained through working on the project can be supported and further developed on their return to the classroom. This process has been an important means of providing on-going training and development in the area of assessment as well as ensuring a source of local advocacy of the procedures at the school and classroom level.

At all stages of the process, teachers working on the development of the procedures have been supported through the availability of teacher release time. This has enabled those interested in the project's work to participate in its development without the added burden of having to counter-balance this with classroom responsibilities. Through negotiations with TESOL Departments at tertiary level, teachers have also had the opportunity to have their contributions accredited to postgraduate studies. This has not only been an important incentive for teachers to become involved in the project, but it has also given some formal recognition to the valuable contribution they have been able to make. Again, it signifies an important link between the work of the schools sector and tertiary institutions in supporting initiatives for development and change.

Factors influencing the design of the assessment procedures

Through the processes outlined in the initial planning phase, several key principles were identified which were to guide the development of the assessment procedures. These have been summarised as follows:

Assessment should be an integral part of the curriculum process

Consistent with South Australian Education Department practices, the assessment procedures should be an integral part of the curriculum process, not something external to it. As indicated earlier, the development and implementation of the procedures should follow a collaborative model, which would mean that the procedures should be derived as far as possible from existing good classroom practice and, that schools and teachers should be involved in the collection and analysis of data for reporting purposes. In this way the development and implementation processes should serve a useful professional development function, both in informing program planning and in enabling classroom teachers at all levels to become more active and skilled participants in the assessment process.

Language assessment should reflect an underlying model of language

The concept of language 'proficiency' underpinning the work of the project has been described in terms of students' performance in using English for particular purposes in the context of mainstream schooling: a model of language in use. As Dwyer notes (1992:29), 'authentic assessment of language performance demands a search for authentic contexts and cross–curricular emphases'. In attempting to refine this construct then, the need to be able to adequately define teachers' expectations about students' language performance was to become a key factor in the development process. Working groups needed to be mindful of the range of purposes for which students use English across the curriculum given the fact that, in learning English and in using English to learn, they are actively engaged in:

> *using language to widen their networks of interpersonal relations; to gain access to, process and use information; to think critically; to reflect; and to express themselves creatively and imaginatively.*
>
> (SAED ESL Curriculum Guidelines 1990 —
> adapted from Scarino et al. 1988)

Format for the procedures

A portfolio approach

Given the above principles, it was decided to adopt a portfolio approach to the assessment process. As Mincham (1992:42) notes:

> *This would be compatible with many teachers' existing assessment practices and would allow them both to gather information over a period of time and to report on it for resourcing purposes in mid-year if required.*

As already indicated, in order to assess 'real' language in use, the procedures would need to be based on authentic classroom activities. A strong practical imperative for this lay in the fact that, in many school situations where ESL specialist teachers were either not available or were on fractional appointments, the assessment procedures would need to be conducted by mainstream teachers in the course of their normal activities. The procedures would therefore need to be seen by teachers to be a relevant and useful addition to their programs.

What should the portfolio include?

In deciding what should be included in the portfolio, it was necessary to be able to specify teachers' expectations of the English language demands of the various curriculum areas at different year levels. To do so, working parties of ESL and mainstream teachers were asked to undertake a detailed investigation of what they considered students needed to be able to do to be successful in the school curriculum. At the same time they were asked to identify the types of learning activities commonly engaged in across curriculum areas at different year levels. The model used for this investigation was an adaptation of the basic framework of the Australian Language Levels Guidelines (1989) which categorises language use into three domains: interpersonal, informational and aesthetic. This framework was intended to ensure that an appropriate balance of language use would be reflected in the assessment activities required for inclusion in the portfolio, at different year levels. The incorporation of activities with a high degree of linguistic and cognitive complexity was also an important consideration. In completing their investigation, teachers drew on departmental curriculum documents from each of the eight required areas of study as well as on their own classroom practice. The resulting statement of 'essential learnings' provided key contextual information for the next stage of the development process.

Guidelines for the collection and analysis of students' work: the development of draft assessment exemplars

For this stage of the project, working parties of ESL and mainstream teachers were convened to develop draft activity-based assessment exemplars which teachers could use as a guide for the collection and analysis of students' work for inclusion in the portfolio. These exemplars drew on the 'essential learnings' statements and reflected a range of oral and written language use across the interpersonal, informational and aesthetic domains. As noted in the introduction, only oral and written activities have been included in the assessment procedures.

The assessment of reading and listening, in addition to other aspects of students' learning, such as attitudes and strategies for learning is, however, considered to be an important part of any assessment program and teachers are encouraged to include their own observations or records of these aspects in students' portfolios. The draft exemplars which were developed were topic or theme-based. Each exemplar stated the specific language objectives which it was designed to assess and contained specifications for the conduct of the procedures as well as detailed assessment criteria.

Initial trialling

Trialling of the draft materials was then carried out by a further group of teachers state-wide. The results of the trialling indicated the need for changes to the way in which the draft exemplars were formulated. As indicated previously, the draft assessment activities had been intended for use as exemplars, not as standard assessment tasks. It had been hoped that teachers in mainstream classrooms would be able to use the activities as models on which to base assessment tasks relevant to their own programs. This proved to be problematic and an alternative, more generalisable framework was sought. In addition, teachers commented on the need to focus more explicitly on the development of criteria which would show how language is shaped according to the context of its use.

Re-drafting: the adoption of a genre-based approach

In order to address these issues, current genre-based approaches to language teaching were explored and an associate program of in-service devised for the working groups. These approaches are grounded in systemic theory which recognises the central role that language plays in the construction of meaning. Systemic theory views language not simply as a means of 'conveying' ideas and information which somehow exist as separate and independent entities; rather language is seen to be the principal means by which we organise and shape our world (Christie 1990:8).

The context of culture

Because language is viewed as a social phenomenon, the ways in which different cultures characteristically construct and interpret meanings vary one from another. While many similarities exist across cultures in terms of the social purposes for which language is used, the ways in which such purposes are realised may vary considerably. (Halliday 1978, 1985a, 1985b; Halliday and Hasan 1985; Martin 1985.) A commonly quoted example of this is the 'shopping exchange' which, in Western cultures, has a very different set of features from that of more 'traditional' cultures in which barter is an essential aspect of goods and services transactions. Each culture, then, has formulated its own ways of achieving particular social purposes through spoken or written language. Such culturally formulated activities are commonly referred to as 'genres'.

The context of situation

Within cultures, language varies not only according to the particular purpose for which it is used, but also according to the specific context in which it occurs. Halliday and Hasan (1985:12) identify three key variables which influence the language choices people make in order to construct and negotiate meaning in socially and culturally appropriate ways. These factors include the experiences they wish to represent (i.e. the field of discourse), the interpersonal relationships that are involved (i.e. tenor of discourse) and the role that language plays in the particular situation, including whether the text is spoken or written (i.e. the mode of discourse).

In Halliday's (1982) view, systemic linguistic theory has much to offer those working in the educational context. Halliday (1982:202) argues that what teachers need is a functional grammar which, 'interprets language as a resource, and specifically as a **resource for meaning**'. Unlike traditional, formal approaches to grammar which are rule-oriented, syntactic in focus and tend to analyse texts at the sentence level rather than at the whole text level, a functional grammar is able to analyse how language is actually **used** by mapping systems of choice.

In discussing text, context and learning, Halliday and Hasan (1985:44–45) point out that:

> *To be able to read a text, or listen to it, effectively and with understanding, we have to be able to interpret it in terms of all (these) metafunctions (the meaning of metafunction being 'that part of the system of a language — the particular semantic and lexico-grammatical resources — that has evolved to perform the function in question'). In other words, anyone who is listening to a teacher, or reading a textbook, has to:*

1a. *understand the processes being referred to, the participants in these processes, and the circumstances — time, cause, etc. — associated with them (experiential);*

1b. *understand the relationship between one process and another or one participant and another, that share the same position in the text (logical);*

2. *recognise the speech function, the type of offer, command, statement or question, the attitudes and judgments embodied in it, and the rhetorical features that constitute it as a symbolic act (interpersonal); and,*

3. *grasp the news value and topicality of the message, and the coherence between one part of the text and every other part (textual).*

In applying systemic functional grammar to the educational context, applied linguists and educators such as Martin (1985), Christie (1990), Painter (1990), Rothery (1989), Derewianka (1990) and others have been able to develop a powerful tool for the analysis of written texts in a range of curriculum areas. The genre-based approaches to the teaching of writing which were being developed particularly by the Language and Social Power Project of the NSW Disadvantaged Schools Program (Callaghan and Rothery 1988) served as a useful model for the redevelopment of the SNAP assessment exemplars. They were particularly exciting for the insights they were able to provide into the language demands of different factual genres across the curriculum.

Following this model, the working parties of ESL and mainstream teachers began by identifying the types of genres which appeared most commonly in the statements of 'essential learnings' they had previously developed. This analysis revealed a similar trend to that shown in early classroom research conducted in NSW by Martin, Rothery and others, viz., that students, especially in primary schools, were writing mainly recounts of personal experience and narratives. The types of factual writing which represent the powerful texts in the academic curriculum, through which information is shaped and exchanged and through which opinions are expressed, were not being explicitly taught. (See Martin 1992 for discussion of these issues.) Based on this information, the working parties reformulated the range of activities to be included in students' assessment portfolios, making sure that there was an appropriate balance of oral and written genres, reflecting 'real' curriculum demands at different year levels (see Figure 1).

Folio suggestions for general assessment and reporting purposes include any combination of the following:

Folio requirements for resourcing purposes include the following:

Reception — Year 2

Oral: 2 samples taken from:
- Retelling a story
- Activity-sharing
- Morning talks

Written: 2 samples made up of:
- Recount <u>and</u>
- Report <u>or</u>
- Procedure

Years 3 - 4

Oral: 2 samples taken from
- Retelling a story
- Activity-sharing
- News

Written: 2 samples made up of:
- Report [required] <u>and</u>
- Narrative <u>or</u>
- Procedure

Years 5 - 7

Oral: 2 samples taken from:
- Retelling a story
- Reporting on a process
- Giving an opinion

Written: 3 samples made up of:
- Recount [required] <u>and</u>
- Hortatory Argument [required]
- <u>and</u> Narrative
- <u>or</u> Report

N.B. Moderated samples of responses for Year 5 - 7 reports are not available at this time, but some guidance may be offered for rating purposes in the comments accompanying the Year 3 - 4 samples.

Figure 1 Suggested assessment activities for student portfolios

---

Years 8 - 12

* required Years 8 - 9
** required Year 10
*** required Years 11 - 12

Oral: 2 samples taken from the suggested list of activites.

Written: 3 samples to be taken from at least 2 curriculum areas.
              The 3 different activities should be selected from the
              following list:
                           • Explanation *
                           • Narrative
                           • Recount
                           • Analytical argument **
                           • Science experiment
                           • Report
                           • Discussion***

N.B. Samples of student responses to specific oral activities for Years 8 - 12 are not available at this time. Instead, a checklist of criteria and a suggested list of activities has been included on which oral assessments can be based.

Because of the intertextual nature of many secondary activities, several genres may occur in any one activity. The activities provided as part of the moderated samples have been selected to cover as wide a range as possible of typical secondary learning tasks and offer a guide to the selection of an appropriate range of student work for inclusion in the folio.

Figure 1 Cont. Suggested assessment activities for student portfolios

Teacher support materials

Detailed descriptions of written text features and accompanying assessment proformas

To assist teachers in working with the genre-based approach, detailed descriptions of a range of written texts were developed, including analysed samples drawn from cross curriculum areas (see Figure 2). Assessment proformas were also drawn up for each genre to assist teachers in assessing the students' work (see

---

DESCRIPTION OF WRITTEN TEXT FEATURES:
HORTATORY ARGUMENT

Purpose
An hortatory argument is a factual genre which is used to *persuade* the reader *to* agree with a proposal put forward by the author i.e. the Thesis. It is usually directed toward seeking change or exhorting action. It is more people oriented than an analytical argument and more active through an appeal to people's emotions and what they see, feel, think and say. An hortatory argument has one point of view as opposed to a discussion which presents both sides of an issue (e.g. letters to the editor, political speeches, debates, sermons etc.).

N.B. The choice between hortatory or analytical argument will be determined by the audience and purpose for writing (e.g. a book review written for a teenage magazine may be more hortatory as opposed to a book review written for a reputable newspaper which may be more analytical).

Schematic Structure
- **Opening statement:**
  - presents information about the current state of affairs
  - previews the issue
  - highlights its significance
- **Thesis:** a statement of position (may be included in the Opening Statement)
- **Arguments:** a range of arguments, with appropriate evidence, is presented to support the thesis or position statement. They are presented in a way which evokes people's emotions and which appeal directly to the reader, challenging her/his perceptions and inviting responses
- **Summary:** a restatement of the arguments to support the thesis and may include an appeal for action

Language Features

> **FIELD**
>
> - **Participants** - focus is on *specific* participants (e.g. The Australian Conservation Foundation, Mr. Walker) and *generalised* participants (e.g. human beings, crops), both human and non-human. When people are referred to it is usually as individuals rather than as professionals (experts).
>
> - **Nominal Groups** - expanded nominal groups are used to give factual information about nouns/things in the text and tend to serve a classifying function (the noun/thing is underlined):
>   e.g. our conservation goals
>   e.g. endangered Australian wildlife
>   e.g. Australia's shameful kangaroo slaughter
>   **(refer to Nominalisation)**
>
> - **Topic specific/technical vocabulary** is used but to a lesser extent than in analytical arguments (e.g. moratorium, conservationists, species)
>
> - **Processes (verbs)** - a range of processes is used, particularly:
>   - *material (action) processes* which relate actions and happenings (e.g. slaughtered, kills, has destroyed)
>   - *verbal processes* which refer to what people say (e.g. agrees, question, are talking)
>   - *mental processes* which refer to what people perceive, think or feel (e.g. believe, like, is concerned, fear,)
>   - *relational processes* which show attribute, identity or possession (e.g. is, features, depends)
>
> - **Circumstances** — circumstantial elements are used to give information about processes (verbs) i.e. the how, when, where, why, with whom etc. (e.g. in May 1985… often painfully… without conscience… during the latest severe drought)

Figure 2   Description of written text features: hortatory argument

TENOR

- **Person** *first, second* and *third* person is used throughout the text. First person pronouns (e.g. we, our) are used frequently to engage the reader thus personalising the text. A sense of ambiguity is also created i.e. does 'we' refer to the author only or the author and reader?

- **Language** is used:
    - to establish a more participatory, interactive writer/reader relationship i.e. of equal to equal
    - in an interactive way through using rhetorical questions, making suggestions and inviting responses (e.g. Can we afford to ignore this destruction of our national symbol?)
    - to evoke people's emotions, attitudes, feelings etc. (e.g. 'killing our kangaroos' as opposed to 'culling the kangaroo population')
    - (optional) poetically through use of literary devices such as alliteration, repetition, metaphor etc. (e.g. trusting targets… grim harvest of death… And is not our nation's pride at risk?)

- **Modality** is used to express obligation on the part of both author and reader. The modal is linked with a personal pronoun (e.g. we must… we need to…) which establishes a relationship of solidarity/equal status with the author.

- **Intensification (emphasis)** of certain points is made through grammatical parallelism (e.g. And what are the implications for the rest of nature, for the bush, for the land, for other animals, for our fellow human beings?) which is a typical oral rhetorical device.

MODE

- **Theme (the first piece of information in a sentence/clause)** is used to structure the text and highlight significant aspects of the message. Varied use of:
    - *human participants* (e.g. We must take action… Australians cannot afford to ignore… Our own Prime Minister recently stated…)
    - *conjunctions* that show logical relationships within the text and which are representative of spoken language (e.g. But we are still unwilling to recognize… Yet this is not the first time… And yet our politicians continue to… So in the end they are ignored.)
    - *nominalised processes (verbs)* occurring in expanded nominal groups (e.g. Many Australian conservationists are aware of the need to… Monitoring of population size is carried out regularly…)
    N.B. Occurs less frequently than in analytical arguments.

- **Nominalisation** is used to pack more information into the text and sequence/structure the information. This is done by changing processes (verbs), adjectives etc. into nouns/things:
    e.g. People are indiscriminately killing our wildlife and it must be stopped.
    e.g. The indiscriminate killing of our wildlife must be stopped.
    N.B. Nominalisation is used to a lesser extent in hortatory than in analytical arguments because the argument is developed in a more interactive, 'spoken' kind of way.

Figure 2 Cont. Description of written text features: hortatory argument

Continued over page

- **Tense** varies according to different stages in the text:
  e.g. Mr Walker <u>announced</u> that the bans would stay in force.
  e.g. We <u>are talking</u> here about something far more serious than a few isolated cases.
  e.g. We <u>must take</u> action before it is too late!

- **Passive voice** is used to manipulate what is placed at the beginning of the clause i.e. put in Theme position. In hortatory arguments passive voice tends to be used to focus on things rather than people and consequently features less in hortatory than in analytical arguments:
  e.g. The ban <u>was lifted</u>.   **(refer to Theme)**

- **Conjunctions** to show logical relationships are mainly:
  - *additive* to include extra information (e.g. and, besides, or, secondly)
  - *temporal* to do with time (e.g. when, now that, since then, as long as)
  - *causal-conditional (consequential)* to show reason (e.g. although, in spite of, however)
  - *elaborative* to exemplify or clarify meaning (e.g. in fact, that is, for example)

- **Complex clauses** are used to provide information and help structure the text (processes are underlined):
  e.g. The Foundation is concerned about the killing of kangaroos and the export pressures [which <u>have built up</u>] [<u>to exploit</u> this species during the latest severe drought.]
  e.g. [When our prime wildlife <u>is killed</u> on such a scale], what are the implications for the rest of our environment?
  e.g. We must take stock of this horrific assault on our wildlife, [whether or not we <u>accept</u> this point of view].

- **Reference items** are used to refer to something previously mentioned in or beyond the text and hence 'hold the text together' (e.g. these, them, this, it's). *Substitution* and *ellipsis* are other means of doing this.
                                                                     (refer to Glossary)

Figure 2 Cont. Description of written text features: hortatory argument

Figure 3 for an example). The proformas contained detailed criteria relating to the schematic structure and language features of the text as well as to aspects such as accuracy and, in the case of the oral activities, what was termed 'communication skills'. In order that the assessment information could be aggregated for system's purposes, a rising scale of one to five was included on each proforma. Teachers were asked to assign a global rating based on their judgment of a student's overall performance on the task.

Finally, guidelines were drawn up for the implementation of the procedures. These guidelines included a Learner Background Profile, together with suggested strategies for identifying students from non-English speaking backgrounds who would then be assessed. As Mincham (1992:42) notes:

Primary Written Language Assessment Activity — ***ARGUMENT***
(Hortatory : persuading to)

Name of Student: **Year Level:** **Class:** **Date:**

Task: **Context:**

Description of activity: The focus is on *persuading* the reader *to* agree with a proposal (i.e. Thesis) put forward by the author. An hortatory argument presents one point of view and is usually directed towards seeking change or exhorting action. It does so through an appeal to emotion rather than to reason and logic, evoking what people see, feel, think and say. Examples include: letters to the editor, articles, advertisements.

Criteria (Tick appropriate box) N.B.: * indicates upper primary level — beginning only at middle primary level	Very competent	Competent	Limited competence	Not evident	Comments
Degree of support required. Did the student:					
• complete the task independently, i.e. with minimal support					
Schematic Structure. Did the student:					
• * make an opening statement previewing the issue					
• make a position statement, i.e. Thesis					
• present relevant arguments to support the position statement					
• support the arguments with appropriate evidence					
• anticipate and refute an opposing viewpoint (optional)					
• summarise evidence and (optional) make an appeal for action					
Language Features. Did the student:					
• focus on specific and generalised participants, e.g. the ban, nets **[F]**					
• use expanded nominal groups, e.g. the **pollution** of our rivers **[F]**					
• use topic-specific/technical vocabulary, e.g. habitat **[F]**					
• use a range of verbs/processes, e.g. is, kill, say, feel, believe **[F]**					
• use a range of circumstances, e.g. how, when, where, why **[F]**					
• vary use of person, e.g. I, we, he, she, they, you **[T]**					
• use language in a personal and interactive way:					
– writer as 'equal', making suggestions/inviting responses **[T]**					
– attitudinal words to evoke emotions, e.g. slaughter, horrific **[T]**					
– literary devices, e.g. alliteration, repetition, etc. (optional) **[T]**					
• use modality to express obligation, e.g. 'we **must**...' **[T]**					
• use mainly human participants and/or conjunctions in Theme position, e.g. '**But we** are worried that...', '**Ms Cox** claims...' **[M]**					
• * use nominalisation, e.g. 'The **production** of wood chips' **[M]**					
• use appropriate tense, e.g. is, used, has, led, will show **[M]**					
• use a range of conjunctions, e.g. and, but, so, yet, although **[M]**					
• * use complex clauses, e.g. 'Rabbit numbers **which are now estimated to be x** will reach...', '**To address this issue** we...' **[M]**					
• use reference items, substitution, ellipsis, e.g. this, its **[M]**					
Accuracy. Did the student:					
• use verbs/tense accurately, e.g. 'There is pollution' not 'There has pollution', 'It is bad' not 'It bad', 'has occurred' not 'has occur'					
• use agreement accurately, e.g. subject-verb, plurals					
• use syntax accurately, i.e. word order (without omissions)					
• use the following accurately (without omissions)					
– articles, e.g. the, a, an					
– prepositions, e.g. 'the parks in our area' not 'at our area'					
– adverbs/adjectives, e.g. 'growing quickly' not 'growing quick'					
• spell accurately					
• use punctuation accurately					
• * use paragraphs appropriately					

General Comments

Global Rating: (Circle) lowest 1 2 3 4 5 highest
[i.e. ability to write appropriately for purpose and audience]

Figure 3 Primary written language assessment activity

> *For resourcing purposes, the procedures require an assessment to be made of the language needs of each student for whom English is a second language, not just those who are recently-arrived or who stand out as needing support. In some cases, children's needs are not identified as being language-related in the first instance, but are thought to be caused by specific learning difficulties or to be the result of poor motivation or behaviour problems.*

Further trialling

The redeveloped exemplars were trialled in a range of schools by mainstream and ESL teachers. Samples of students' performance were gathered from the full range of students including English background speakers. Oral language samples were audio-taped and later transcribed. These oral and written samples were assessed and rated individually by teachers. During the rating process, teachers were asked to comment on the format of the proformas, as well as on the criteria and to suggest possible changes. These suggestions were incorporated into the final proformas. When individual marking was completed, a group moderation process was used to ensure consistency in the final ratings given. These moderated samples will become an important part of the final assessment package, serving as a means of standard-setting, ensuring commonality of teacher expectations across locations and across the range of teacher experience and expertise.

Some comments on the procedures

While not yet formally implemented, the draft procedures are currently being used by many mainstream and ESL teachers for general assessment and reporting purposes in classroom contexts at primary and secondary level. A number of teachers have commented on the usefulness of the procedures, indicating that, by making explicit the criteria to be used in the assessment of a range of typical classroom activities, they have provided teachers with valuable tools for analysing the English language performance of **all** students, not just those from non-English speaking backgrounds.

The following comments by teachers (Mincham 1992:45) involved in the development and trialling processes reflect some of the positive aspects of this approach to assessment.

Focus on a predetermined set of criteria helped me in becoming more aware of learners' individual needs.

Without the criteria it was easy to revert to assessing surface features such as spelling, rather than (focusing) on the ways in which students are learning to make meaning.

The focus on genre-based activities was relevant to primary classroom activities and easy to fit in.

I recognised some characteristics of individual children I hadn't quite been able to put my finger on before.

Decided I must do more oral work, particularly in small groups.

I now have higher expectations of what young children are capable of achieving in a range of writing.

In terms of training and development, the approach taken in the Student Needs Assessment Procedures has been supported by several state-wide conferences on literacy, genre and social justice organised as a joint ESL initiative by the state and independent schools' systems. In addition, a genre-based approach to the teaching of writing has been incorporated in a major training and development initiative of the ESL Program (the ESL in the Mainstream Teacher Development Course) which has provided in-service to more than 2000 mainstream teachers to date. Future initiatives which will support on-going assessment work, include a proposal for a functional grammar course for teachers in the ESL Program.

Conclusion

The approach taken to language assessment outlined in this chapter has attempted to address the need for assessment procedures which are capable of serving a range of purposes at classroom, school and system level. Brindley (1989:44) suggests that there are a number of key characteristics that are essential if assessment procedures are to inform teachers' decision-making, be useful in reporting on students' achievements and provide evidence of the outcomes of learning for accountability purposes. To fulfil these three requirements, procedures should be explicit, criterion-referenced, standardised, relevant and task-based. The ESL Student Needs Assessment Procedures exhibit such characteristics.

The procedures have already proved to be a powerful tool in achieving curriculum change. Through participation in the development and trialling processes, teachers have had opportunities to re-evaluate their classroom practice and to experiment with a range of factual writing at all year levels. They have been actively engaged in assessing students' performance in a range of activities in very specific ways. Through this process both teachers and students have come to a clearer understanding of how language can be used as a resource for making meaning in socially and culturally appropriate ways, particularly in the context of the 'valued' school curriculum. In becoming aware of the ways in which language can be constructed for particular purposes in particular social contexts within a culture, students are being 'apprenticed' into that culture. As Christie (1990:1–22) points out, in becoming sensitive to the ways in which a society transmits its attitudes, values and beliefs through language, students have the potential to critically evaluate those attitudes, values and beliefs; to think, create, question and so move society beyond its present bounds.

References

Bachman, L.F. 1990. *Fundamental considerations in language testing.* Oxford: Oxford University Press.

Biber, D. 1986. Spoken and written textual dimensions in English: resolving the contradictory findings. *Language* 62:384–414.

Brindley, G. 1986. *The assessment of second language proficiency: issues and approaches.* Adelaide: National Curriculum Resource Centre.

Brindley, G. 1989. *Assessing achievement in the learner-centred curriculum.* Sydney: National Centre for English Language Teaching and Research.

Brindley, G. and S. Hood. 1990. Curriculum innovation in adult ESL. In G. Brindley (ed.) *The second language curriculum in action.* Sydney: National Centre for English Language Teaching and Research.

Callaghan, M. and J. Rothery. 1988. *Teaching factual writing: a genre-based approach.* Sydney: Metropolitan East Disadvantaged Schools' Program Literacy Project.

Campbell, W.J. and M. McMeniman. 1984. *A review of the Commonwealth ESL Program.* Canberra: Commonwealth Schools Commission.

Christie, F. 1990. The changing face of literacy. In F. Christie (ed.) *Literacy for a changing world.* Hawthorn: ACER.

Collier, V. 1987. Age and rate of acquisition of second language for academic purposes. *TESOL Quarterly* 21, 4:617–641.

Cummins, J. 1979. Cognitive/academic language proficiency, linguistic interdependence, the optimum age question and some other matters. *Working Papers on Bilingualism* 19:121–129.

Cummins, J. 1981. Age on arrival and immigrant second language learning in Canada: a reassessment. *Applied Linguistics* 2:132–149.

Cummins, J. 1984. *Bilingualism and special education: issues in assessment and pedagogy.* Clevedon, England: Multilingual Matters.

Cummins, J. 1991. Conversational and academic language proficiency in bilingual contexts. In J.H. Hulstijn and J.F. Matter (eds) Reading in two languages. *AILA Review* 8:75–89.

Cummins, J. and M. Swain. 1986. *Bilingualism in education: aspects of theory, research and practice.* London: Longman.

Derewianka, B. 1990. *Exploring how texts work.* NSW: Primary English Teachers Association.

Dwyer, J. 1992. System-wide assessment: profiling performance in literacy evaluation. In C. Bouffler (ed.) *Issues and practicalities.* NSW: Primary English Teachers Association.

Fullan, M. 1982. *The meaning of educational change.* Toronto: Ontario Institute for Studies in Education.

Halliday, M.A.K. 1978. *Language as a social semiotic: the social interpretation of language and meaning*. London: Edward Arnold.

Halliday, M.A.K. 1982. A grammar for schools. *Australian Journal of Reading* 5, 4:202–205.

Halliday, M.A.K. 1985a. *Spoken and written language*. Geelong: Deakin University Press.

Halliday, M.A.K. 1985b. *An introduction to functional grammar*. London: Edward Arnold.

Halliday, M.A.K. and R. Hasan. 1985. *Language, context and text: aspects of language in a social-semiotic perspective*. Geelong: Deakin University Press.

Martin, J.R. 1985. *Factual writing: exploring and challenging social reality*. Geelong: Deakin University Press.

Martin, J.R. and P. Peters. 1985. On the analysis of exposition. In R. Hasan (ed.) *Discourse on discourse*. Occasional Papers No. 7. Applied Linguistics Association of Australia.

Martin, J.R. 1992. *English text: system and structure*. Amsterdam and Philadelphia: Benjamins.

Mincham, L. 1990. *Draft ESL student needs assessment procedures R–12*. Adelaide: SA Education Department.

Mincham, L. 1992. Assessing the English language needs of ESL students. In C. Bouffler (ed.) *Literacy evaluation: issues and practicalities*. NSW: Primary English Teachers Association.

Painter, C. 1990. Spoken and written language: implications for language programming. Paper presented at the *ATESOL Conference*, Brisbane.

Rothery, J. 1989. Learning about language. In R. Hasan and J.R. Martin (eds) *Language development: learning language, learning culture. Meaning and choice in language*. Norwood, NJ: Ablex.

Scarino, A., D. Vale, P. McKay and J. Clark. 1988. *Australian language levels guidelines*. Canberra: Curriculum Development Centre.

Skutnabb-Kangas, T. and P. Toukomaa. 1976. *Teaching migrant children's mother tongue and learning the language of the host country in the context of the sociocultural situation of the migrant family*. Helsinki: The Finnish National Commission for UNESCO.

4 Exrater: a knowledge-based system for language assessors

Chris Corbel

Introduction

This paper describes the rationale, development and implementation of Exrater, a computer program to assist language assessors. It begins by describing the use in Adult Migrant Education Service (AMES) Victoria of the Australian Second Language Proficiency Ratings (ASLPR), a scale used in the direct assessment of language proficiency. It then introduces a type of computer program called a 'knowledge-based system', and describes the building of a knowledge-based system, Exrater, for users of the ASLPR. The paper then examines the extent to which Exrater meets the needs for which it was built. It concludes with a consideration of the wider implications of the use of Exrater.

The ASLPR

The Australian Second Language Proficiency Ratings (ASLPR) (Ingram and Wylie 1984) is a rating scale and procedure which provides a means of describing practical language proficiency.

Use

The ASLPR has been widely used in the Australian Adult Migrant English Program (AMEP) for about a decade. In Victoria, which accounts for about a third of the national AMEP activity, prospective students are given an ASLPR rating to assist in placement in classes. Classes are organised on the basis of a number of factors, an important one of which is the ASLPR rating of potential participants (McIntyre, this volume). Teachers in the program assign ASLPR ratings to all students in their class on exit from courses. This proficiency statement serves also by implication as a statement of achievement, as there is no other regular assessment of course achievement. It is estimated that over 30,000 ratings were done in the state of Victoria alone in 1989 (AMES 1989).

Description

The ASLPR was developed from the Absolute Language Proficiency Ratings of the Foreign Services Institute (FSI), which was seen by the authors of the ASLPR to be 'the most widely accepted and most thoroughly researched performance based scale available' (Ingram 1980:49). The ASLPR scale has nine described levels, the six defined FSI levels having been expanded at the lower end of the scale to make it more applicable to the needs of the AMEP, where there are more lower level learners than in the FSI context. It is also possible for plusses to be added to Levels 2, 3 and 4 to indicate proficiency above the base level but falling short of the next.

The scale is presented in three columns, the first providing a General Description, the second, Examples of Specific Tasks, and the third, Comments. (For a full description of the development and trialling of the scale see Ingram 1984.) Underhill (1987) groups rating scales according to whether or not their levels are defined, and whether or not they make reference to specific tasks. The ASLPR, in his terms, is both Defined General (in its Description column) and Defined Specific (in its Examples column).

The rating process

An ASLPR rating is arrived at on the basis of observation of learners' performance on sample activities for the macro-skill being rated. In the case of speaking, this is an oral interview, usually conducted by one rater, and following a general pattern of increasing difficulty. After the interview the rater assigns a rating in the form of an ASLPR level.

The rater assigns the level that most nearly describes the ratee's language behaviour. This is in contrast to the FSI system which adopts a 'threshold' approach. According to Lowe (1988:23) '... a threshold is a perceptual gestalt, a figure or a constellation of factors that are clearly present to perform the function(s) in question when the major border between levels is crossed'. He contrasts the threshold approach, in which a 'perceptual gestalt' is strongly present just on entry to a new level, with a midpoint system, in which the perceptual gestalt is weak at the entry to a level. The preparedness of raters in practice to continually subdivide levels suggests that a strong threshold gestalt does not exist for ASLPR levels. This view is supported by the authors of the scale who state that: '... language behaviour... is related to the point on the scale which most nearly describes it' (Ingram 1980:51), and '... the learner is assigned to the one (level) which his performance most closely resembles' (Ingram 1980:52). Both these statements appear incompatible with a threshold system.

The ASLPR is a compensatory scale. It acknowledges that an individual may exhibit 'minor but compensating' variations in one or more of the components of language performance. An individual's syntax or vocabulary, for example, may more closely resemble the descriptions of syntax or vocabulary at a higher or lower level than the global level actually assigned.

The ASLPR takes a global approach to rating, that is, it presents its rating as a single value for each macro-skill. Although the ASLPR focuses on the assessment of overall performance, it acknowledges the influence of the components of that performance on raters' decisions. It tries to enhance intuitive judgments 'by directing the observer's attention towards relevant criteria' (Ingram 1979:C5), presumably through the presentation of statements about these various criteria within the descriptions for each level. However, these criteria or components are not presented separately or isolated in any way, although this was considered to be a possible future development (Ingram 1979). Thus, although the scale implicitly acknowledges an analytical element in the process of arriving at a rating, it does not overtly direct raters' attention to the components of the performance nor expect them to be rated separately.

Issues in the use of the ASLPR

Reliability

Since the ASLPR relies largely on a structured oral interview for the elicitation of language behaviour, it is essential that the interview be carried out in such a way as to ensure consistency and thus to enhance inter-rater reliability. Raters need to be trained and competent, and they need to be able to refer to the scale as necessary.

Since every teacher in AMES Victoria is also a rater, the task of ensuring consistency is a substantial one. Although training sessions are carried out, there are still many reports of inappropriate ratings being made. The scale is available to raters, but its size and layout makes access to detail and comparison between levels difficult. The level descriptors can be as long as twenty lines, and the complete scale covers eighteen printed pages. Clearly it is not intended that such a scale be memorised. In addition, the large amount of detail can make it difficult to get an overview of a level. Although single sentence summary statements are provided for each level, they provide only a minimal indication of the content of the description of the level. The scale groups the descriptions of the four macro-skills at a level together, making comparisons between levels for a macro-skill difficult.

Information

An ASLPR rating in itself carries little meaning to people who are not familiar with the scale; it needs at least to be accompanied by the ASLPR description of the relevant level. However, since the ASLPR is a compensatory scale, it is possible that an individual may not exhibit all the characteristics of a level, but may in fact exhibit elements that occur in a higher or lower level. These variations will not be revealed in the ASLPR rating, even if it is accompanied by a description of the ASLPR level. Thus the ASLPR is unable to provide the kind of detail that is of interest to teachers and learners for diagnostic purposes, and to external audiences such as employers who may wish to have a detailed profile of an individual's proficiency.

Discrimination

The need to discriminate between learners with low proficiency levels led to the creation of additional levels at the lower end of the ASLPR scale. The use of plusses at the upper end of the scale is recommended as this also allows for finer discrimination. Even so, in practice, users informally make finer distinctions than those allowed. Ingram (1985), in referring to the reported difficulties in discrimination, draws attention to the difficulty of finding a way to describe accurately any further intermediate levels. In addition, he suggests that the addition of levels is likely to have a negative influence on reliability.

Ingram (op. cit.) points out that this issue may arise from a confusion of achievement and proficiency. However, the use of the ASLPR as an indicator of achievement as well as proficiency is strongly entrenched in AMES Victoria. As a result, AMES Victoria is not able to show improvements in language levels for many of the participants in its courses, since many do not move from one ASLPR level to another in the period of a typical course.

Exrater

We have seen that the use of the ASLPR in AMES Victoria raises issues to do with the training and moderation of raters, the provision of detailed information about individual proficiency, and the need to discriminate more finely between individuals (see McIntyre, this volume). We now turn to an examination of the development of Exrater, a 'knowledge-based system' intended to address these issues.

Expert systems and knowledge-based systems

Expert systems are computer programs that solve problems by emulating human experts. They have been the subject of intensive research and development efforts for several decades. Although expert systems have not become as widespread as had been predicted, they are in use in a wide range of business areas (Fiegenbaum et al. 1988), and to a lesser extent in other fields, including education.

An example from an educational context is SNAP (Smart Needs Assessment Program) 'which helps teachers mainstream students with disabilities into regular education classes' (Pilato and Malouf 1991). As Pilato and Malouf (1991:49) explain:

> *A consultation with the SNAP System is similar to a problem solving meeting with a human expert. A teacher responds to questions which analyse a problem that students are having and helps the teacher clarify the problem. The System only requests information it needs to recommend teacher actions. At the end of a SNAP consultation, the program recommends a set of training options from the System's collection. The process of using the system then shifts to actual implementation of one or more of the recommended training options.*

Increasingly attention has been focused on small expert systems that are intended to enhance the work of individuals by making information more readily available to them, rather than by attempting to emulate an expert. These small expert systems are referred to as 'knowledge-based systems', since they attempt to capture knowledge and expertise and make it available to others (Bowie and Arnold 1990), or 'intelligent job aids' (Harmon 1987; Harmon and Sawyer 1990), since they are intended for use in the process of everyday work, in the way one would use a phone book, as a source of information. An attraction of knowledge-based systems is that they can be built in-house by non-programmers using relatively cheap programming tools.

As Bowie and Arnold (1991) state, knowledge-based systems are appropriate when there is a need:

* to improve access to information;
* to improve the speed, consistency and quality of decisions;
* for training of staff;
* to shift responsibility from one or two highly knowledgeable individuals to others.

Knowledge-based systems are particularly appropriate to supporting tasks in which, as Harmon (1987) states:

* response speed is less important than accuracy;
* the task is infrequently performed;
* reading instructions won't interfere with performance;
* many steps or a complex decision-making process is involved.

However, as Bowie and Arnold (1991) point out, the task needs to be one in which:

* the knowledge needed to carry it out is well defined and narrow;
* the task does not rely on common sense and intuition;
* someone exists who already knows how to do it;
* the task takes no longer than twenty minutes for the expert.

Support for ASLPR raters seemed to be an appropriate application of the knowledge-based system concept: the accuracy of the rating was important, the rating task was carried out infrequently, and the task involved a complex decision-making process. In addition, the 'knowledge' already existed in the form of the ASLPR itself, ratings are based on the descriptions in the scale rather than personal knowledge, and there are many teachers proficient in its use. There was also a possibility of cost savings in in-service training.

Description

Development began in 1988, using KnowledgePro, an expert system development tool. KnowledgePro was chosen on the grounds of low cost and greater flexibility, particularly in its support of hypertext (see below), than comparable tools. It allows unlimited free distribution of applications that it is used to build, and runs on standard IBM-compatible PCs (see Freedman 1987; Bowie and Arnold 1991, for more detailed comparisons between knowledge-based system tools). Work was carried out by the author as part of regular duties. The resulting program is called Exrater, short for Expert Rater. Corbel (1990) presents a more detailed discussion of program concepts.

Exrater does not attempt to identify a ratee's ASLPR level through a computer-mediated question and answer 'consultation', since it would have been too time consuming to capture all the possible combinations of elements in an example of language performance in the form of expert system rules, given the compensatory nature of the ASLPR. Instead Exrater presents elements of the ASLPR descriptions to the rater under various rating categories. The categories for speaking, for example, are range, fluency, intelligibility, appropriacy, grammar and discourse, and vocabulary. The rater selects the statement in each category which most closely matches the language behaviour of the ratee. Figure 1 (see below) shows the selections available on the screen the user sees for the Range category of the speaking macro-skill. Screens for the other categories are similar.

This presentation allows the user to compare levels without the distraction of detail. However, detail is immediately available if required to help distinguish between levels. It will be seen in Figure 1 that some of the words and phrases are underlined. Figure 2 (see below) shows the result of selecting the word 'Effective'. Additional information about the selected item appears on a pop-up screen. Selecting any of the other words or phrases will present a similar expansion or explanation.

Thus the full ASLPR is available for immediate reference. In addition, some technical terms, such as 'discourse', which occur in the ASLPR unglossed, are

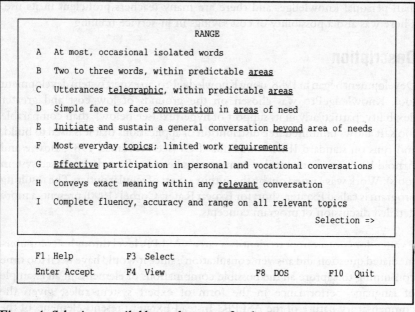

```
                              RANGE
   A   At most, occasional isolated words

   B   Two to three words, within predictable areas

   C   Utterances telegraphic, within predictable areas

   D   Simple face to face conversation in areas of need

   E   Initiate and sustain a general conversation beyond area of needs

   F   Most everyday topics; limited work requirements

   G   Effective participation in personal and vocational conversations

   H   Conveys exact meaning within any relevant conversation

   I   Complete fluency, accuracy and range on all relevant topics

                                                    Selection =>


   F1  Help            F3  Select
   Enter Accept        F4  View           F8  DOS        F10  Quit
```

Figure 1 Selections available on the screen for the Range category

linked to definitions and examples. In Figure 2, for example, selecting the word 'circumlocution' provides a definition of the term. This three-dimensional presentation of text is known as hypertext (see Tsai [1988] for an overview of the development of the hypertext concept). The use of hypertext means that the program automatically adjusts to the rater's level of knowledge and experience, since it presents as little or as much detail as required. The rater can get immediate detail to assist in deciding between levels without having to internalise the whole scale, and without being distracted by detail when seeking an overview of levels and categories.

A potential problem with this presentation is that users will simply make all selections at the same level, without checking the detail. This is referred to as the halo effect (Yoruzuya and Oller 1980). The presentation of each of the rating category subscales on a separate screen, the use of descriptive statements which draw attention to the specific skill being evaluated, and the use of a letter rather than a number to indicate the rater's selection, all are intended to overcome any potential halo effect in the rating process.

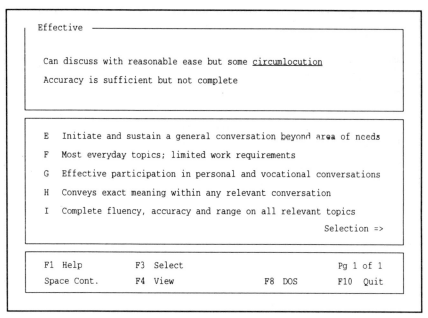

```
  Effective  ──────────────────────────────────────────────

     Can discuss with reasonable ease but some circumlocution

     Accuracy is sufficient but not complete


    E    Initiate and sustain a general conversation beyond area of needs

    F    Most everyday topics; limited work requirements

    G    Effective participation in personal and vocational conversations

    H    Conveys exact meaning within any relevant conversation

    I    Complete fluency, accuracy and range on all relevant topics

                                                     Selection =>


    F1  Help          F3  Select                       Pg 1 of 1

    Space Cont.       F4  View           F8  DOS        F10  Quit
```

Figure 2 Additional information that appears on a pop-up screen

After having made a selection from each of the categories, the rater is presented with a profile of the ratee, containing the selections made in each of the categories, a profile total, and an ASLPR level. The profile total is automatically calculated by the program on the basis of a value assigned to each of the selections. There is no weighting of the categories, so each contributes equally to the total. The ASLPR level is obtained automatically by the comparison of the profile total with a predetermined scale of values. All or some of the profile can then be printed out. Figure 3 (see below) shows an example of a full printout. This can be accompanied by a guide to the profile rating categories, and a full version of the relevant ASLPR description if required.

It should be noted that at present Exrater is not used during an ASLPR interview itself, for two reasons. Firstly a lack of computers makes it impossible for all raters to have a computer for personal use. More importantly, it is seen as inappropriate for the rater to refer to the computer during the interview, since this may have a negative influence on the ratee. This situation might perhaps be reconsidered if small, less obtrusive notebook computers were to replace the desktop computers now in use.

```
                              EXRATER


ASLPR Speaking Profile of Juan Esposito
Done on 26 May 1992
By Chris Corbel



                          SPEAKING PROFILE
(The number after each statement is its ASLPR level)
Range:
Initiate and sustain a conversation beyond areas of need (1+)


Fluency:
Good rate of utterance; confident though still hesitations (2)


Intelligibility:
Reasonably comprehensible to native speakers, with repetition (1+)


Appropriacy:
Few skills in specialist register; some social expressions (1)


Grammar and Discourse:
Common tenses; most question forms; basic cohesion; some modifiers (1+)


Vocabulary:
Limited range; much hesitation and circumlocution (1+)


Comments:



ASLPR Rating:  1+
Profile Total: 24
Profile Key:
3 or less = 0, 4 to 10 = 0+, 10 to 15 = 1-, 16 to 21 = 1, 22 to 27 = 1+
28 to 33 = 2, 34 to 39 = 3, 40 to 45 = 4, over 45 = 5
```

Figure 3 Example of a full printout

Implementation

Exrater was introduced informally to a small number of AMES Victoria staff during its development. When a fully functional, (though not yet error-free) version was ready it was installed on computers at the AMES Victoria centres which had them. Several short in-services have been held, and interested teachers have been given copies to install at home. Exrater has not been made compulsory in any sense, and there remain many teachers who have not yet seen it.

One of the major problems in the uptake of Exrater has been the actual availability of computers. There is a relatively small number of computers available for teacher use, rarely more than one or two in a teaching centre. The decision to develop a computer-based application was made on an assumed progressive increase in computer availability, which, although it has taken place, has not kept pace with demand. A second problem is time. The computers available have tended to be low-level machines suitable for CALL and text-based word processing. Although Exrater is very limited in its requirements (it does not need graphics or even colour) the trial version does tend to run slowly. This, combined with accessibility, has meant that Exrater, while well received by those who have used it, is not yet an established part of most teachers' work.

Evaluation of Exrater

Exrater was developed to meet specific organisational needs concerning the use of the ASLPR. In this section we will consider the extent to which Exrater has met these needs, as well as some unexpected uses to which it has been put.

Reliability

It was intended that Exrater would improve reliability by enhancing the training and moderation of raters, and by improving their competence as raters through the presentation of the scale in a more accessible way. In the case of training, it was envisaged that Exrater could be used by new staff members as an introduction to the ASLPR, in addition to more formal in-service sessions. Although Exrater is a part of an ASLPR kit being developed in AMES Victoria, its use at this stage is only recommended, and there has been no attempt to investigate its effectiveness as an adjunct or alternative to other forms of training.

In the case of moderation sessions, however, informal observation of a small number of teachers indicates the potential of Exrater in this area. Three pairs of teachers who had co-taught a course, and who had already assigned an end-of-course ASLPR rating to course participants, were asked to profile those students using Exrater. As they carried out the profiles they were forced to identify explicitly the elements of their students' performance on which they based their decisions. The teachers were thus made more aware of each other's decision-making processes and opinions. What had been routine became overt and, in a sense, problematic, particularly when they disagreed on an aspect of the profile or with Exrater's ASLPR rating.

On the issue of the effect of access to the scale on reliability, more information is available. Corbel (1992) found that in certain cases the Exrater rating was more accurate than a global ASLPR rating. A group of AMES Victoria teachers (n=18) was shown a video of four learners and asked to rate each globally and using Exrater. The global ratings were more accurate (i.e. agreed with the average rating) for lower level ratees, whereas the Exrater ratings were more accurate with the higher level ratees. It was thought that the extent to which Exrater improved reliability might be linked to the degree of familiarity of the raters with the ratee level. Tentative support for this suggestion comes from the ratings of a video of a mid-level learner (ASLPR 2) by three other groups (n=18, 30, 9) each of which was progressively more familiar with higher level learners. For each of the groups the global ratings and Exrater ratings became progressively closer.

It should be pointed out, however, that this work was done using paper-based versions of the Exrater categories. As such it offers evidence relating mainly to the use of analytical scoring methods in direct assessment, that is, methods which explicitly state the categories on which marking is to be based, and which mark each category separately, rather than on the effectiveness of a computer-based version. The findings are, in fact consistent with work in the rating of writing. Huot (1990:338) found that 'in comparison studies, analytic scores have proven to be the most reliable of all direct writing assessment procedures'. Whether this is also the case for the direct assessment of speaking it is not known, although the use of an analytic checklist in the FSI rating procedure to resolve discrepancies between raters (Wilds 1975) suggests that this might be the case.

It is not possible to say to what extent raters use the hypertext options in Exrater, since, as was noted earlier, these trial groups used a pen and paper version of the program that did not have the additional detail. No observations have yet been made of users in the field, nor comparisons done of the reliability of users of paper-based and computer-based versions of the program.

Information

As can be seen from Figure 3, Exrater is able to provide more individualised information than a simple ASLPR level, even when the rating is accompanied by its description. Exrater produces a profile, with details about a ratee's performance in a number of categories. It also shows in which categories an individual is strong or weak. There is potential for the use of these profiles by teachers and learners in the discussion of learning goals. There is also the possibility of the comparison of profiles at different times, which could provide evidence of slight improvements in proficiency which might otherwise not be identified (see below).

There is an issue to do with the reliability of these category ratings, however. An analysis of the rating category subscales for the first group of teachers referred to above showed that there was very little complete agreement between raters on all their subscale selections, although to expect a high degree of agreement is probably unrealistic. The advantage of the subscales is that the score they produce tends to average out the variations in the scores for the separate categories and present a more balanced result. Using Exrater, it is not possible for the rater to allow a personal feeling about the importance of one category to override the other categories. This produces consistency, but whether it is consistent with construct validity is another matter. However, in the absence of strong evidence for the weighting of categories, the simplest approach, as taken by Exrater, seems the best. In addition, the possibility of two people at one proficiency level having two different profiles is not at all inconsistent with a compensatory scale like the ASLPR.

Nunan (1987) expresses concern about the accuracy and stability of profiles. The profiles generated by Exrater are not without the kinds of uncertainties that all such profiles have, but they do provide far more information than is available at present. Whether this information should be made available to an external audience is another issue. One view is that external audiences (employers, funding agencies) should be provided with as much information as possible to show them how complex language and language learning is (Spolsky 1990). A contrary view is that these audiences are not interested in detail and are only interested in the bottom line — the mark or score or rating itself— or aggregated versions of them (Alderson 1991).

The experience of AMES Victoria in providing ASLPR ratings for an external audience (the Commonwealth Department of Education Employment and Training) supports the latter view. Though full profiles were initially provided, this was discontinued on request. The recipients reported having no time to read them and not being able to interpret the language used (which is unchanged from the ASLPR) when they did.

The provision of detail to an external audience has been significant on at least one occasion. An ASLPR rating was done on an individual in a workplace who faced lack of promotion on vague grounds relating to her language. The detailed Exrater profile demonstrated that she was very strong in all categories but one, and this one was influencing her overall level of competency. In other words, what seemed to be a major language problem was identifiable as just one element of the person's performance. The evidence that there was a specific issue to be addressed led to management's acceptance of a learning plan for the worker. Whether a general ASLPR rating would have provided such relevant, personal information is less certain.

However, there have been ethical issues raised concerning the divulging of detailed information about individuals to external audiences, particularly employers, since it is feared that it may be used as the basis for dismissal if it is considered unfavourable. This is a particular concern when AMES Victoria carries out language audits in workplaces. It should be noted that Exrater does in fact allow for confidentiality in printing profiles by allowing the user to omit any of the details that are considered confidential. Overall, AMES Victoria has worked closely with representatives of unions as well as management in the use of Exrater, as in all aspects of workplace language assessment. Provided confidentiality is safeguarded, the union view has been that any attempts to improve the rating process are to be supported.

Discrimination

Exrater allows finer discriminations to be made between ASLPR levels, through its use of a profile total, than is otherwise possible. As can be seen in Figure 3, there is a range of six points between each described ASLPR level. It is therefore possible to identify an improvement in an individual's profile total, even if the overall ASLPR level has not changed. An attraction of this approach is that it enables points between levels to be identified, without the necessity of actually describing additional levels, yet in an overt, described way. Thus a profile total at the upper end of a range for a level can be considered, for example, a 'good' 1+, yet the actual elements that make up the 'good' 1+ are observable. This feature has proved attractive to teachers who continually feel the need to talk about finer divisions than the scale allows.

This element of Exrater has attracted interest from AMES Victoria program planning and monitoring staff as well. Several comparisons have been made of Exrater profiles of groups of learners at the beginning and end of courses. These suggest that Exrater is indeed more effective at showing changes in proficiency in the period of a typical AMES Victoria course than is the ASLPR.

In a review of Exrater, Davies (1991:7) suggests that a

> *major contribution to the ASLPR that Exrater appears to make is that it allows proficiency growth to show itself... If this sensitivity of Exrater can be shown to correspond to external criteria establishing growth it will be an important aspect of the claims of Exrater to validity.*

Other applications

Anecdotal reports from centres and programs where Exrater is in use indicate additional uses to which Exrater has been put.

Learner self-assessment

A group of higher level learners was shown how to use the program, and used it to self-assess. Teachers reported a positive response from users, with the only criticism being that the program did not actually do the assessing.

Support for 'naive' raters

The Exrater category subscales (Figure 1 shows one of these) were given to a small number of visitors to a centre, who were then asked to use them to rate participants in an informal social setting. The 'naive' raters were found to have rated more harshly both globally and using the Exrater categories than did the teachers.

Task analysis

As part of a language audit, AMES Victoria was asked to comment on the competency-based task descriptions of an industry curriculum document. AMES had been asked to say what ASLPR level would be necessary for each task. By profiling each task using Exrater it was possible to show that the tasks comprised elements from a wide range of ASLPR levels and that it was unlikely that the tasks, as they were described, could be carried out by any NESB worker. Management agreed to a modification of the tasks to bring them more into line with ASLPR levels, and more attainable by NESB workers.

Course planning

Teachers at a centre used printouts of the Exrater categories to assist in course planning.

Conclusion

It is not possible at this early stage to say conclusively whether Exrater has met its aims. Indications are that it is has the potential to meet the needs for improved reliability, information and discrimination. As computer access improves, this potential may be met. Although the improvement in reliability noted above could perhaps have been achieved with a paper-based version of the program, the computer is clearly an advantage in creating profiles, and quantifying the values of the category selections, thus improving discrimination.

A report on Exrater by Davies (1991) recommends the writing of a manual, and the use of Exrater for self-assessment by learners. The writing of a manual is presently underway, and a project to develop a more learner-friendly version of Exrater is planned. The following issues for investigation, also identified in the report (Davies 1991:6), await attention.

• Field validation of Exrater categories through the comparison of the categories with an appropriate external criterion of proficiency.

- Distinguishing rating categories (including the weighting of categories) through, for example, factor analysis and Item Response Theory test analysis.

- The improvement in reliability offered by Exrater — does it persist over time, or will over-familiarity of raters with the categories lead to a need to extend or replace them?

- The role of the computer in Exrater delivery — is it more than simply 'the sense of being up-to-date in a sophisticated and modern world'?

To this list might be added an investigation of the extent to which users make use of the hypertext facilities, and the effect, if any, on reliability. This would be an interesting addition to work in the rapidly expanding area of the investigation of cognitive and performance aspects of hypertext use.

We have also seen that Exrater has been used in unanticipated ways. There may yet be others. One of the most useful side-effects of Exrater, from a professional development point of view, has been the 'problematising' of language proficiency in general, and the ASLPR in particular, that has resulted from its development and use. Although the ASLPR has been in use in AMES Victoria for a decade, it has never been subject to such scrutiny as it has been by Exrater users. Users are looking at the detail of the scale in a way that they haven't had to before. This has led to questioning of the content of the scale, the ways in which teachers use it in planning, teaching and assessment, and, more generally, the nature of the construct of language proficiency (see also McIntyre, this volume). Davies (1991) suggests that the link between Exrater and the ASLPR should be regarded as 'a two-way relationship', with the ASLPR being able to benefit from the work on Exrater.

The success of Exrater has raised other types of issues relating to knowledge-based systems. Should a knowledge-based system assist non-specialists to make decisions that are the professional domain of specialists? Should an organisation capture expertise in a way that makes it available to its competitors? These issues led to an AMES Victoria decision (subsequently reconsidered in response to market pressure) not to make Exrater available outside the Adult Migrant English Program. However, Exrater has shown that a knowledge-based tool in the hands of a non-programmer can result in the development of useful applications at very minimal cost. In addition, the very process of building the system has resulted in a greater awareness of the complexity of the content that the system is trying to capture. Although it is clearly in need of refinement and further work, Davies (1991:13) concludes that 'Exrater is an important development, both in its contribution to the defining of language proficiency and in providing a methodology for the more efficient assessment of proficiency'.

References

Alderson, J.C. 1991. Bands and scores. In J.C. Alderson and B. North (eds) *Language testing in the 1990s*. London: Modern English Publications and the British Council.

Adult Migrant Education Service Victoria. 1989. *Annual Report*. Melbourne: Adult Migrant Education Service Victoria.

Bowie, J.S. and W.R. Arnold. 1990. *The intelligent PC*. Englewood Cliffs: Prentice Hall.

Corbel, C. 1990. An expert support environment for language teachers. In A. McDougall and C. Dowling *Computers in education*. Amsterdam: North–Holland.

Corbel, C. 1992. *Improving global rating reliability with a category-oriented, hypertext-based profiling instrument*. MA thesis, University of Melbourne.

Davies, A. 1991. *Report to AMES Victoria on examination of Exrater*. Melbourne: University of Melbourne/NLLIA Language Testing Centre.

de Jong, J.H.A.L. and D.K. Stevenson (eds). 1990. Individualising the assessment on language abilities. Clevedon: Multilingual Matters.

Fiegenbaum, E., P. McCorduck and H.P. Nii. 1988. *The rise of the expert company*. London: Macmillan.

Freedman, R. 1987. Evaluating shells. *AI Expert*, September.

Harmon, P. 1987. Intelligent job aids: how AI will change training in the next five years. In G. Kearsley (ed.) *Artificial intelligence and instruction: applications and methods*. Reading, Mass.: Addison Wesley.

Harmon, P. and B. Sawyer. 1990. *Creating expert systems for business and industry*. New York: Wiley.

Huot, B. 1990. The literature of direct writing assessment: major concerns and prevailing trends. *Review of Educational Research* 60, 2:237–263.

Ingram, D.E. 1979. Introduction to the Australian second language proficiency ratings (ASLPR). A paper in the *AMEP Teachers manual*. Canberra: Australian Government Publishing Service.

Ingram, D.E. 1980. A performance-based approach to the measurement of second language proficiency. *Australian Review of Applied Linguistics* 3, 1:49–62.

Ingram, D.E. 1982. *Report on the formal trialling of the Australian second language proficiency ratings (ASLPR)*. Canberra: Australian Government Publishing Service.

Ingram, D.E. 1985. Assessing proficiency: an overview of some aspects of testing. In K. Hyltenstam and M. Pienemann (eds) *Modelling and assessing second language acquisition*. Clevedon, Avon: Multilingual Matters.

Ingram, D.E. and E. Wylie. 1984. *Australian second language proficiency ratings (ASLPR)*. Canberra: Australian Government Publishing Service.

Lowe, Jr, P. 1988. The unassimilated history. In P. Lowe, Jr and C.W. Stansfield *Second language proficiency assessment: current issues*. Englewood Cliffs: Prentice Hall.

Nunan, D. 1987. The ghost in the machine: an examination of the concept of language proficiency. *Prospect* 2, 2:153–169.

Pilato, V. and D. Malouf. 1991. Expert systems in schools: solving the implementation paradox. *Educational Technology*, August.

Spolsky, B.A. 1990. Social aspects of individualized assessment. In J.H.A.L. de Jong and D.K. Stevenson.

Thompson, B. and B. Thomson. 1988. *KnowledgePro*. Nassau, NY: Knowledge Garden.

Tsai, C-J. 1988. Hypertext: technology, applications and research issues. *Journal of Educational Technology Systems* 17, 1:3–14.

Underhill, N. 1987. *Testing spoken language*. Cambridge: Cambridge University Press.

Wilds, C. 1975. The oral interview test. In R.L. Jones and B. Spolsky *Testing language proficiency*. Washington: Centre for Applied Linguistics.

Yorozuya, R. and J. Oller. 1980. Oral proficiency scales: construct validity and the halo effect. *Language Learning* 30, 1:135–153.

5 Language assessment and real-life: the ASLPR revisited

Philip McIntyre

Introduction

It is precisely because of the impact that the (ACTFL proficiency) guidelines and the OPI have had on foreign language learning in the past decade that it becomes of the utmost importance to pause and assess their contribution critically and openly.

(Shohamy 1990:385)

The exhortation contained in this quotation is equally relevant to the Australian second-language learning context, and in particular Adult Migrant English Services (AMES), where the oral proficiency interview (OPI) has been the major assessment tool used since 1979, the year the Australian Second Language Proficiency Ratings Scale (ASLPR) was introduced (Ingram 1979, 1980; Ingram and Wylie 1982, 1984). This scale, designed to describe the development of 'general proficiency', views language proficiency as a unitary ability and expresses scores as a global rating in each of four macro-skill areas of speaking, listening, reading and writing. It is used by all state AMESs, except NSW, where a 'component ability' (Bachman 1990:44) scale is used, in which the macro-skill of speaking is broken down into five factors — vocabulary, fluency, syntax, comprehension and effect on listener (Brindley 1986).

In Victoria, an informal review of uses and perceptions of the ASLPR across AMES was carried out in 1988 by the present writer, entitled *ASLPR revisited*, (referred to throughout this paper as 'the 1988 review'). This review raised a number of issues and proposed a number of recommendations for further investigation and research, which have led to a number of research studies over the past three years. This chapter discusses the review, its recommendations and the outcomes of these recommendations in the light of questions raised by Shohamy (1990) and Bachman (1990), about the validity and reliability of assessment procedures such as the ASLPR which aim to replicate 'real-life' language use.

Background use of ASLPR in AMES: the historical context

In 1978, the Joint Commonwealth-States Committee of the Adult Migrant English Program (AMEP), acting on a recommendation of the Galbally Review (1978) developed 'on-arrival' English courses for migrants and refugees in the first months after their arrival in Australia. It was in this context that the ASLPR was developed:

> *It was hoped that such a description of proficiency development would help meet the demands of the Galbally review for learners to be informed of the goals they could expect to achieve in the courses.*
>
> (Galbally 1978:44)

> *To provide an overarching framework of proficiency development within which ESL programs could be planned.*
>
> (Ingram 1980)

The ASLPR obviously fulfilled a need in AMES for a language assessment that would reflect the broader view of language that was the engine of change in teaching approaches at the time, for which discrete-point tests were no longer serving the purpose. Pre-course interviews of an ad hoc nature had been instituted in 1977. The advent of ASLPR and its proposals for a more structured interview procedure, therefore, achieved an early face-validity amongst teachers in that it confirmed the practice, it appeared appropriate (Savignon 1983) and looked as though it measured what it was supposed to measure since

> *the learner is given the opportunity to display his (sic) full proficiency in situations that replicate as closely as possible those of real life.*
>
> (Ingram 1979 based on Clark 1972)

Its claims of validity were perceived as further enhanced with the publication of a report on extensive reliability studies (Ingram 1984). Its content validity was never really established though, in Victoria, some attempt was made to include in the OPI tasks which required other types of language interactions, representative of the larger set of tasks of which the test was supposed to be a sample (Savignon 1983).

Over the more than ten years of its life, ASLPR has indeed provided a *lingua franca* for teachers to talk about proficiency. Classes are mostly designated in terms of ASLPR levels in place of the previous terms of 'beginner, elementary, intermediate, advanced' concepts which could vary in relation to the range of classes which existed in a given centre or program. An interesting example of this common language is that teachers usually use a one-digit description to describe students or classes e.g. 'Oh, she's a 1-', or 'I'm teaching the 1+ group this time', which in their opinion referred to **speaking** level. However, most teachers if presented with four-digit ratings like these:

(S)	3	(L)	4	(R)	1+	(W)	0+
	1+		1		2		2

have no hesitation in describing the likely learner and personal profiles.

The role of intuition in rating

There is a good deal of evidence to suggest that teachers have developed certain intuitions in their use of the scale. Indeed, in interviews for placement and within-class assessments, intuition may even play the largest role in assessing proficiency. Further evidence for the role of intuition appears in Ingram's 1984 reliability study which states that the reliability of the intermediate levels 2+, 3+, and 4+ is an important question, but sidesteps the issue by noting that there was 'no sign that learners were rated more or less reliably than at the described levels' (1984:16).

Most teachers rate intuitively because of time pressures — it is simply quicker than reading long descriptions. In addition they have probably become more familiar with the scale and comfortable with the position of interviewer, thus fulfilling the prophecy made by Ingram (1980:18) that:

> *It is possible that, as more experience is gained with the ASLPR and the*
> *assessment techniques, interview times can be reduced.*

In one sense, the rating by intuition could be perceived as a strength, as teachers have internalised what certain ASLPR levels mean with a fair degree of consistency for purposes of streaming and placement, at least within one teaching centre. Common understanding of the meaning of different levels can be achieved at the local level. However, inter-rater reliability may suffer across centres and across other ESL providers whose intuitions may not match since there is no common point of reference. An additional problem, as Brindley (1986) points out, is that there is a loss of information when users do not refer to the scale descriptions when rating.

Use of ASLPR in AMES

ASLPR and placement assessment

Assessment of proficiency in AMES is generally used for purposes of placement of students in appropriate learning arrangements. All applicants for classes are interviewed by a team of trained assessors, to assess their proficiency level and also to gain a profile of personal information for a computer data-base and educational information for the eventual teacher.

Towards the end of each class, students are again assessed in ASLPR terms, this time by the class teachers themselves. These so called 'end-of-course' assessments, while to some extent indicating progress (see **Language gains** section below), more importantly serve to indicate the next most appropriate learning arrangement for each learner, both within and across centres and providers. Thus the ASLPR again serves as a placement tool.

As mentioned, interview and assessment procedures have been somewhat curtailed and samples of language elicited at performances somewhat limited. Yet, used for such placement purposes they have been found adequate, since placement of students seems to be about eighty to eighty-five per cent acceptable. For those students who are less-than-reliably assessed, no significant disadvantages accrue since in AMES' multi-class centres, such students can easily be transferred to a more appropriate class. Bachman (1990:330) acknowledges this:

> *The RL approach has proven to be a useful means for classroom teachers and for many other testing situations in which the decisions to be made about individuals are not irreversible or of monumental importance, this approach is perhaps sufficient. It provides a relatively easy way to develop tests that 'look good' and may have some predictive utility.*

Language proficiency, however, is only one of the factors which need to be considered in streaming; others include age, aptitude, goals and aspirations, differential macro skill development, education and first language (Ingram 1980), in addition to everyday matters such as family and life commitments, personal worries, time practicalities etc. It is this broader profile which has become increasingly important in defining learning pathways in the AMEP. Placement into the AMEP Learner Pathways Framework (Lipa 1993) is now determined by learner goals and learning pace as well as by ASLPR level.

Reliability across providers

In the current climate of increasing unemployment, many more potential students are competing for entry into high level special purpose programs beyond ASLPR 2, the exit point from the AMEP. It is here that possible disadvantages may accrue from varying ASLPR assessment made by teachers who are referring learners to classes beyond the AMEP which require a level of 2 or 2+. Ingram (1980:21) foresaw this when he noted the need for intermediate points on the scale:

> *It is becoming clear that additional intermediate points at 2+, 3+, and 4+ are desirable... 2+ is emerging as a crucial point as the desirable minimum level before entering into 'special purpose' programs.*

However, students' further progress may be hampered if, having received a 2+ rating from AMES, the tertiary provider to which they are referred assesses them at just Level 2. On the other hand, a person assessed at 2- by AMES may gain acceptance into such a course. Hence the 1988 review recommended that:

> *Across AMES and other providers, inter-rater reliability studies are needed to give credibility, assist referral processes and to begin defining these other levels that are being used. We need to work with RMIT initially to try to get a description*

available for Level 2+. This level is allowed for in the introduction by David Ingram and is used by teachers in AMES, RMIT and TAFE providers, and it's about time it was described.

In order to address the question of inter-rater reliability across two institutions, the assessments made by one AMES centre (Myer House Day Centre) and one AMEP tertiary provider (RMIT Centre for English Language Learning [CELL]) were examined for correspondence or variation, in one term for each of the past three years, covering Levels 1+, 2-, 2, 2+ and 3. The results (see Figure 1 below) show an increasing rate of correspondence but still significant occurrence of variation. Here the exit assessments (AMES) are for the most part higher than those at entry (RMIT CELL). The most significant correspondence, however, was shown in the figures for Term 3 1990, when assessments were carried out a few weeks after teachers from both centres had attended a moderating session, watching videotapes of interviews at relevant levels, rating performances for listening and speaking levels, and discussing their ratings and perceptions of the performances in order to arrive at a consensus in ratings.

Date	Correspond				Differ				M.H. Higher				CELL Higher				N
	S	L	R	W	S	L	R	W	S	L	R	W	S	L	R	W	
Term 1 '89	10	6	5	15	21	25	25	16	13	24	14	11	8	1	11	5	31
Term 3 '89	22	13	*	16	13	22	*	19	5	13	*	4	8	9	*	15	35
Term 3 '90	29	23	4	2	3	9	2	*	3	7	1	*	—	2	1	*	32
Term 2 '91	13	13	11	12	9	9	11	9	8	8	10	8	1	1	1	1	22

S — Speaking, L— Listening, R — Reading, W— Writing, * — not tested

Figure 1 The results of the assessments made by two institutions

Regular moderating sessions for users of the ASLPR are not only necessary to achieve inter-rater reliability, but may also help to maintain fairness (Savignon 1983). Occasionally, learners have gained acceptance into courses due to a number of profile factors, personal qualities, or because of class numbers, despite a slightly lower ASLPR rating, while others rated higher have not. Yet almost inevitably the acceptance or non-acceptance of a learner is perceived by teachers to be determined by assessment of proficiency.

Moderating sessions also serve to maintain face validity by focusing attention on interviewer behaviour (Shohamy 1990), that is, whether the test appears to be testing communicative language. The interview format used by both providers requires the teacher to adopt the dual roles of assessor of proficiency and obtainer of information, which may well involve only one type of communication.

The ASLPR is an example of what Bachman (1990:363) refers to as the 'real-life' (RL) approach. Claims for validity are based on the surface resemblance of test tasks to real-life tasks. Bachman (1990:323) claims that the 'real-life' approach to authenticity is primarily about face validity and predictive utility. Within such approaches, relatively little attention is given to establishing content validity, that is, the extent to which the test samples the tasks that the testee will have to perform. The comparative study of assessments cited above revealed low face validity of the assessments amongst teachers of the two institutions and their students. However, the real cause may lie in the fact that the two assessments of proficiency are based on different performances by the same learners, elicited by different types of interviews and testing instruments. In other words, the ASLPR interviews are sampling different things for different purposes. Those of the tertiary provider are designed to obtain a profile of greater predictive utility for learners going into special purpose programs, whereas those of the AMES centre studied are testing for 'general proficiency' (if indeed such a concept can exist — see following section) and thus less concerned with predictive utility. Indeed, one frequent comment by teachers in AMES is that they would like a test that provided greater predictive utility than can be provided by ASLPR assessments which in their view do not indicate possible learning potential.

Such problems may be peculiar to the specific interface between the two centres quoted above, but may also be due to the influence of the principles which underlie the construction of the ASLPR, that is:

- at lower levels, the major parameter of change is the range of situations in which the language can be used;

- at the middle levels, once sentence formation is more or less complete, discourse development becomes pivotal;

- at upper levels, register flexibility assumes increased importance.

It is reasonable to place 'middle' as 1 to 2 and upper as 2+ to 5. Therefore, as long as the intermediate levels remain undefined, the interface of 2/2+ remains very hazy because the tertiary providers consider mostly specific registers and purposes, while AMES considers mainly language for general registers and purposes.

Factors perceived as affecting reliability of ratings

The 1988 review in considering the extent to which AMES teachers applied the ASLPR scale consistently, reported that:

> *Most AMES teachers can provide an anecdote or two about students who were 'badly' rated or placed but it is probably because placement according to ASLPR appears to be about eighty to eighty-five per cent appropriate, that the inaccurately-placed ones are prominent in everyone's memory.*

These apparently high levels of agreement between raters are in line with Ingram's (1984:13) studies:

> *The (inter-rater) reliability correlations… are high, being at or beyond the 0.001 significance level suggesting a high level of agreement in interpreting and applying the scale.*

Teachers attributed unreliable or 'poor' ratings to a number of factors:

* **Halo effect.** One factor affecting over- or under-rating was the overall class level.

> *To teachers in a centre with classes consistently in the ASLPR 0 to 1 range, a better performing learner can appear many times better and attract an over-rating. By the same token, in centres with classes constantly in the Level 2 and above range, a weaker learner may appear doubly weak and attract an under-rating, unless attention is again paid to the descriptions.*

- **Potential.**

  Sometimes an interviewer may form an opinion that the learner might have some so-called 'passive knowledge' of the language, (ability not elicited), a conclusion arrived at from seeing reading/writing ratings in excess of oral ones, and sometimes from other features of the personal profile, thus rating the potential rather than the actual proficiency at interview. Whether this potential is in fact realised later is dependent on circumstances, and indeed may not develop at all, (or may not even be there) which again can be detrimental to the perceived validity of the ASLPR scale.

- **The necessity to show progress.**

  There was an unwritten and unstated belief that because of classes being designated in ASLPR terms, learners had to 'go up' a level in one course or else teachers may be thought not to be doing their job effectively. This practice also harmed learners in the long run.

However, to a large extent these perceived problems have been rectified by having been brought to notice. The influence of the first factor has been diminished by all centres having a full range of classes. The second problem has been addressed by including a comment about opinions of the potential in the comments column of the application forms. This serves to alert teachers to the need to watch for any development. The third problem has largely disappeared due to the decreasing importance of numbers of courses taken as a priority criterion for re-entry. AMES is also developing alternative ways of describing language gains, which will be discussed later in this paper.

- **Differential weighting of rating criteria: 'structural' versus 'communicative'.** The ASLPR descriptions contain a wide range of communicative criteria ranging from sociolinguistic appropriateness to grammatical accuracy. An overall rating may depend on the relative weight given to these criteria, as the 1988 review noted:

  Stemming from debates in literature and practice on teaching approaches, the inclination of the interviewer can skew intuitive ratings. There is some evidence that many teachers give undue weighting to grammar in interpreting the scale descriptions, despite statements about ability to perform tasks with certain allowances for inaccuracies and a developing system of accuracy. There has sometimes been confusion for example about how to rate a long-term resident's speaking proficiency because of fossilised inaccuracies (Vigil and Oller 1976), which nevertheless do not interfere with an interlocutor's understanding nor affect the participation in any degree.

The question of what is an 'accurate' rating of the language proficiency of long-term residents particularly the relative roles of fluency and accuracy still remains. The issue assumes particular importance at placement, as a lower rating can lead to such people being most inappropriately placed in a class of newer arrivals. This may frustrate the long-term resident and overwhelm the newer arrival. The case of the 'fractured but fluent' learner may also pose a challenge to theories of language proficiency which downplay the importance of communicative effectiveness. If, at interview, it is possible to understand the person so readily that the rater can at the same time focus on the exact nature of the linguistic errors made, it must mean that the people are communicating very efficiently i.e. meaning does not need to be negotiated. On the other hand if all the negotiation of meaning is due to inability, confusion or inaccuracy with the language, then the rater will not be able to pick up specific inaccuracies.

- **Rating from general descriptions or sample tasks.** The 1988 review suggests that ratings may vary according to the part of the ASLPR scale that raters focus on:

    Interestingly, teachers who rate from the sample tasks column seem to rate higher than those who rate from the general descriptions. There may be some mismatch in these, or in our perceptions of what's required by specific tasks. Thus it may be a relevant time to look into what language is required, how well the tasks suggested fulfil the descriptions, update and extend the examples of tasks.

Improving reliability

The investigation of these factors affecting the reliability of ratings led to a number of recommendations by the 1988 review for moderating use of the ASLPR and standardising ratings across providers:

- *To improve consistency across centres and programs — sessions with regular interviewers were needed to state perceptions, accompanied by reliability studies and training in interview procedures.*

- *To improve consistency across AMES and other providers — inter-rater reliability studies are needed to give credibility, assist referral processes and to begin defining these other levels that are being used.*

It would also be interesting to research the correlation between:

- *class teacher assessing from knowledge of students and independent assessment using the scale;*

- *interviewers' intuitive assessments after three to four minutes and those of interviewers using the scale and complete interview;*

- *rating within the interview and rating by observation live and video.*

A small-scale research project was also envisaged in which experienced users would be asked to provide data in ratings made by reference only to the descriptions or only to the tasks.

Identifying training needs

Within AMES, inexperienced raters receive induction training in the use of the ASLPR. Centres and programs have instituted a process for moderating their teachers' ratings, and begun to meet with other centres in order to moderate ratings across programs. In addition, some centres have joined with their neighbouring TAFE ESL provider in order to moderate ratings, while other TAFE providers have received training sessions from experienced AMES staff. This has gone some way towards standardising agreement and increasing reliability of ASLPR assessments, one of the problems highlighted by Brindley (1986). Further investigation needs to be carried out, however, of other forms of reliability, especially test-retest and parallel form reliability (Shohamy 1990).

The development of Exrater

Exrater (Corbel 1990) was the first attempt in AMES to define a component ability scale (Bachman 1990) from the ASLPR. Aimed at simplifying access to the ASLPR and identifying the heuristics underlying it, it was directly prompted by teacher perceptions of the scale in the 1988 review and accompanying recommendations:

- *ASLPR descriptions are too dense and need to be rewritten or simplified. A commonly-occurring complaint! There is a need to delineate key words / pointers within a description to help rate more quickly — to try to state the intuitive or actual factors we use to match the description to language used. It could end up being a set of aspects rather like those developed for a COPQ test of speaking proficiency for Foreign Medical Professionals by McNamara (1990) which lists a number of factors, each on a continuum, such as:*

  - **intelligibility**, *from intelligible to unintelligible;*
  - **fluency**, *from even to uneven;*
  - **comprehension**, *from complete to incomplete;*
  - **appropriateness of language**, *from appropriate to inappropriate;*
  - **resources of grammar and expression**, *from rich, flexible to limited; leading to*
  - **overall communicative effectiveness**, *from near-native flexibility and range, to limited. (I think they're actually in the descriptions anyway.)*

  Finer variations within ASLPR levels may need to be developed as the current levels are too broad. Why is this perceived to be so? It appears to be due to supply and demand for classes at certain levels. In centres where there is a great pressure on numbers at certain levels, we form sub-categories of the one level in order to make separate classes or select a certain number of students, and selection may be affected by whether there are more students at the 'upper' part of a level than the 'lower' or vice versa. The problem is that these 'upper' or 'lower' parts have not been defined, with consequent detrimental effects on teachers' perceptions of reliability of ratings according to the ASLPR.

  In some areas of the program, alternative sub-categories, goal-related ones such as 'intending further study', or 'employment focus', 'specific skill classes', or 'faster' or 'slower' or 'older learners' may be used, and are probably preferable. However, how is a 'faster' learner identified?

- *Draw out the 'strands' of development of elements of language proficiency from various levels, and see how the continuum works.*

- *Can we identify the elements of proficiency and the sub-skills over a number of performances at interview to verify their existence and usefulness?*

Interestingly, the developer of the ASLPR, in one of his earliest articles about the scale, had originally suggested that better access to the descriptions might be obtained by a factor approach (Ingram 1979:C13):

> *A further table of value to the tester would be a summary table providing for each major factor in proficiency (e.g. pronunciation, syntax, vocabulary, discourse, register flexibility, function mastery, fluency, comprehensibility and comprehension) a one-line description of it at each level.*

Exrater (Corbel, this volume) was based on an analysis of the 'speaking' descriptions in an attempt to produce such one-line descriptions, and identified factors of Production, Intelligibility, Fluency, Accuracy, Vocabulary and Appropriacy. Pronunciation was also identified, but was later deleted after trials showed it was not considered effective in assisting raters, who found it was incorporated in the 'Intelligibility' factor. Similar analysis was later carried out on the other three macro-skills. The decision to computerise the program was first taken as a convenient way for newer staff to train themselves in rating with ASLPR on an individual basis, but it has also sparked interest amongst teachers experienced in ASLPR by providing an 'expert system' against which to test their intuitive assessments. Interest has also been shown by teachers in the program's potential for use as a diagnostic tool, as advocated by Shohamy (1990:388) who states that:

> *An oral test... will contain a random sample of a number of speech interactions which may require different criteria along with their contextualised variables... Such an assessment can be diagnostic, that is, ample information is supplied about various dimensions such as fluency, accuracy pragmatics, register use, accent, grammar, or whatever dimension is relevant.*

Having gained experience in rating with component ability scales, both Exrater and the McNamara (1990) scale, I believe that the factors may be very useful in identifying strengths and weaknesses of various learners, and in delineating class and course types more appropriately than when the review comments were made. Bachman (1990:329) also, in proposing the interactive/ability approach (IA) reminds us that language proficiency is too complex, implying a large number of behaviours, for any single criterion measure to be adequate for predictive utility:

> *If one chooses to define language proficiency in terms of component abilities... then... we should attempt to measure these component abilities and report scores for the measures separately.*

While Exrater does provide a global rating, based on averaging the scores for each component ability, it also provides an overall points score, indicating whether the rating is lower or higher within the global level. Finally, it provides the user with a profile of each of the component scores.

Interview procedures

Interview materials

One of the major criticisms of the 'real–life' approach concerns the lack of standardisation or variability in test procedure (Quinn and McNamara 1987; Brindley 1986; Bachman 1990). To address these concerns, in 1982, a 'Black Box' kit of guidelines for the development of the OPI had been produced by AMES Victoria together with related materials for varying tasks, such as role–play, dialogue interchanges from photographs, picture descriptions, small news items for reporting and giving opinions etc. Over time, however, the use of these materials lapsed owing to a number of factors, which were summarised thus in the 1988 review:

- *Time constraints on interviews — fifteen to twenty minutes per person to test all four macro-skills, obtain and give information, discuss problems etc. — have led to listening and speaking being rated simultaneously.*

- *The need to gather accurate information for the national computer data-base and assess proficiency levels at the same time may affect the interview. A performance may be affected by whether the interviewer fills in the form as the interview progresses or has an already-completed form, as the interviewer has to cover similar areas for something to talk about anyway.*

- *It is also necessary to begin needs analysis, to indicate possibilities for and impediments to learning, as information gained at interview is vital to pre-course planning. It is felt currently, that this information is helpful to principals in getting classes together, and to other administrative personnel, but little of this information, aside from the usual factors in the personal profile, gets to the actual teacher.*

- *It appears that teachers may rate intuitively in the first three to four minutes of the interview, and not change that rating significantly, if at all, even after much more time at interview. This may again be due to time constraints and the fact that ratings sufficiently accurate for placement may be obtained*

Given the realities of the interview procedure, extra time on tasks at interview clearly would not elicit significant extra information on which to base the oral ratings. In addition, the overly cumbersome format of the kit meant it was bypassed or that items were misplaced. However, reading, which is always tested as part of the interview, is also perceived as another language interaction task, since comprehension is assessed by discussion. This of course can also produce problems of reliability in rating reading, which will be discussed further on.

Variability in ASLPR interviews

The range of procedures used in the OPI can lead to varying questions — some predictable, some complex — and some variation in the instruments used. This can lead to considerable variation in performance as Quinn and McNamara (1987:8) comment:

> *A major weakness… is its (ASLPR) built-in tendency to become a variable instrument… Although all instruments contain measurement error, it is especially important with the interview-based approach to establish the validity of the rater's interview and the accuracy and consistency of his or her ratings.*

On this point, the 1988 review made the following recommendations:

- *Examine interviewers' questions and identify degrees of difficulty in understanding them and responding.*

- *Check the intention and any cultural bias of various questions and the 'expected' responses.*

- *Review the original 'kit' interviews and materials for possible updating.*

- *In-services on 'standard' and alternative questions, interview development, how to note listening, timing and ratings, hints for drawing out students etc.*

The outcome was a small-scale project examining the form and procedures of interviews (McIntyre 1989), which surveyed the procedures in fourteen AMES programs for enrolment and placement. In addition, twenty interviews were audiotaped from four programs, fifteen transcribed for detailed analysis, five used as corroborative evidence, ranging from ASLPR 0 to above 2. Among the findings were:

- In roughly half the programs surveyed, interviewers had to complete the computer information forms and assess proficiency simultaneously, while in the other half, the interview was conducted with the forms already completed. This led to differences in the types of questions asked, the former showing more open and information-seeking questions, the latter more closed or confirmatory questions. Furthermore the order of development of topics in interviews seeking information tended to follow that required by the forms, and was not always cohesive orally, whereas in other interviews the development followed responses given, though not consistently. Both interview types however included almost the same range of topics, addressing mostly personal, family and work or study backgrounds, collapsing the 'exploratory and analytical' categories of the original ASLPR interview guidelines (Ingram 1980, 1984).

- Time taken for interviews ranged from ten to thirty minutes. This was dependent on the ability level of the learners, and the need to check information relevant to attendance, such as commitments, family or other problems, or to learner pathways. This sometimes required the help of interpreters.

- Analysis of miscued responses showed that many were related to the pragmatics of the interview, such as illogical sequence of topic development mentioned above; questions repeated after the information had been provided; questions reworded before responses to the originals could be given; and excessively wordy questions.

- As anticipated, no separate listening tasks were evident. Both listening and speaking were rated from the interview interaction in general.

- It appeared that many interviewers use the customary introductory comments and questions not only as the good testing practice of lowering the test-taker's anxiety (Bachman 1990), but also to make an intuitive exploratory rating of roughly above or below ASLPR 1, in order to pitch the level of their subsequent interview.

The study established a need for sessions moderating interview procedures. Meanwhile, further studies are needed to examine how intuitive ratings are made. These would include ratings made to establish the 'pitch-level' of the interview, and comparing those made to establish the 'pitch-level', those made intuitively after three to four minutes and those made after full interview from the scale descriptions, in order to ascertain if these are consistent or change significantly.

Validity issues

The results of this study also raise some concerns about the content validity of the AMES interviews as a sample of learners' proficiency. Shohamy (1990: 386–7) concludes that:

> *Clearly an oral interview cannot be a valid measure of a test-taker's oral proficiency... the test samples must be based on a variety of language interactions...*

Clearly in AMES, the only evidence of any interaction type other than the interview question and answer format is by and large that of reporting on a text which, while ostensibly to test reading, also serves as further evidence of oral proficiency. Shohamy et al. (1986) (op. cit.), however, found only moderate correlation between interviews, discussions, reports and role-plays.

The validity of the ASLPR interview is further called into question by van Lier's (1989) implication that it may well be difficult to predict a candidate's performance in any interaction other than the interview context itself, though perhaps because AMES interviews are for the purposes of pre-course placement, such a context may predict sufficiently well for classroom interactions which, like interviews, are examples of what van Lier refers to as 'asymmetrical interaction'. This asymmetry in interactions was particularly in evidence in interviews in the AMES study, where the interviewer controlled the beginnings, topics and endings and the one-way question-answer interaction. Indeed only two of the interviewees who were recorded responded to an invitation to ask questions towards the end of the interviews, which may indicate that interviewees do not see asking questions as their right.

On the question of the interview as an adequate sample, van Lier (1989:469–501) comments that:

> *the ostensible aim is to have a good interview, not to have a good conversation...*
> *if this is communicative competence as expressed in conversation, the interview*
> *must strive to become a conversation in order for the information to be valid*

and notes that it may indeed be possible for the interview to become a conversation at specific points. However, the data from the project revealed the disappointing fact that the one or two likely points which could have led to real negotiation of meaning occurred after the closing of the interview, when trying to fit times of classes with interviewees' personal commitments. In other words the one 'real' conversation did not form part of the assessment.

Authenticity in the OPI

Bachman (1990:317) has argued that the authenticity of a test lies not only in its surface resemblance to real-world language use but also in the extent to which test tasks sample different areas of language skills and knowledge:

> *Test authenticity thus becomes essentially synonymous with what we consider*
> *communicative language use or the negotiation of meaning.*

Bachman (1990:357) also highlights the necessity to sample a sufficiently wide range of language to generalise about ability and calls for an integration of the 'real-life' approach with the interactional/ability approaches for

> *designing a wide range of test tasks according to specifications of language abilities*
> *and test method facets, followed by a program of construct research validation.*

While such a brief may not be necessary in the context of ASLPR use for class placement purposes, it may well be possible and indeed essential with the advent of other high-stakes purposes for which ASLPR ratings are used. These are outlined in the following section.

Assessments external to AMES

Real-world criteria and language assessment

Since real-life testing in general makes claims about performances in actual or simulated setting or, as in the case of ASLPR, aims to assess proficiency in situations that replicate as closely as possible those of real-life (Ingram 1979), it is surprising that the crucial field of assessments carried out by non-ESL personnel in non-test real-life situations has been so little investigated as a way of investigating the validity and reliability of language assessments.

In 1989, a small-scale research project was carried out in AMES (Lipa 1989) in which learners in an employment-oriented course took part in simulated job-interviews. These were taped and rated by their peers, other AMES teachers and (volunteer) personnel officers from a variety of workplaces. The study revealed that teacher assessments were higher than those of the workplace assessors. On the one hand, this could be construed as confirming the notion that ESL teachers make greater allowances in their assessments of non-native speakers; on the other hand, it could be that workplace personnel who assess such performances are focusing on the interview as an indication of the suitability of the person whose English is being assessed for actual employment.

Further such investigation is important in these times of high unemployment, especially as 'jobseekers' are being increasingly targeted by the AMEP. Employment-oriented courses are now a regular feature of the work of AMES and the study described could be replicated in order to obtain much broader data. Although the scale used was modelled on the subscales of the Occupational English Test in speaking for foreign health professionals (McNamara 1990), the subscales developed for Exrater by Corbel (this volume) from ASLPR descriptions could perhaps be used in the replications, although some of the specifically linguistic terminology used in the Exrater descriptions may not be appropriate for lay assessors.

Using the ASLPR for external assessment

An important initiative in the use of ASLPR has been the recent establishment of an External Assessments Unit in AMES, engaged in auditing the language and literacy needs of workplace staff, a part of government, employer and union agreements on award restructuring for industry. AMES is being contracted to carry out assessments of non-English speaking background (NESB) workers, in order to establish the language training they will need if they wish to access workplace training schemes and attain skill levels to which salary increases are linked. Because of a number of ethical and social justice issues, the validity of testing procedures and the reliability of ratings become crucial in this field. A group of experienced assessors have, therefore, undergone an 'Advanced

Training Certificate in the Use of ASLPR', conducted by one of the co-developers of the scale, and have carried out assessments both in workplaces and for the CES.

In the first of these language audits in a business enterprise, assessors have investigated the interactional domains, consultative practices and documents for disseminating information on site with a view to:

• preparing appropriate interview tasks and testing instruments for individual ASLPR assessments of the English language proficiency of non-English speaking background staff;

• assessing the language of information documents and training materials in ASLPR terms;

• establishing levels of effective participation in workplace interactions.

To meet the first two of these objectives, the unit trialled a set of guidelines (see next section) for tasks used for reading and writing in ASLPR — for the evaluation of existing ones as well as the selection and development of new ones. Once again, such a project had been suggested in the 1988 review which recommended the following action:

• *Collate all centres' and programs' instruments for assessing reading and tasks for writing.*

• *Moderate the reading passages and show how they equate with the descriptions. What language, textual, context and content features make the various passages similar or dissimilar, related to various levels?*

• *Establish whether the passages show any cultural bias or topics which may be 'unavailable' to students.*

• *Collate and investigate questions used by teachers in conjunction with these passages.*

• *Examine the writing tasks and see if they are appropriate to each level, but also investigate **what's involved in doing them**, to identify the elements* *of the writing process that we focus on in order to say that a performance fulfils the task and to what extent our perceptions of these vary, e.g. spelling is one element, the relative importance of which is variously perceived. (The 'Reading and Writing Assessment Kit' [Hood and Solomon 1989] could help considerably here.)*

- *Define tasks that could be done which either stem from or hinge upon the reading tasks already undertaken. The problem with some of the writing done at present is that it is undirected, and non-contextualised.*

- *Disseminate the information discovered and moderate people's perceptions of reading and writing performance against the ASLPR scale*

Developing guidelines for assessing reading and writing texts and tasks

A project carried out as part of NCELTR's special project program funded by the Commonwealth Department of Immigration and Ethnic Affairs, (McIntyre, 1994) initially aimed to collect materials currently in use in the AMEP, Australia-wide, categorise them, identify gaps in provision and and develop a range of supplementary materials. In the event, the collection indicated a need for criteria against which existing or potential materials could be considered rather than the development of supplementary materials *per se*. This was also in line with the advice of the developers of the ASLPR scale which encourages raters to assemble more localised kits of testing instruments, ostensibly so that the learners' language behaviours may be observed in situations that replicate as closely as possible those of real-life (Ingram 1979, 1980; Ingram and Wylie 1982), and that the effects of variables such as unfamiliar contexts, cultural aspects, local conditions may be minimised. Thus, it is hoped the primary validity concerns of real-life testing, those of content validity and authenticity, which Bachman (1990) raises, will be addressed in the varying venues in which AMEP programs are available.

The scale descriptions of reading and writing were therefore investigated in order to identify the types of documents and tasks suggested as appropriate for each level and criteria for their selection. The resulting matrix consists of a number of cells, each of which addresses a document type at a particular level (mentioned in the ASLPR), together with criteria from the scale against which proposed documents might be compared and suggestions for tasks or materials prompted by data in the collected documents. The cells are explained by McIntyre (1994) in Figure 1.

The administration of the ASLPR reading tasks relies on a different macro-skill (speaking) to establish comprehension. In addition, no standardised tasks are provided. As indicated, these factors have an influence on the reliability and validity of assessments.

The research reported above suffers from a number of limitations. Foremost among these is the lack of a workable model of levels of complexity in language used in documents, the inter-relationship between text and task complexity, types of writing tasks and the way they are specified. Research into this last point, reported in Huot (1990) is inconclusive concerning the effects of topic selection and rhetorical specification — in particular that of audience — on writing quality. However, it is worth noting that the studies outlined were mostly conducted on native-speaking schoolchildren, whereas the writing of adult second-language learners may be more markedly affected by the task format. Further investigation into this and the other questions outlined above needs to be undertaken.

Assessing language gains

Other recommendations from the 1988 review addressed the question of how to show learner progress and language gains from courses, typically expressed in questions such as the following:

- *How long does it take students with differing profiles to reach particular levels?*

- *How long does it take them to increase one level?*

Suggestions for addressing these questions included:

- *Follow three groups of students over a period of six or twelve months and plot their language gains in terms of ASLPR.*
  - *one from Level 0 onwards;*

The criteria headings have been drawn up from the following questions which need to be asked of each piece of material being considered. The first two criteria — **Identify document** and **Format/context** — address the 'reality' of documents. The boxed criteria — **Distance, Complexity, ASLPR performance** and **Conditions** — are those described in the wording of ASLPR. The **Tasks** and **Materials** are from the collected documents (and some further suggestions).

Identify document   What exactly is the document?

Format/context   Is it in 'real-life' format, (print, style, colour etc.) with contextual features (photos, graphics, etc.)?
If not, is it recognisable as the original?
Do you have the original for viewing?

Distance   How familiar/close to test-takers is it likely to be?

Complexity   How simple/complex is the language used?

ASLPR performance   What do we expect the clients can do at this level?

Conditions   How do we expect them to do it?

Tasks*   What will we ask them to do with this material?

Materials   How might we enhance current materials?
What other documents/materials could be used?

*As the ASLPR developers state that reading is a part of the interview, many of the reading documents collected did not show reading tasks, relying simply on discussing what was read with the interviewee. (This practice is under debate, because checking reading comprehension orally may not allow an interviewee to show his or her full potential.) In line with current use then, forms of questioning are not specified, however some indications lie in the ASLPR descriptions e.g. '… Can summarise key points… ' (R 3) which may determine what is asked or discussed. Aside from these, the aim of the questioning would be to elicit whatever information the interviewers might wish to know were they in the role of a person wanting information from the document read, in line with the 'realistic' aim outlined by the scale developers mentioned above.

The guidelines are based on the interview as it exists now. However questions of whether there should be standardised tasks, what types are suitable for the range of backgrounds, cultures and standards of education of students in the AMEP, how instructions for these might be given, and the usefulness of these writing tasks themselves, are acknowledged.

Figure 1 Explanation of the cells

      –   *one from Level 1 onwards;*
      –   *one from Level 1+ onwards.*
     (this may carry over to other providers)

- *Pre-employment students subsequently employed, might be interviewed and rated after a time length in that employment equivalent to the course they had.*

- *I am able to contact quite a few of the Galbally Rec 13 course people from the 1980 course. It would be interesting to rate their English ASLPR now as well as finding out:*
  - *how they have fared since leaving the course;*
  - *what they are doing now;*
  - *what steps and stages they had to go through to get there;*
  - *what part the course played in their development;*
  - *at what point they felt their language was good enough for their profession.*

Surveys of language gains of learners across AMES Victoria, using data extracted from the computerised Adult Migrant Information System (AMIS) indicate that learning gains are relatively rapid at the lower ASLPR levels (0 to 1), but progress slows considerably at Levels 1+ and 2. This suggests that the intervals between lower levels are not commensurate with those at middle levels, (and even less so at upper levels of the scale, from 2 to 3 to 4 etc.).

The method of data-collection, however, has not permitted questions such as numbers of hours needed by varying types of students to bridge these intervals, to be addressed. The other longitudinal and retrospective studies recommended above will be necessary in establishing the degree of influence of formal instruction in eventual language proficiency and in the success or otherwise of migrants in pursuing both work and mainstream study goals.

Affective factors in ASLPR rating

In the 1988 review a variety of affective and social factors of communication were identified as having an impact on ratings:

It (the ASLPR) rates one specific performance at one particular time and relies on one specific rater's interpretation or impression of that one performance. That performance may impress or depress the rater according to:

(Interviewers)
- *our mood and ability to concentrate;*
- *our nervousness or confidence;*
- *the length of time available/unavailable;*
- *the pressure of numbers of interviews;*
- *how many 'awkward' ones we've had today;*
- *our attitude to, or energy spent on, the interviewee just completed;*
- *subconscious attitudes to certain interviewees, (e.g. accent, tone, forms).*

(Interviewees)
- *their mood/ability to concentrate;*
- *presence of children, extraneous noise, interruptions etc.;*
- *the degree of their nervousness;*
- *the pressure of their day;*
- *their previous experiences at interviews;*
- *their personality e.g. the 'charmer' with little language;*
- *the degree of worry about getting a class;*
- *whether they feel that a 'too good' or 'too bad' performance will disqualify them from getting a course;*
- *whether a class is available now or not etc.*

The gender and age of both the interviewer and interviewee are other factors which can have a significant effect on the interaction (McIntyre 1988). Yet such social-psychological variables, which for several years now have been recognised as important in language learning, are only now belatedly working their way into language testing research (Shohamy et al. 1986).

Hymes' (1972:288) broader concept of communicative competence includes attention to the social dimension and 'sociolinguistic interference' in the relationship between theory and practice. Recalling his 1961 paper, he writes:

New speech habits must be introduced necessarily by particular sources to particular receivers, using a particular code with messages of particular forms via particular channels about particular topics in particular settings — and all this

> *from and to people for whom there already exist definite patternings of linguistic routines, of personality expression via speech, of uses of speech in social situations, of attitudes and concepts towards speech.*

I believe that this is a most important area of linguistic investigation which in time may well redefine the current notions of performance, communicative effect, language ability, as well as affecting the construct validity of tests of language proficiency.

Canale (1984:81) argues that adequate tests of communication must first be based on 'a sound description of communicating and proficiency in communicating'. Since ASLPR and other real-life tests rely on a **performance** from which to assess language proficiency, and provide no explicit model of ability, the possibility of separating language from communication often mentioned by assessors still remains debatable.

The question of construct validity of RL tests thus remains problematic. Continuing research into the social and affective dimensions of language performance will be required in order to build a comprehensive model of language ability that encompasses both 'language' and 'communication' in the broader sense intended by Hymes.

Future directions

As will be evident from this overview of assessment practices in AMES, significant research and development in relation to the use of ASLPR has been carried out. However, much still needs to be done.

First, and most importantly, the sampling of language performance on the basis of which ASLPR assessments are made, is very limited at present. This is due to time constraints, to the lack of any perceived detrimental effects that may result from less reliable ratings and the acknowledged difficulty in incorporating a range of tasks in interviews assessing 'general proficiency' of people who may or may not be familiar with the possible range of contexts that could be included (especially recent arrivals and those at lower levels). Nevertheless, broad sampling is important, as Shohamy et al. (1986) have shown in their experimental test for EFL Oral Matriculation in Israel. While reservations could be expressed about the appropriacy of one of their tasks (role-plays) for recently-arrived migrants, there may well be other types that could serve AMES purposes. Trialling of alternative oral tasks needs to be undertaken to investigate to what extent they produce the same results as those obtained at present.

A project has been proposed to update and expand the 'sample tasks' columns in the ASLPR scale, and further light may be shed on the issue of task expansion by the development of particular testing instruments in workplaces by the External Assessments Unit. This leads to the development of a variety of tests incorporating a range of tasks. This will, as Shohamy (1990) acknowledges, help to ensure that the right test is used for the right purpose.

Second, ways of documenting learners' ongoing language use need to be explored. The larger the sample of language on which assessments are based, the greater will be its predictive utility. Anticipating teachers' naive queries about the introduction of the ASLPR in 1979, Clark (1978:223) observed that:

> *The most direct procedure for determining an individual's proficiency… would simply be to follow that individual surreptitiously over an extended period of time… clearly impossible or at least impractical to administer a test of this type in the usual language learning situation.*

However, at teaching institutions such as AMES, there is the possibility of compiling on-going assessments from a larger range of interactions than is possible at interview. While teachers as assessors of their own learners may not be seen as ideal by some, they nonetheless are the ones who have the largest number of real-life interactions with them. These include conversations in private, out of class, face-to-face or by telephone about such matters as absences, illness, learning problems or progress, homework, personal problems, goals for learning, places to shop, TV programs, news items; giving support about transport, approaching employing authorities, difficulties with government departments and so on, all of which require real negotiation of meaning. In addition, teachers often observe learners' peer interactions on a range of topics. If teachers were encouraged to keep a more formal journal of these interactions, they could perhaps prove untapped sources of language for more precise, on-going assessments which could be documented in the form of progress profiles or portfolios.

Third, further investigation of actual interviews is needed to establish which areas could be turned to conversation, as van Lier (1989) suggests, together with moderating sessions for interviewers, to match more closely their interviewing styles and to achieve a closer simulation of real-life interaction. The importance of this for external assessments is paramount.

Fourth, work on subscales, component ability scales and factor scales need to be continued because of their importance in assessments beyond AMES and their potential as diagnostic tools within AMES. There are difficulties with interpreting the wording of some of the 'simplified' descriptions and these may have to be reworded, not only to enable teachers to differentiate between certain level statements, but also to enable further comparative work on ratings by workplace personnel and teachers to be carried out, to provide more useful profile information, and to make assessments more intelligible to people outside the linguistic and language teaching professions.

Fifth, wording within the descriptions of the ASLPR regarding both the issue of familiarity or distance of contexts may need further definition by reference to sample tasks. Wording such as 'situations of immediate need' (Level 0+, 1+); 'common everyday events or topics' (Levels 1-, 1); 'in their everyday lives' (Levels 1, 2) may vary from person to person interviewed. If one wishes to assess 'general proficiency' in RL tests, then it will be necessary to identify the choices or ranges of real-life contexts or situations relevant to each particular level and to attempt to classify these in terms of difficulty. On the other hand, it could be argued that there is no such thing as 'general proficiency' — there is only proficiency in specified domains. In the words of Bachman (1990:310–311):

> *What any attempt to define authenticity by sampling 'real-life' language use fails to recognise ultimately, is that instances of language use are by definition context dependent and therefore unique.*

Finally, in reading and writing assessments, the inter-relationship between the complexity of texts and complexity of tasks will need to be identified. ASLPR statements about linguistic complexity are at best vague. As Ingram and Wylie (1982) state for example:

- *short, simple sentences and short, syntactically simple texts;*
- *sentences of greater complexity;*

- *structurally complex forms; unusually complex structures;*
- *more complex discourse; forms 'remote' from normal discourse;*
- *routine, uncomplicated;*
- *directly stated; clearly presented; meaning clearly spelt out;*
- *simple stylised forms;*
- *low frequency idiom.*

The reading documents collected for the NCELTR project need to be examined in greater detail for instances that explicate these statements, providing further guidance for users. Similarly, oral proficiency performances need to be further examined to establish to what extent the utterances of interviewees match wordings in the descriptions (such as *developing spontaneity*) that are currently open to interpretation.

Conclusion

Bachman (1990) suggests that the notion of authenticity in RL tests is problematic, as it involves the context in which the testing takes place, the qualities of the test taker, and the nature of language itself. However, despite these difficulties, Bachman (1990:313) admits that it has been a useful means of test development, by providing a 'relatively easy way to develop tests which "look good" in society at large'. More tellingly, he chides critics who 'have not, in my opinion, provided a viable alternative'.

I believe that AMES, teaching as it does adults who need to function in society at large, must persevere in the RL direction it has taken thus far, as its learners will be assessed in real-life terms by their interactants in society. However, the construct validity of the ASLPR remains open to question and the only evidence provided so far is circular as the following statement by Ingram (1984:4) demonstrates:

> *Test-retest reliability was likely if construct validity was assured and if other forms of reliability were found to exist... reliability coefficients are high. It was argued earlier that construct validity was probable, therefore test-retest reliability seems likely to exist.*

Establishing predictive ability is also problematic but necessary, since predicting how adults will manage interactions in real-life is important. To do this a wider range of interactions and more precise criteria for assessing them will be required, thus leading perhaps to the development of different tests for different purposes. From a theoretical point of view, what is needed, as Bachman (1990:357) points out, is a synthesis of the RL and interactional/ability approaches which would involve the specification of tasks of the kind used in the ASLPR underpinned by a framework of language ability. By proceeding in this way, it may be possible to ensure that assessments in AMES not only reflect real-life language use but also are based on an explicitly defined construct of language ability.

References

Bachman, L.F. 1990. *Fundamental considerations in language testing*. Oxford: Oxford University Press.

Brindley, G. 1979. *Assessment of ESL speaking proficiency through the oral interview*. Sydney: Adult Migrant English Service.

Brindley, G. 1986. *The assessment of second language proficiency: issues and approaches*. Adelaide: National Curriculum Resource Centre.

Canale, M. 1984. Testing in a communicative approach. In G.A. Jarvis (ed.) *The challenge for excellence in foreign language education*. Middlebury, Vt.: The Northeast Conference Organisation.

Clark, J.L.D. 1972. *Foreign language testing: theory and practice*. Philadelphia, Pa.: Centre For Curriculum Development Inc.

Clark, J.L.D. 1978. Interview testing research and educational testing service. In J.L.D. Clark (ed.) *Direct testing of speaking proficiency: theory and application*. Princeton, NJ: Educational Testing Service.

Corbel, C. 1990. *Exrater: a computer program to assist in the rating of language proficiency*. Melbourne: Adult Migrant English Service Victoria.

Department of Immigration and Ethnic Affairs. 1984. *Australian second language proficiency ratings (ASLPR)*. Canberra: Australian Government Publishing Service.

Galbally Review. 1978. *Review of post-arrival programs and services for migrants*. Canberra: Australian Government Publishing Service.

Huot, B. 1990. The literature of direct writing assessment: major concerns and prevailing trends. *Review of Educational Research* 60, 2:237–263.

Hymes, D.H. 1972. On communicative competence. In J.B. Pride and J. Holmes (eds) *Sociolinguistics*. Harmondsworth: Penguin.

Ingram, D.E. 1979. Introduction to the Australian second language proficiency ratings (ASLPR). A paper in the *AMEP Teachers' Manual*. Canberra: Australian Government Publishing Service.

Ingram, D.E. 1980. The Australian second language proficiency ratings — their nature, development and trialling. Paper presented at the *1980 RELC Regional Seminar*, Singapore.

Ingram, D.E. 1982. *Report on the formal trialling of the Australian second language proficiency ratings*. Canberra: Adult Migrant Education Program, Department of Immigration and Ethnic Affairs.

Ingram, D.E. and E. Wylie. 1982. *Australian second language proficiency ratings (ASLPR) revised*. Canberra: Australian Government Publishing Service.

Ingram, D.E. and E. Wylie. 1984. *Australian second language proficiency ratings (ASLPR)*. Canberra: Australian Government Publishing Service.

Lipa, L . 1989. Job interview rating scale: trial on pre-employ*ment courses in AMES Victoria*. Unpublished manuscript. Melbourne: Adult Migrant English Service Victoria.

Lipa, L. 1993. *Learner pathways in the AMEP*. Research Report Series 4. Sydney: National Centre for English Language Teaching and Research.

McIntyre, P. 1988. *'ASLPR revisited'*: *a review of thoughts, comments and recommendations after a term's moderating sessions with AMES centres and programs.* Unpublished manuscript. Melbourne: Adult Migrant English Service Victoria.

McIntyre, P. 1989. *The ASLPR interview in AMES: an examination of its forms and procedures.* Unpublished manuscript. Melbourne: Adult Migrant English Service Victoria.

McIntyre, P. 1994. *Moderating materials — guidelines for the selection of texts and tasks for reading and writing assessment with the ASLPR.* Unpublished manuscript. Sydney: National Centre for English Language Teaching and Research.

McNamara, T.F. 1990. *Assessing the second language proficiency of health professionals.* Unpublished PhD thesis, University of Melbourne.

Quinn, T.J. and T.F. McNamara. 1987. Australian second language proficiency ratings. In J.C. Alderson, K. Kranke and C. Stansfield (eds) *Reviews of English language tests.* Washington: TESOL.

Savignon, S.F. 1983. *Communicative competence: theory and classroom practice.* Reading, Mass.: Addison Wesley.

Shohamy, E. 1990. Language testing priorities: a different perspective. *Foreign Language Annals* 23, 5:385–394.

Shohamy, E., T. Reves and Y. Bejarano. 1986. Comprehensive test of oral proficiency. *ELT Journal* 40, 3:212–220.

van Lier, L. 1989. Reeling, writhing, drawling, stretching and fainting in coils: OPI as conversation. *TESOL Quarterly* 23, 3:489–508.

Vigil, N.A. and J.W. Oller. 1976. Rule fossilization, a tentative model. *Language Learning* 26, 2:281–295.

6 Competency-based assessment in second language programs: some issues and questions[1]

Geoff Brindley

Introduction

Competency-based models of vocational education and training have in recent years dominated the educational landscape in Australia, the UK and New Zealand. They have also begun to exert a significant influence in the field of language learning. In the UK, the Royal Society of Arts (1987, 1988) developed Profile Schemes in Practical Skills and ESL which were based on explicit specifications of learning outcomes in the form of Profile Sentences (stated in terms very similar to what are now called competencies or units of learning) and which incorporated various forms of criterion-referenced assessment. More recently, also in the UK, the Languages Lead Body (LLB) (1992) has produced a competency-based National Language Standards framework for the use of foreign languages at work, aimed at providing a 'common specification which can be used by training providers, employers and individuals when considering levels of language skills and training required'. In Australia, the *Certificate in Spoken and Written English (CSWE)* (Hagan et al. 1993), a comprehensive accredited CB framework for adult ESL, along with an accompanying set of *Assessment Guidelines* (Burrows 1993a, 1993b, 1993c), has recently been adopted in a wide range of publicly and privately funded adult ESL programs and 'may act as a model for the teaching of other languages' (Candlin and Strong 1993:i).

CB approaches are thus beginning to become firmly established in the field of adult language learning as a basis for curriculum design, assessment and reporting. The stakes associated with assessment are at the same time becoming higher, with the advent of accreditation and certification. Because of the rapidity with which these changes have come about, however, as Bottomley et al. (1994) note, there has been relatively little public discussion of the implications for language teaching and assessment.

The aim of this paper is, therefore, to briefly survey a number of key issues and questions surrounding the role of assessment in CB approaches to language learning. Many of these issues have been discussed at some length by writers in both general education (e.g. Wolf et al. 1991; Moss 1992; Mehrens 1992; Worthen 1992) and language testing (e.g. McNamara 1990; Bachman 1990; Shohamy 1993a, 1993b; Bachman and Palmer, forthcoming) in the context of ongoing debates about the merits and feasibility of performance assessment. The issues are worth revisiting, however, in order that the strengths and potential weaknesses of current approaches to CBA may be evaluated and areas identified where further research and development are needed.

Criteria for evaluating CBA

Assessment procedures are conventionally evaluated in terms of their validity, reliability and practicality; that is, to what extent do they assess what they claim to assess, to what extent do they produce consistent results and to to what extent can they be feasibly implemented given the prevailing institutional conditions and the resources available? Although there is some debate in the literature surrounding the extent to which performance assessment (of which CBA is an example) should be evaluated according to these traditional criteria (cf. Linn et al. 1991), they are sufficiently broad to cover most areas of concern and will therefore be used as a loose organising framework for the discussion which follows. For reasons of space, I will focus principally on the first two issues, however. Discussions of practicality issues can be found in Worthen (1992) and Nuttall (1992).

Validity issues in CBA

In the context of competency assessment, validity concerns embrace a number of key issues. These are summarised as follows by Mehrens (1992:7):

In studying the validity of performance assessments, one should think carefully about whether the right domains are being assessed, whether they are well defined, whether they are well sampled, whether — even if well sampled — one can infer to the domain, and what diagnostically one can infer if the performance is not acceptably high.

This statement highlights a number of important points about CBA. First, it emphasises the fact that there needs to be a clear conceptualisation of the domains being assessed before valid assessment instruments can be designed. In the context of language learning, this means that competency specifications and assessment criteria must begin with the definition of a construct. This involves an explicit attempt to address the question, 'What does it mean to know how to use a language?' for the target population.

The second related point is that CBA involves *inference*. As Gonczi et al. (1993:6) point out:

Performance is what is directly observable, whereas competence is not directly observable, rather it is inferred from performance. This is why competencies were defined as combinations of attributes that underlie successful performance.

CBA does not, in other words, begin and end with the assessment of isolated performances. Assessment is also concerned with the extent to which the knowledge, skills and other attributes of individuals enable other similar performances to be carried out. This is the view which is consistently taken in both the assessment of vocational and professional competencies (Masters and McCurry 1990:39; Gonczi et al. 1993:11) and in the field of language and literacy assessment (Ingram 1984:11; Cope et al. 1993:70; Griffin and McKay 1993:16), where specific tasks are seen as indicators of underlying ability. The way in which competencies are described in the CSWE ('... expressed in general terms', '... able to be adapted to a number of contexts' [Hagan et al. 1993:5]) implies, similarly that performances are seen as indicators of generalisable abilities.

The third point follows from this — in order to establish the validity of inferences based on assessments, we need to know to what extent performance on one task generalises to other similar kinds of tasks: it thus becomes important to sample performances across a range of tasks and contexts.

The final point that the author makes about performance assessment is that its validity derives in part from its diagnostic value — to what extent can the information provided by the assessment be used to alert the learner to what aspects of the performance need to be improved if a performance does not meet the required standard?

Investigating the validity of CBA

Validity is defined by Messick (1989:13) as:

> *an integrated evaluative judgement of the degree to which empirical evidence and theoretical rationales support the* adequacy *and* appropriateness *of* inferences *and* actions *based on test scores or other modes of assessment.*
>
> (author's emphases)

Validating an assessment procedure thus requires the collection of evidence that would justify the interpretation and use of the information yielded by it. Such evidence, in the case of standardised tests, has frequently taken the form of statistical information on the extent to which a test has measured a construct independently of other constructs and on the relationship between performance in a test and in other similar kinds of tests. Recently, however, there have been calls to expand the range of validation evidence to include a wide range of other non-statistical methods ranging from ethnographic investigation to self-reports from test-takers (Moss 1992).

Given the recent advent of CBA, there has been little time to accumulate validity evidence of any kind so it would be inappropriate at this stage to attempt to evaluate the validity of CBA schemes in terms of the criteria outlined above. I will therefore restrict myself to raising some key issues and problems involved in establishing the construct, content and predictive validity of CBA and suggest some lines of investigation that might be opened up in order to gather relevant data.

Construct validity

One of the key questions in CBA that needs to be addressed is that of construct validity: how adequate is the assessment as a measure of what it is supposed to assess? This entails an investigation of the extent to which the construct that is defined reflects current theoretical understandings of the attributes or qualities being tested.

Construct validation, however, is a very complex issue, since to a large extent validity judgements will depend on the way that those designing the assessment procedures choose to define the construct in question, that is, language ability. This will determine which competencies are identified, the terms in which they are described and, by extension, the nature of the criteria which are used to assess performance. Consequently, differing constructs are likely to result in quite different assessment criteria. For example, the performance criteria to be demonstrated for Competency 4 at Stage 3 of the CSWE, 'can negotiate complex/problematic exchanges', are as follows:

Competency 4. Can negotiate complex/problematic spoken exchanges for personal business and community purposes.
- *Achieves purpose of exchange and provides all essential information accurately.*
- *Uses appropriate staging for text e.g. opening and closing strategies.*
- *Provides and requests information as required.*
- *Provides and requests goods and services as required.*
- *Explains circumstances, causes, consequences and proposes solutions as required.*
- Sustains dialogue e.g. using feedback, turn taking, seeking clarification and understands statements and requests of the interlocutor.

(Hagan et al. 1993:76)

It is interesting to contrast this set of performance criteria with the following example taken from the Royal Society of Arts Practical Skills Profile Scheme which provides a method for assessing work-related and non-vocational courses in Communication, Numeracy and Process Skills:

PROFILE SENTENCE : C12 *Participate effectively in negotiation*
Performance criteria (the student has demonstrated the ability to:)
- *Define own preferred outcome in given situation*
- *State own needs/wishes clearly in language appropriate to listeners*
- *Express disagreement sympathetically*
- *Consider sympathetically suggestions of others*
- *Suggest new ideas to solve temporary difficulties*
- *Contribute to discussion freely and clearly without dominating the meeting.*

(Royal Society of Arts 1988:41)

Differing constructs, differing criteria

The lack of commonality between these two sets of criteria illustrates graphically how the perspective of the test designer can influence the way that competencies are described and hence assessed. In the first case, it is primarily *language* that is the object of assessment (staging of discourse, conversational strategies, information-giving etc.). In the second, it is interpersonal communication skills in a more general sense and non-linguistic, social and affective factors (intentionality, sympathy, empathy) have a much greater role.

In the context of this discussion, there is a good deal of evidence to suggest that disciplines outside applied linguistics interpret 'communication' or 'communicative competence' quite differently to language testers and hence employ different criteria for assessment (cf. Haddon 1991; Elder 1993). Communication theorists, for example, accentuate criteria such as *empathy, behavioural flexibility* and *interaction management* (Wiemann and Backlund 1980) and emphasise the role of non-verbal aspects of communication. In other fields, such as organisational management, communicative ability is seen very much in terms of 'getting the job done' and the success of communication is thus judged primarily in relation to how well the outcomes are achieved rather than on specific linguistic features (Brindley 1989:122–23). McNamara (1990) makes this point in relation to doctor-patient communication, noting that in the medical profession 'there is a concern for the communication process in terms of its outcomes'. He comments (1990) that 'sociolinguistic approaches to "communicative ability" are indeed narrow, and narrowly concerned with language rather than communicative behaviour as a whole'.

Investigating criteria for communicative success

The question, 'How valid is CBA?', then, needs to be considered in terms of the claims that are being made on the basis of the assessment and the way in which users of assessment information interpret it. If the 'can-do' statements in CBA schemes are intended to be meaningful and generalisable beyond the classroom, however, then there may be a case for operating with a broader definition of language ability than has conventionally been the case in language assessment.

Whether to incorporate non-linguistic factors such as those mentioned above is clearly a very complex issue, as McNamara (in press) points out:

The incorporation of affective and other non-linguistic variables in a model of second language communicative ability may be problematic in that such a rich picture of the assessment situation may make drawing inferences from it difficult. Yet there is a need for a model that is rich enough to enable conceptualisation of all the issues involved in second language communicative performance situations... Having constructed a model, it is then necessary to determine what is appropriate and possible to assess in a given test situation.

In order to be able to take these suggestions further, however, more information is needed on the relationship between overall communicative success and specific linguistic behaviour. A useful starting point might be to examine instances where learners are deemed to have fulfilled the overall task requirements in CBA schemes but to have failed to meet one or more of the performance criteria. Such an investigation would be useful in two ways: first, it would assist in identifying potentially problematic performance criteria; second, it might give an indication of those non-linguistic factors which facilitate the performance of certain tasks and in this way generate hypotheses concerning factors which might legitimately be taken into consideration in the assessment of some competencies. At the same time, it would be useful to gather data on the way in which information on language competencies is being interpreted and used by relevant third parties outside the classroom. This would assist in establishing whether the 'can-do' statements embodied in competency statements were being interpreted in the broad sense described above and at the same time provide data which could be used to examine the predictive validity of CBA.

Performance criteria and scoring methods

Also of relevance in the construct validation of CBA is the relationship between construct definition and scoring methods. In CBA, the method for assessing attainment of competencies differs somewhat from that which is used in traditional language proficiency assessment. In the latter case, a scalar judgement is usually made, along some kind of continuum from 'zero' to 'native-like' proficiency. In CBA, however, assessment is on a yes/no basis, that is, the assessor is required to make a binary judgement as to whether or not the learner demonstrates the behaviours specified in the performance criteria. In addition, each of the criteria has to be fulfilled in order for the learner to qualify for the award of the competency.

The obligatory nature of performance criteria forces developers of CBA schemes to make strong claims concerning the mandatory elements of communicative acts. Thus in the RSA scheme, the LLB framework and the CSWE, certain obligatory features of oral and written discourse are identified and these features then serve as the basis for the criteria according to which the quality of a language performance is evaluated. In the RSA and LLB schemes, no information is provided on the theoretical basis of these criteria. Nor is there any specific guidance to assessors on how to apply them. The CSWE, on the other hand, is quite explicit about its theoretical underpinnings which derive from a genre-based approach to the definition of competencies. The theoretical rationale has its roots in Halliday's (1985) systemic-functional linguistic theory 'which systematically relates language to the contexts in which it is used' (Hagan et al. 1993:1) and draws on applications of genre theory in other educational contexts (see Martin 1993 for an overview). The basis of the competency specifications is the language user's knowledge of the relationship between text and context which is used 'to predict the language likely to be used in any given situation' (Hagan et al. 1993:9). The elements and performance criteria are accordingly described according to four broad descriptive categories: *purpose of text*; *discourse structure*; *grammar/vocabulary* and *phonology/graphology* (Hagan et al. 1993:7–8). The text is seen as an encounter involving a number of successive stages in which certain linguistic features are mobilised to achieve the social purpose of the task.

A number of writers, however, have questioned the extent to which it is possible to unequivocally specify the elements of oral and written texts. Bottomley et al. (1994:21) comment that the 'presentation of text types (in the CSWE) tends to gloss over the difficulty of capturing with certainty the elements of (particularly spoken) discourse'. In this regard, Kress (1993:28), claims that genres are not fixed and in constant evolution:

> *while generic conventions provide certain dimensions of constraint, generic form is never totally fixed, but is always in the process of change — for example, a job interview in 1992 is very different from a job interview in 1932.*

Willing (1992:20) expresses doubts about application of the term 'genre' to oral discourse:

> *What is understood, structurally, and substantively, about genres in the literary sense, and what is understood about the schematic scripting of oral interactive*

> *encounters, are at present incommensurate. Indeed it is premature to suppose that there could ever be enough common conceptual and analytical ground to warrant extending the term 'genre', other than very metaphorically, to the conceptualisation of oral interactive discourse.*

He quotes Levinson (1979:294) to the effect that:

> *Conversation is not a structural product in the same way that a sentence is — it is rather the outcome of the interaction of two or more independent goal-oriented individuals, with often divergent interests.*

In a similarly cautious vein, Murray (1994) points out that the text-based approach relies on the availability of very comprehensive descriptions of different oral and written genres and puts the view that 'full descriptions of the structures of most oral and written genres have yet to be developed'. She notes that for this reason she has chosen to use criteria for portfolio assessment in the form of an assessment guide based on the more 'subjective, general features of written texts'.

Commenting on the problems involved in validating performance assessments, Messick (1992:9) notes that there is a

> *need to move beyond traditional professional judgement of content to accrue construct-related evidence that the ostensibly sampled processes are actually engaged by respondents in task performance.*

In the context of CBA this suggests that further research needs to be undertaken into the way that authentic discourse (particularly oral discourse) functions to achieve certain social purposes (Burns 1993; Corbel 1993; Gollin 1994) before competencies derived from text analysis can be exhaustively specified with confidence. Such research will hopefully assist in throwing more light on those features that are obligatory and those that are optional and thus help to inform the criteria that are used to evaluate communicative performances in CBA schemes.

Authenticity and generalisability

One of the most attractive aspects of CBA is that it enables the teacher to focus on communicative activities resembling the authentic use of language and to use similar tasks for assessment purposes. In fact, it might seem reasonable enough to assume that assessments based on authentic-looking communicative tasks are valid by definition since they attempt to replicate 'real-life' language use situations, which is ultimately what communicative language teaching and assessment are concerned with.

However such assumptions have been questioned by many writers in both general education and language assessment on a number of grounds. In the first place, an assessment activity is by its very nature an artificial situation: no matter how 'life-like' the task is, people still know they are being assessed under special conditions. As Spolsky (1985:36) comments:

> ... *We are forced to the conclusion that testing is not authentic language behaviour, that examination questions are not real, however much like real-life questions they seem, and that an examinee needs to learn the special rules of examinations before he or she can take part in them successfully.*

A second problem with 'authentic' assessment tasks is the difficulty of generalising from a one-off performance to other situations of language use. Commenting on the tendency of some language testers to claim validity on the basis that their tests reflect real-life settings, Skehan (1984:208) comments:

> *This viewpoint confuses naturalness of setting with sufficiency. A large part of the problem in testing is in sampling a sufficiently wide range of language to be able to generalise to new situations. Merely making an interaction 'authentic' does not guarantee that the sampling of language involved will be sufficient, or the basis for wide-ranging and powerful predictions of language behaviour in other situations.*

Bachman (1990) has also cautioned against the acceptance of authentic-looking 'direct' assessments such as the oral interview as automatically valid measures of ability. He points out (1990:309) that such procedures confuse the observation of a performance with the ability itself and are limited in their generalisability beyond the specific context in which testing takes place. Bachman proposes a somewhat different approach to authenticity by suggesting that authenticity lies not only in the surface resemblance between assessment tasks and real-world behaviour but also in the extent to which different areas of language skills and knowledge are sampled in the task. This is what Bachman (1990:317) refers to as *interactional authenticity*:

> *In summary the IA (interaction/ability) approach views authenticity as residing in the interaction between the test taker, the test task and the testing context.*

In order to construct valid 'authentic' tests of communicative language ability Bachman (1990:322) argues that we have to

> ... *construct or select tests or test tasks that reflect our knowledge of the nature of language abilities and language use. Both the development and selection of authentic language tests is thus based on a theoretical framework that includes the language abilities of the test taker and the characteristics of the testing context.*

Summing up this discussion, what Bachman and others are arguing is that authenticity in the sense of surface resemblance to target language use situations is a necessary but not sufficient condition for test and task validity.

In order to be able to generalise beyond a particular instance of language use, what is needed is a principled way of specifying the abilities that assessment tasks are tapping and a sampling frame which enables a multidimensional picture to be built up of the way in which these abilities are being assessed, using a range of different tasks using different assessment methods. One of the most consistent findings from recent American research performance assessment in general education is that performance appears to be highly task–dependent (Brandt 1992; Linn et al. 1990). The same picture is beginning to emerge in language assessment (Pollitt and Hutchinson 1987; Shohamy and Inbar 1991; Swain 1993). This underlines the necessity of using multiple tasks and multiple assessment formats.

As Murray (1994) points out, one of the advantages of this multidimensional approach in the context of classroom assessment is that it naturally lends itself to profiling approaches which enable teachers to build up samples of different types of student work which reflect progress over a period of time.

At this point in the evolution of CBA, there is a lack of data indicating the degree to which it is possible to generalise from the performance assessments that are being conducted to other contexts of language use. In order to gather evidence on generalisability, studies are needed of the relationship between performances on different kinds of assessment tasks accompanied by an examination of the extent to which they draw on common underlying abilities. Empirical techniques such as Rasch analysis and generalisability theory can be used to examine the relationships between performances across a range of tasks (Pollitt and Hutchinson 1987; Bachman 1990). This would help to clarify the somewhat murky relationship which currently exists between ability and competencies.

Reliability issues in CBA

CBA relies heavily on teachers' subjective judgements of language performance. In the interests of fairness to learners, it is important that these judgements are seen to be consistent. As more and more rating tools are developed to assess competencies, teachers will therefore need to be trained to interpret and apply performance criteria in a consistent way. Rater training involving familiarisation with the criteria and practice in applying them to samples of performances across a range of ability levels has long been standard practice with proficiency rating scales and it has been claimed that high levels of inter-rater agreement can be obtained in this way (Dandonoli and Henning 1991).

However the feasibility of obtaining inter-rater reliability with respect to language performance has come increasingly under question. Research in language testing has shown that despite training, 'significant and substantial differences between raters persist' and that rater behaviour can change significantly over time (Lumley and McNamara 1993). North (1993:45), in a comprehensive survey of the whole field of subjective judgements in rating concludes that 'judge severity is relatively impervious to training and that people rate in different ways'. This is of course, is hardly surprising given the complexity of the interaction between the language behaviour being rated, the personal characteristics of both the rater and the candidate and aspects of the setting in which the rating takes place. However, it leaves the assessor in a dilemma: if variability in rater behaviour is the norm then what can be done to reduce the error in rater judgements? Should we simply learn to live with lower levels of reliability as some testers have suggested (see, for example, Swain 1993) and try to convince consumers of test information that it is not realistic to expect human judges to agree?

Although innovations in measurement technology in the form of many-faceted Rasch analysis (Linacre 1989) have proved of considerable benefit in resolving problems of rater disagreement in standardised proficiency tests (Wigglesworth

1993), such technology would not be either easy or practical to apply in the context of CBA. Institutions will still have to find ways of trying to achieve consensus on the qualities of learner performance. In this regard the collection and analysis of 'benchmark' performance samples has proved a useful way of focusing raters' attention on key aspects of task performance at different levels (Burrows 1994). Another way of trying to accommodate for rater severity without the benefit of technology is outlined by North (1993:45). He describes a procedure for oral assessment using two assessors, one who knows the class in question (high sensitivity) and one who is familiar with the whole range of the level (low sensitivity). Ratings are carried out independently using both holistic and analytical marking 'with negotiation over grades between the two assessors as a final step to adjust for severity' (ibid).

In the context of CBA, preliminary research conducted by Burrows and Jones (1993) into rater consistency in judging attainment of competencies in Stage 2 of the CSWE indicates quite high levels of overall rater agreement (calculated in terms of percentages) for most competencies. The study also provides useful data on the interpretation and application of performance criteria. For example, the competency 'can understand and give spoken instructions' proved problematic to assess for some teachers since it requires the simultaneous assessment of listening and speaking. At the same time, some of the relativistic terminology used to describe performance ('mostly appropriate', 'mostly correct spelling' etc.) was difficult for some assessors to interpret. Another interesting outcome of this investigation was the fact that teachers reported that they found some texts difficult to assess because they did not conform to the specified text type ('this task does not generate a recount') and thus could not be marked according to the given performance criteria. This highlights the importance of ensuring that assessment tasks are aligned to the performance criteria so as to allow the testee to demonstrate all of the behaviours described. Given what might seem to be the subtle differences between some text types, this may not always be easy for teachers to do and strengthens the case for further development of banks of fully piloted assessment tasks.

Data of the kind provided by this study are useful in establishing the extent to which CBA can meet acceptable standards of reliability and validity. Further such investigations could profitably be conducted to focus more closely on some of the issues which are emerging. Of particular importance in the context both of construct validity and reliability is the way in which individual performance criteria function. Since agreement is only deemed to occur when all of the performance criteria are achieved, overall agreement figures only give a partial picture. Of equal interest is the question of the extent of agreement on each criterion. If it can be shown that some criteria produced more consistent agreement than others, then steps could perhaps be taken to re-examine and re-order criteria so as to retain only those on which acceptable levels of consistency can be obtained. In investigating this question, indices such as Cohen's k*appa* (Chaudron et al. 1988) are likely to provide more a reliable indication of consistency than percentage agreement which fails to take chance agreement into account (Page and Iwata 1986).

Conclusion

Reports on the implementation of CBA indicate that it has already demonstrated a number of positive benefits (cf. Bottomley et al. 1994):

- Teachers' and learners' attention becomes more focused on language as a tool for communication rather than on language knowledge as an end in itself.

- Assessment is integrated into the learning process through the use of attainment targets which are directly linked to course content and objectives.

- Learners are able to obtain useful diagnostic feedback on their progress and achievement since explicit criteria are provided against which they can compare their performances.

- Better communication between users of assessment information and educational institutions is established through the use of various forms of outcome reporting which are couched in performance terms and are hence intelligible to non-specialists.

In order to demonstrate that CBA is a viable alternative to other 'traditional' forms of language assessment, however, it will be necessary to continue to collect evidence on the way it is implemented and used. To this end I have suggested a number of avenues of investigation which could productively be pursued in order to address some of the more important unanswered questions raised in this paper. As more research evidence comes to hand, it will become clearer to what extent the obvious educational utility of competency-based approaches can be supported by the technical quality of the assessment procedures which underpin them.

Notes

1   This chapter is reprinted with permission from *Prospect* 9, 2, 1994.

References

Bachman, L.F. 1990. *Fundamental considerations in language testing.* Oxford: Oxford University Press.

Bachman, L.F. and A.S. Palmer. Forthcoming. *Language testing in practice.* Oxford: Oxford University Press.

Bachman, L.F. and S. Savignon. 1986. The evaluation of communicative language proficiency: a critique of the ACTFL oral interview. *Modern Language Journal* 70, 4.

Bottomley, Y., J. Dalton and C. Corbel. 1994. *From proficiency to competencies: a collaborative approach to curriculum innovation.* Sydney: National Centre for English Language Teaching and Research.

Brandt, R. 1992. On performance assessment: a conversation with Grant Wiggins. *Educational Leadership,* May.

Brindley, G. 1989. *Assessing achievement in the learner-centred curriculum.* Sydney: National Centre for English Language Teaching and Research.

Brindley, G. 1991. Defining language ability: the criteria for criteria. In S. Anivan (ed.) *Current developments in language testing.* Singapore: Regional Language Centre.

Burns, A. 1993. Spoken discourse in the TESOL classroom. *TESOL in Context* 3, 1.

Burrows, C. 1993a. *Assessment guidelines for the Certificate in Spoken and Written English. Stage 1*. Sydney: NSW Adult Migrant English Service.

Burrows, C. 1993b *Assessment guidelines for the Certificate in Spoken and Written English. Stage 2*. Sydney: NSW Adult Migrant English Service.

Burrows, C. 1993c. *Assessment guidelines for the Certificate in Spoken and Written English. Stage 3*. Sydney: NSW Adult Migrant English Service.

Burrows, C. and M. Jones. 1993. *Investigating consistency in assessment in the Certificate in Spoken and Written English*. Draft project report. Sydney: NSW Adult Migrant English Service.

Burrows, C. 1994. The AMEP meets CBT: a literature review. *Prospect* 9, 2:18–29.

Candlin, C.N. and R. Strong. 1993. Foreword. In Hagan et al.

Chaudron, C., G. Crookes and M. Long. 1988. *Reliability and validity in second language classroom research*. Technical report No. 8. Centre for Second Language Classroom Research, Social Science Research Institute, University of Hawaii.

Cope, W., M. Kalantzis, A. Luke, R. McCormack, B. Morgan, D. Slade, N. Solomon and N. Veal. 1993. *Communication, collaboration and culture*. Canberra: Department of Employment, Education and Training.

Corbel, C. 1993. From literacies to oracies. *TESOL in Context* 3, 1.

Dandondi, P. and G. Henning. 1991. An investigation of the construct validity of the ACTFL proficiency guidelines and oral interviews procedure. *Foreign Language Annuals* 23, 1.

Elder, C. 1993. How do subject specialists construe classroom language proficiency? *Language Testing* 10, 3.

Gollin, S. 1994. Some insights from the NCELTR Spoken Discourse project. *Interchange* 23.

Gonczi, A., P. Hager and J. Athanasou. 1993. *The development of competency-based assessment strategies for the professions.* Canberra: Australian Government Publishing Service.

Griffin, P. and P. McKay. 1992. Assessment and reporting in ESL language and literacy in schools project. In *NLLIA ESL development: language and literacy in schools project report. Volume II.* Canberra: National Languages and Literacy Institute of Australia.

Hadden, B. 1991. Teacher and non-teacher perceptions of second language communication. *Language Learning* 41, 1.

Hagan, P., S. Hood, E. Jackson, M. Jones, H. Joyce and M. Manidis. 1993. *Certificate in Spoken and Written English.* Sydney: Adult Migrant English Service NSW and the National Centre for English Language Teaching and Research.

Halliday, M.A.K. 1985. *An introduction to functional grammar.* London: Edward Arnold.

Ingram, D.E. and E. Wylie. 1984. *Australian second language proficiency ratings (ASLPR).* Canberra: Australian Government Publishing Service.

Kress, G. 1993. Genre as social process. In B. Cope and M. Kalantzis (eds) *The powers of literacy: a genre approach to teaching writing.* London: The Falmer Press.

Languages Lead Body. 1993. *Introduction to the national language standards.* London: Languages Lead Body.

Levinson, S. 1979. Activity types and language. *Linguistics* 17.

Linacre, M. 1989. *Many-facet Rasch measurement.* Chicago: MESA Press.

Linn, R.L., E. Baker and S. Dunbar. 1991. Complex, performance-based assessment: expectations and validation criteria. *Educational Researcher* 20, 8.

Lumley, T.J.N. and T.F. McNamara. 1993. Rater characteristics and rater bias: implications for training. Paper presented at *Language Testing Research Colloquium*, August, University of Cambridge.

McNamara, T.F. 1990. *Assessing the second language proficiency of health professionals.* Unpublished PhD thesis, University of Melbourne.

McNamara, T.F. In press. *Second language performance testing: theory and research.* London: Longman.

Martin, J.R. 1993. Genre and literacy. In W. Grabe (ed.) *Annual review of applied linguistics 1992*. Cambridge: Cambridge University Press.

Masters, G.N. and D. McCurry. 1990. *Competency-based assessment in the professions.* Canberra: Australian Government Publishing Service.

Mehrens, W. 1992. Using performance assessment for accountability purposes. *Educational measurement: issues and practice* 11, 1.

Messick, S. 1989. Validity. In R. Linn (ed.) *Educational measurement*. Washington: American Council on Education and National Council on Measurement in Education.

Messick, S. 1992. The interplay of evidence and consequences in the validation of performance assessments. Paper delivered to the annual meeting of the *National Council on Measurement in Education*, April, San Francisco.

Moss, P. 1992. Shifting conceptions of validity in educational measurement: implications for performance assessment. *Review of Educational Research* 62, 3:229–258.

Murray. 1994. Using portfolios to assess writing. *Prospect* 9, 2:56–69.

North, B. 1993. *The development of descriptors on scales of language proficiency.* Washington, DC: The National Foreign Language Center.

Nuttall, D. 1992. Performance assessment: the message from England. *Educational Leadership*, May.

O'Neil, J. 1992. Putting performance assessment to the test. *Educational Leadership*, May.

Page, T. and B. Iwata. 1986. Interobserver agreement: history, theory and current methods. In A. Poling and R. Fuqua (eds) *Research methods in applied behavioral analysis*. New York: Plenum.

Pollitt, A. and C. Hutchinson. 1987. Calibrating graded assessments: Rasch partial credit analysis of performance in writing. *Language Testing* 4, 1.

Royal Society of Arts. 1988. *Practical skills profile scheme*. London: Royal Society of Arts.

Royal Society of Arts. 1989. *English as a second language — dual certification*. London: Royal Society of Arts.

Shohamy, E. 1993a. Competency-based assessment: an outsider's perspective. Presentation at *NCELTR National Assessment Workshop* July 15–16, Macquarie University, Sydney.

Shohamy, E. 1993b. Competence and performance in language testing. Paper presented at the *Cambridge Summer Institute in English and Applied Linguistics*, July, Downing College.

Shohamy, E. and O. Inbar. 1991. Validation of listening comprehension tests: the effect of text and question type. *Language Testing* 8, 1:23–40.

Skehan, P. 1984. Issues in the testing of English for specific purposes. *Language Testing* 1, 2.

Spolsky, B.A. 1985. The limits of authenticity in language testing. *Language Testing* 2, 1.

Swain, M. 1993. Second language testing and second language acquisition: is there a conflict with traditional psychometrics? *Language Testing* 10, 2.

Wiemann, J.M. and P. Backlund. 1980. Current theory and research in communicative competence. *Review of Educational Research* 50, 1.

Wigglesworth, G. 1993. Exploring bias analysis as a tool for improving rater consistency in assessing oral interaction. *Language Testing* 10, 3.

Willing, K. 1992. *Talking it through: clarification and problem solving in professional work.* Sydney: National Centre for English Language Teaching and Research.

Wolf, D., J. Bixby, J. Glenn and H. Gardner. 1991. To use their minds well: investigating new forms of performance assessment. *Review of Research in Education* 17.

Worthen, B. 1992. Critical issues that will determine the future of alternative assessment. *Phi Delta Kappan*, February.

7 Assessing achievement in English for professional employment programs

Ruth Clarkson and Marie-Therese Jensen

Introduction

Background and rationale

In 1990–91 the Royal Melbourne Institute of Technology (RMIT) Centre for English Language Learning (CELL) undertook an NCELTR project on monitoring and evaluating learner achievement. The purpose of the project was to identify procedures and tools for assessment that might be useful in providing information on progress and outcomes to learners, teachers and eventually, perhaps, external parties such as course funding authorities or employers.

The achievement of learners in an English for Professional Employment (EPE) course was chosen as the focus of the project. This course was selected for study for two main reasons. First, it is well established at CELL, where it has been offered for about seven years. The course syllabus is stable and the teachers are experienced in dealing with the specific needs of clients from a wide range of professional backgrounds. Second, the EPE course has the advantage of being representative of a number of such courses currently available in Australia to adult migrants of non-English speaking background in the Adult Migrant English Program (AMEP) and in Colleges of Technical and Further Education (TAFE). If a way of evaluating learner achievement could be found for one course of this kind, it might be transferable to other English for Occupational Purpose (EOP) courses.

Theoretical issues in language assessment

In deciding the form that assessment should take it was first necessary to consider the nature of the EPE course and its syllabus. The EPE is a short (six-week) intensive course, which aims to prepare learners to gain professional employment in a situation as close as possible to the work previously done in the learner's country of origin. The course also provides some orientation to the Australian workplace. The EPE course syllabus is based on a number of tasks which are set throughout the course. Learners prepare these tasks with the help of the teacher. The final draft of a written task, or the video recording of an oral task, are performances which are readily assessable by the teacher. These recorded performances are also available to the teacher for diagnostic purposes if time permits further polishing.

Given the task-based nature of the course, an achievement test based directly on the objectives of the EPE course seemed to be the most appropriate way of assessing course outcomes, provided that the objectives of the course were explicit enough. The test would need to be direct in so far as learners would have to demonstrate the skills that the teacher wished to measure (Hughes 1989). Of course the question of authenticity becomes relevant, that is, the question may be raised whether the skill identified by the teacher/course designer is the same skill sought by employers in the world outside the classroom. However, since this question involves broad-ranging issues of curriculum design as well as assessment, it will not be discussed in detail here.

Achievement tests take a variety of different forms (Hughes 1989). A standard achievement test requires a standard syllabus for a wide range of learner groups. However, the EPE course, like many courses in the Adult Migrant English Program, has a particular syllabus which expresses the need of its client group. This made the development of this kind of test impracticable.

Achievement can also be demonstrated by monitoring learners' gains using a rating scale at entry and exit. The Australian Second Language Proficiency Rating Scale (ASLPR) is used for selection of clients on the EPE course, along with a set of selection criteria, such as readiness for employment, which are applied by the course teacher. Normally clients are accepted at Level 2+ (Speaking and Listening Skills). This proficiency scale, however, is insufficiently fine-tuned to account for achievement in learning over the brief period of six weeks.

Since the assessment was to be syllabus-based, a close examination of the EPE course syllabus was undertaken in order to establish exactly what should be assessed. Our examination revealed that all course tasks must be performed satisfactorily by all learners, that is, each learner must show that they can (or can not) perform a task. Students are selected for the course on the assumption that they will be able to acquire the skills required for each task. For example, each student needs to write a *professional profile* in order to introduce themselves to, and to gain acceptance by, work experience employers. The successful performance of this task will then enable all students to gain experience during the four weeks of attachment to a relevant professional workplace. However, a given student sometimes meets the objectives of the EPE course in an outstanding way, and it was felt that any assessment procedure should acknowledge this.

What was required, therefore, was a form of assessment which allowed task achievement to be assessed against defined criteria for success. In this case, some kind of criterion-referenced assessment seemed to match the syllabus of the EPE course. Hughes (1989:18) explains criterion-referenced assessment in the following way:

> *The tasks are set, and the performances are evaluated. It does not matter in principle whether all the candidates are successful, or none of the candidates is successful. The tasks are set, and those who perform them satisfactorily 'pass'; those who don't, 'fail'. This means that students are encouraged to measure their progress in relation to meaningful criteria, without feeling that, because they are less able than most of their fellows, they are destined to fail.*

So that explicit criteria may then be applied at the assessment stage Brindley (1989) points out that teachers need to plan in terms of specific objectives. The question of who sets the objectives thus becomes crucial to the matter of assessment. As will be shown below in the description of the development process of the EPE Rating Scale, it seems that learners are less well equipped than EOP teachers in setting detailed and achievable objectives.

The development process: description and analysis

The development process began with a detailed examination of the EPE course structure, which features a range of written and oral tasks. Within this range of tasks, a progression from simple to complex was noted. For example, a number of tasks prepare for the *standard chronological resume*, namely a preliminary *profile* of a class member, then the individual profile of each learner prepared for employers who may offer professional attachment. Clients who complete the standard resume well before the end of the course will go on to write a *'functional'* resume, that is, a resume which can be adapted to a range of different job applications which the client is likely to make.

Time did not allow for development of an assessment of performance on all course tasks. Six tasks were therefore selected, most of which were identified as essential to successful participation on the EPE course. These were:

Written tasks
- professional profile;
- standard letter of application;
- resume.

Oral tasks
- telephone call for job description;
- short talk on professional experience;
- simulated job interview (video).

All three written tasks and the *job interview* lead the course participants directly to meeting their aims of obtaining a professional attachment and subsequent employment, and were chosen for this reason. The other two tasks are representative of less essential course tasks, and their selection may be less justifiable. (*Phone calls*, for example, are not made by all learners during the course, while the *short talk* is an activity which prepares clients for the job interview but does not lead directly to obtaining employment.)

Defining the objectives and assessment criteria

Since language performance is judged by a number of audiences who may exercise different criteria, it was decided to seek input from learners, teachers and employers. It was hoped that this would help to define the objectives of each course task, and simultaneously, the criteria by which successful performance of each task would be measured.

Employers

Employers complete a questionnaire at the end of the four-week professional attachment period. This deals with overall performance of the course participant and includes an assessment of English language use. In fact, employer questionnaires by definition provide an evaluation of learner performance during the professional attachment period rather than during the language course. Thus employers have experience of only one course task, the *professional profile*, which enable them to decide whether to offer professional attachment of an AMEP client. Unfortunately no data was gathered on assessments by employers of the profile of the client assigned to them. The input of employers was therefore limited in usefulness.

Learners

Extensive input from learners was gathered in the earlier stages of the project. In Week One of each of the two EPE courses, learners were familiarised with the course tasks and asked to identify their own strengths and weaknesses for three tasks. However, it appeared that not all of them understood that they were being asked to identify specific language-related factors. Of the relevant answers, many focused on psychological strengths, such as 'energy and enthusiasm' and weaknesses, such as 'nervous(ness)'. However, some weaknesses identified were linguistic, such as 'I don't know what kind of question I can expect'; 'Adapting the resume to the specific selection criteria'; 'I don't know formal expressions commonly used in resumes' and 'Not vast professional vocabulary'.

Two further questions were asked:

1. What should we look for to measure improvement in the three tasks after the six weeks of the EPE course? and

2. What is **enough** improvement? (How will you recognise that you have achieved your aims?)

These questions were answered in detail by only about half of the thirty or so learners, many of whom did not give direct answers. For example, one learner answered Question 1 concerning how improvement in job interview performance could be measured as follows: 'To record at least twice, one at the beginning or as soon as possible and the other at the end'. The following student answer to Question 2 is similarly general and not particularly helpful for purposes of establishing assessment criteria: 'Satisfy the interviewer fully during the simulated interview'. Many of the answers to Question 2 were of the 'make or break' variety, that is, learners perceived improvement in terms of their life goals rather than their language goals. For example, one learner wrote: 'If I find a job I'll recognise that I have achieved my aims'. This kind of response highlights the fact that learners need training to set themselves achievable goals for a short EOP course.

In Week 4 learners were involved in drafting criteria for describing level of performance in the key task, the simulated job interview. For this task, learners were asked to individually list the criteria by which they could measure successful performance. The list was compared with one developed by the Public Service Board, NSW, which the teacher used for teaching the task. Virtually all the criteria named by the two learner groups were included in the NSW list. This overlap suggested that teachers and learners were in agreement on their performance criteria.

The learners then worked in groups of three to define three levels of success for each criterion. They later watched a number of video taped simulated job interviews of themselves and their course colleagues and were asked to award marks to themselves and to each other for each criterion for each interview. Learners expressed appreciation and even enjoyment of this activity, particularly the awarding of marks and did not object to being assessed by their peers. The training in self-assessment which accompanied the video viewing was in fact the most positive outcome of this data gathering exercise.

The teacher

Analysis of task components

The input from the class teacher as 'expert judge' proved most valuable in formulating the criteria for assessing learner achievement. Drawing on her experience with a number of such courses, she noted the components required for successful completion of each of the six tasks, along with a summary of what overall task fulfilment would be in each case. The task components, along with the abilities they were considered to draw on, are listed in Appendix A (p. 180). these components were then organised as far as possible into Bachman's (1990) categories of language competence, broadly expressed as organisational and pragmatic competence. No weighting was given to relative components of the tasks, since it was felt that virtually all components were essential to successful completion. It was noted that for oral tasks, particularly the job interview, certain non-linguistic components were necessary for successful performance, e.g. dress, posture, eye contact.

This analysis of components could serve as the basis for goal-setting and discussion with learners when setting goals at the beginning of the course. It could also serve as a checklist of points to consider when learners prepare to perform oral tasks and to draft written ones. Furthermore, it could assist learners to assess their own performance, even while bearing in mind that the global task is more than the sum of its parts.

Developing rating scales for the tasks

The linguistic task components which by now had become criteria for assessing learner achievement, were then summarised as global statements of achievement in the form of rating scales for each task at three different levels from A (excellent) to C (unsatisfactory). These scales are included in Appendix B (p. 188). It was felt by the teacher that all components must be present for the task to have been achieved. At first it seemed that only one level of achievement might be enough: either the student can or cannot write a competent resume, to take one example. However, in order to provide a more nuanced assessment for the benefit of the learner or any other audience, it was decided to grade levels of achievement by indicating when performance of a task was excellent, and describing what a typical inadequate performance might be. The detailed descriptions of levels of performance meant that the rating scales could be applied during the course.

End of Course Certificate

What the teacher had formulated as 'overall task fulfilment' was restated as the objective for each task. The End of Course Certificate (Appendix C, p. 193) was then worded in terms of the level of success at which the objective for each of the six tasks had been met. The rating scale for the six tasks was intended as a more comprehensive explanation of the short statement on this certificate.

Reliability

A set of performances by twelve EPE course participants at CELL was selected for each of three course tasks. These tasks were:

- letter of application;
- resume;
- simulated job interview.

Teachers of similar EOP or EPE courses conducted by AMEP tertiary providers in five states were asked to rate all twelve student performances in three tasks according to the EPE Rating Scale. Ratings from three teachers have been analysed here in terms of the agreement between raters (inter-rater reliability). Because of the small number of subjects rated, it was not appropriate to use a more usual statistical analysis for measuring correlation such as Pearson's r. It was decided to use a calculation suggested by Brown (1990) for determining consistency of classification over two administrations of a criterion-referenced test. (Pairs of raters would be considered as two administrations of the test.) If the raters assigned Levels A or B of the EPE Rating Scale, the performance was considered to be at *Mastery* level. If Level C was assigned, the performance was considered to be at *Non-Mastery* level. In the following table, (Table 1), three figures are given for each pair of raters:

- *P o* or percentage agreement;
- *P chance* (probability of raters agreeing by chance);
- *K*, or *kappa coefficient*, which 'reflects the proportion of consistency in classification beyond that which would occur by chance alone' (Brown 1990).

Comment

In the absence of a single global coefficient of rater agreement, the data above are not simple to interpret. It is difficult to know how high K needs to be in order to establish consistency of agreement, although Chaudron et al. (1988) refer to 'a rule of thumb statement by Hartman that kappa should be larger than 0.6... which has been used in some SL research reports'. In any event, it seems at first glance that the inter-rater agreement is higher for assessment of the two written tasks (the Letter of Application and the Resume) than for that of the spoken task (the Simulated Job Interview). At least two reasons might exist for the seemingly relatively low agreement of raters for the Interview. Firstly, it was not possible to train the raters in a moderation session that would bring them all together. Secondly, since the EOP courses with which the raters are familiar vary so much (in length, proficiency level of students at entry, area of specialisation if any, etc.)

Agreement between raters on three tasks
for the English for Professional Employment course

Task One: The Letter of Application

Raters 1, 5, 6*

Raters	Percentage Agreement	P chance	K
1 and 5	.83	.54	.63
5 and 6	.83	.54	.63
6 and 1	.67	.51	.33

Range for values of K: .33 to .63

Task Two: The Resume

Raters 1, 5, 6

Raters	Percentage Agreement	P chance	K
1 and 5	.83	.72	.39
5 and 6	.92	.78	.58
6 and 1	.75	.67	.36

Range for values of K: .36 to .58

Task Three: Simulated Job Interviews

Raters 1, 5, 6

Raters	Percentage Agreement	P chance	K
1 and 5	.75	.75	0
5 and 6	.75	.75	0
6 and 1	.83	.63	.54

Range for values of K: 0 to .54

Table 1

the raters inevitably apply local standards when deciding on their assessment level for each student performance. There also remains the problem of whether performance in the 'real world' is the standard being applied (or indeed whether it should be applied).

Validity

Does the Rating Scale really assess whether learners have achieved the aims of the EPE course, and what do potential users of such an assessment procedure think of the scale? The first of these questions is about the content validity and the second about the face validity of the rating scale. Clearly, the two are closely related.

Content validity

It could be argued that the achievement of students in the EPE course will be ultimately tested in the real world, in terms of whether the course participants succeed in gaining employment in their professional area. While this is true, the EPE Rating Scale sets out only to assess their achievement during the course, and not to predict eventual success, in terms of employment outcomes.

The EPE Rating Scale is therefore an assessment based on the successful completion of a number of tasks which will assist the learner to enter a period of professional attachment in the first instance, (and eventually to gain employment in his or her own professional area). The content validity of the scale derives from the tasks themselves which constitute a representative sample of tasks which are essential in obtaining an attachment and eventually employment. Performance of authentic tasks such as writing a resume, or of simulated tasks such as a job interview is what is being assessed according to criteria which are either fulfilled or not. These criteria are in fact the components of each task as analysed by the course teacher (see Appendix A) and can also be seen as objectives, so that successful completion of task components is the same as achievement of course objectives. (This assumes that there is no major difference between the whole task and the sum of its parts; this assumption seems not unfair, given the help provided to each learner to develop the skills necessary to perform each task.) In this way the assessment of achievement is also tapping the key components of proficiency.

Face validity

EOP course teachers were the group chiefly targeted in order to investigate the face validity of the scale. Teachers working in EOP courses run by tertiary providers in the AMEP were asked to give their opinion as to the usefulness of the EPE Rating Scale, either directly or as a model of an assessment procedure. A questionnaire was circulated, which included information about the following aspects of the RMIT CELL course:

* six course tasks;
* the components of each task;
* the rating scale for each task.

Teachers were asked to indicate which tasks, as well as which task components, were included in their own courses. This *de facto* course design survey had as its aim to establish the transferability of the rating scale. If the scale were seen by teachers on other EOP courses as transferable, its face validity would be high. At the same time, the context of the rating scale would become clear in such a way that teachers could comment on its usefulness as a model even if their own courses differed substantially in approach.

Questionnaires were completed by seven teachers in three states, and the responses were as follows.

Tasks

The number and percentage of teachers who presented tasks similar to the six detailed in the questionnaire, were as follows:

Profiles	4 (57%)
Standard letter of application	7 (100%)
Standard chronological resume (or 'core' resume writing task)	7 (100%)
Telephone call for a duty statement	5 (71%)
Short talk on professional experience	3 (42%)
Standard job interview	7 (100%)

The reasons for the tasks being perceived as less that 100 per cent transferable include the following:

- *Profiles* are not applicable to a number of courses which are longer than the RMIT EPE Course, as there is sufficient time for a full resume to be prepared and sent as part of the approach in organising a professional attachment.

- One course only operated in a Self Directed Learning (SDL) format (ten hours a week) so the *telephone call* and *short talk* were not included. Also the course participants had a higher ASLPR rating than the CELL learners (i.e. ASLPR 3+ instead of 2+), so were more concerned with acquiring appropriate register than with acquiring job seeking skills.

- The *short talk* was specified as being related to course participants' professional experience and while most teachers cover oral presentations in their course they may not be on this topic.

These finding confirmed the prediction that the core tasks common to EPE type courses are the *letter of application*, the *resume* and the *simulated job interview*. For this reason only the rating scales relating to these three 'expected' core tasks were considered in detail by all respondents to the questionnaire.

Task components

Profiles

The four teachers who presented profiles in their courses agreed on five out of the thirteen components listed as being necessary for satisfactory performance of the task (Appendix A). These components included no errors of syntax or spelling; inclusion of appropriate information on qualifications and employment history; and use of technical terminology appropriate to profession.

Three out of four agreed on five of the components as applicable: dates in years only; inclusion of personal details; adaptations of profile to the type of professional attachment being sought; information selected to impress or interest employers and titles of qualifications and positions in equivalent Australian terms.

Spacing and alignment of information according to a suggested format applied in two instances. Only one of the four teachers required that the profile be presented as printed on a word processor.

Standard letter of application

Of the thirteen components for the standard letter of application (Appendix A) all seven teachers agreed on all the items, except three teachers who replied that they did not present the 'heading' for the letter, and one who did not feel that it was essential for the letter to be word processed.

Standard chronological resume

As in the case of the *letter of application*, there was substantial agreement between the seven teachers on all of the thirty-three components of the task which were deemed necessary to complete a standard or 'core' resume (Appendix A). However, three did not require the inclusion of personal 'interests'; two did not require 'performance verbs', a personal signature or 'attachments' (i.e. Appendices to the resume); one did not specify dates in years; and another did not request 'tertiary' qualifications as not all of their clients necessarily possessed these.

Telephone call for a duty statement

Five out of the seven teachers who included this task in their course, included nearly all of the fourteen components (Appendix A). Only two questioned 'avoiding an informal telephone interview', (in place of this component one teacher thought that course participants could be asked to provide a brief summary of qualifications and experience over the phone). One teacher did not require 'Titles of qualifications and positions in equivalent Australian terms'.

Short talk on professional experience

Each of the four teachers who included this task in their courses included the sixteen components listed (Appendix A). However, two stated that they did not require the oral presentations to be on this particular topic, and one indicated that they included two major oral presentations in their course.

Simulated standard job interview

Although this was a relatively complex task requiring the integration of a number of skill components, all seven teachers agreed to all twenty-seven of the components listed for this task (Appendix A).

Usefulness of rating scale

Of the seven teachers surveyed, all except one agreed that the End of Course Certificate (Appendix B), expressed the levels of achievement on the six tasks (or those that they included), for learners in their EOP course. The one who disagreed did so on the grounds that most of their students began the course with ASLPR 3+, so that while most of the course participants might begin at Level C, they would end at a level which the teacher defined as B+. A greater definition of scale would need to be provided between Levels B and A of the Scale for this class.

All of the seven teachers surveyed stated that this model was useful as a tool either in its present form for assessing learner achievement of the tasks presented or adapted to other core tasks in their EOP courses. The only comments made were that it would be useful to use the scales from the beginning of the course as a point of reference for course tasks, and as something to aim for by the end of the course though not necessarily at the highest level of achievement: a basic satisfactory or Level B of performance was seen as acceptable. The only other comment was that similar criteria would need to be developed for the other tasks that are normally included in an EOP course.

Conclusion

To summarise, of the six tasks teachers were questioned about as to their inclusion in their courses, those normally seen as essential in an EOP course i.e. the *standard letters of application*, the *standard chronological (or 'core') resume* and the *simulated job interview* were presented in each course. For each of these three tasks there was substantial agreement as the the components that are essential for satisfactory performance of the task. Finally there was unanimous agreement as to the usefulness of the rating scale in its application to the courses surveyed apart from one SDL course for clients with a higher language level than normal.

From the generally favourable response to the questionnaire, it can be concluded that the EPE rating scale is seen by EOP teachers to be an effective way of measuring learner achievement in a task-based course such as the English for Professional Employment course at CELL. Although its face validity remains to be established with learners, initial informal surveys of student opinion also indicate a positive reaction. Further research will be required to establish the extent to which the scale can meet the information needs of other external audiences.

References

Bachman, L.F. 1990. *Fundamental considerations in language testing*. Oxford: Oxford University Press.

Brindley, G. 1989. *Assessing achievement in the learner-centred curriculum*. Sydney: National Centre for English Language Teaching and Research.

Brown, J.D. 1990. Short cut estimators of criterion-referenced test consistency. *Language Testing* 7, 1.

Chaudron, C., G. Crookes and M. Long. 1988. *Reliability and validity in second language classroom research. Technical report No. 8*. Centre for Second Language Classroom Research, Social Science Research Institute, University of Hawaii.

Hughes, A. 1989. *Testing for language teachers*. Cambridge: Cambridge University Press.

Appendix A

EPE Course: Task Components

1. Professional Profile

The profile is the equivalent of a **Career Digest**, or the summary of a long resume. Written in the first week of the EPE course, it serves to introduce applicants to potential work experience employers.

Objective
The profile will clearly and accurately communicate to the work experience employer who the applicant is and what professional qualifications and experience they possess.

1.1 Organisational Competence

1.1.1 Grammatical Competence
Dates in years only
No errors of syntax
No spelling errors
Layout
Printed on word processor (WP skills acquired on course)
Spacing of information according to suggested format
Alignment

1.1.2 Textual Competence
Rhetorical Organisation
Conventional Order of Content:
Personal details
Qualifications: dates, titles, name of institution, location
Employment history: positions held, including levels, names of employers, locations
Adaptations as appropriate to professional attachment (work experience) sought

1.2 Pragmatic Competence

1.2.1 Illocutionary Competence
Information presented, selected to interest/impress potential employers

1.2.2 Sociolinguistic Competence
Titles of qualifications and positions in equivalent Australian terms

Technical terminology appropriate to profession

2 Standard Letter of Application

Objective
To write an application letter which is well presented, with appropriate style and level of detail to provide a suitably impressive introduction of the applicant.

2.1 Organisational Competence

2.1.1 Grammatical Competence
No errors of syntax

No spelling errors

Words and expressions used appropriate to the application letter genre

Layout

Typewritten or word processed

Business letter format

Format of application letters

2.1.2 Textual Competence
Rhetorical Organisation

Conventional Order of Content:

Heading

Separate paragraphs for:

- The main purpose of the letter
- Qualifications and past work experience
- Expressing interest in the particular position and what the applicant can offer
- Concluding remarks

Length regulated by careful selection of detail as the letter is an introductory 'summary' of the applicant

2.2 Pragmatic Competence

2.2.1 Illocutionary Competence
Information presented, selected to interest/impress potential employers

2.2.2 Sociolinguistic Competence
Titles of qualifications and positions in equivalent Australian terms
Technical terminology appropriate to profession
Register
* Objective in presentation of facts
* Neutral in presenting oneself
* Polite

3 Resume

Objective
To write a well formatted resume which gives the most important items prominence and pays attention to selection of appropriate details to provide:
* Ease of access to information for employer
* Optimal representation of the applicant

3.1 Organisational Competence

3.1.1 Grammatical Competence
No errors of syntax
No spelling errors
Words and expressions used appropriate to the resume genre
Use of performance verbs for tasks undertaken
Layout
Typewritten or word processed
Spacing of information across and down the page
Alignment of information including duties/responsibilities listed in point form

Use of text type and underlining to highlight main items, headings and subheading
Dates on the left hand side in years only

3.1.2 Textual Competence
Rhetorical Organisation
Conventional Order of Content:
Personal details — Minimum amount of information
Qualifications — Tertiary education only
* Name of institution and location
* Specialist subject areas/titles of theses
* Specialist courses
* Level/status of recognition of qualifications
Membership of professional association
Employment history:
* Title and level of position
* Organisation, location and brief description if relevant
* Duties and responsibilities
* Professional activities
End section:
* Interests
* Additional skills and courses
* Referees
* Signature and date
* Attachments

3.2 Pragmatic Competence

3.2.1 Illocutionary Competence
Sufficient inclusion of detail for interpretation of overseas qualifications and experience
Headings chosen to be impressive in one's specialist field
Use of performance verbs for tasks undertaken
3.2.2 Sociolinguistic Competence
Titles of qualifications and positions in equivalent Australian terms
Technical terminology appropriate to profession

Degree of detail and information chosen to communicate in one's profession
Objective report style language
Use of summary form only

4 Telephone Call for a Duty Statement

Objective
To make a simple telephone call to obtain a duty statement for an advertised position.

4.1 Organisational Competence

4.1.1 Grammatical Competence
Correct grammatical forms for the functions listed below
Correct words and formulaic expressions for making a phone call
Pronunciation intelligible (stress, intonation)

4.1.2 Textual Competence
Rhetorical Organisation
Performance of Sequence of Functions:
Greeting and identification
Statement of purpose
Exchange of information, including spelling name and address
Final thanking and farewell

4.2 Pragmatic Competence

4.2.1 Illocutionary Competence
Convey request in such a way as to obtain the promise of a duty statement

4.2.2 Sociolinguistic Competence
Polite register
Titles of qualifications and positions in equivalent Australian terms
Technical terms correct and language appropriate to profession

4.3 Strategic Competence (where applicable)
Politely avoid an informal telephone interview OR
Respond to unexpected questions i.e. informal interview

5 Short Talk on Professional Experience

The short talk on the student's professional experience is an activity which is undertaken in the third week of the EPE course. It is a preparation for the simulated job interview in the fourth week, because it requires oral presentation of the key elements of the experience of the job applicant.

Objective
To deliver a short talk about the speaker's professional experience which is well organised, interesting and easily understood by the listener.

5.1 Organisational Competence

5.1.1 Grammatical Competence
Errors of syntax do not seriously impede communication
Accurate use of professional terminology
Some use of expressions which typically introduce, maintain and conclude a short talk
Spoken delivery
Medium pitch
Audible
Clear articulation
Suitable rate
Pronunciation does not impede understanding: accent, stress, intonation
Fluent

5.1.2 Textual Competence
Rhetorical Organisation
Logical, coherent organisation
Has recognisable main points and subpoints
Timing controlled

5.2 Pragmatic Competence

5.2.1 Illocutionary Competence
Establish credibility by displaying familiarity with material
Information chosen is relevant to purpose of the task, the topic chosen and the audience.

5.2.2 Sociolinguistic Competence
Formal register
Of interest to a group of mixed professionals

6 Simulated Standard Job Interview

Objective
To perform well at a simulated professional employment interview, by
- Communicating with the interviewer
- Showing evidence of being well-prepared by relating one's skills and experience to employment selection criteria

6.1 Organisational Competence

6.1.1 Grammatical Competence
Errors of syntax do not seriously impede communication
Accurate use of professional terminology
Intelligibility: pronunciation, stress and intonation do not impede communication
Fluency: connected smooth speech
Ability to Answer Questions
Understand questions asked; answer immediately or clearly ask for repetition/rephrasal
Answer questions directly with a short answer, followed by one to five sentences of appropriate explanation or example
Answers contain sufficient detail and are not too long
Responds appropriately, tailoring answers to selection criteria
Ability to answer designated prepared questions
Asking of own prepared questions

6.1.2 Textual Competence
Identify and respond appropriately to the characteristic stages of interview discourse:

- Opening, introductions
- Discussion of details on resume
- Asking questions about the position
- Closure of interview

Demonstrate knowledge of interview genre including, turn-taking, length of response, chit-chat, dealing with humour, topic closure

Demonstrate some ability to encode and decode the meaning in the interview (e.g. by command of important functions in the interview setting including seeking clarification, interpreting questions and expressing intentions)

6.2 Pragmatic Competence

6.2.1 Illocutionary Competence
Use of verbal and non-verbal strategies which contribute to successful management of the interview (e.g. eye contact, posture, fillers and back-channelling)

6.2.2 Sociolinguistic Competence
Show understanding of Australian accent and idiom
Register: Appropriate level of formality in form of address, general word choice, greeting and farewell
Sound natural, not stilted
Respond to humour

6.3 Preparation (Non-Linguistic)
Selection of ad for an appropriately identified position including level
Resume available
Job description obtained or 'composed'
Preparation of standard answers and own questions
Awareness of interview procedure
Demonstrate a knowledge of the advertised position, the company and the profession in Australia
Show evidence of matching the requirements of the position as expressed in the advertisement and duty statement.

Physical Presentation
Appropriate dress, posture, gestures, eye contact, occasional smiles
Appear reasonably confident

Appendix B

The EPE Rating Scales for Six Course Tasks

Please note that in the following rating scales, Level A is excellent, Level B is equivalent to satisfactory performance of the task and Level C is unsatisfactory.

Rating scale for the professional profile (career digest)

A. Client presented a profile free of spelling and grammatical errors. Layout was according to the set proforma and accurate in presentation of all required components. Details were appropriately selected and key information was provided in equivalent Australian terms. Client displayed some ability in adapting information to positively present self.

B. Client able to present a profile with no errors, after some revision of spelling, grammar and equivalent Australian terms for key information. Some adjustment was needed to layout. Further discussion may have been required on selection of information for inclusion. Limited or no ability to adapt information for presentation of self.

C. Client required frequent redrafting to correct errors of spelling, grammar and transferring of key information into equivalent Australian terms. Layout may still require further adjustments to conform to the proforma. Client may require additional explanations and directions to make improvements to the main items and details. Inclusion of inappropriate material. Overall presentation not likely to represent the client well.

Rating scale for the standard letter of application

A. Client presents a standard letter of application which reflects the conventions of layout of standard business letters. Content has been selected and organised into appropriate paragraphs. The letter has correct spelling, is grammatically accurate and uses accepted English expressions. Register has the expected degree of formality and objectivity. The letter is a concise summary of relevant details only. Language used and details chosen reflect some individuality. Information selected to create a positive introduction of the applicant.

B. Client presents letter of application which reflects the conventions of layout of standard business letters after some modifications. Content has been organised into paragraphs in such a way as not to detract from the purpose of the letter. After some adjustments the letter has correct spelling, is grammatically accurate and usually used appropriate expressions. Correct register is sustained throughout most of the letter. Content may include some slightly irrelevant information and details included may be sketchy. Style of presentation is predictable: overall impression is of a competent letter, but with no items of notable interest.

C. Client presents a letter of application not conforming to the conventions of business letter layout. Indicates an inability to select and arrange content into appropriate paragraphs. Still has intermittent errors in spelling, grammar and English expression. Uses register inconsistently or inappropriately. Unable to select and summarise detail to act as an introduction. Poor performance creates a negative impression.

Rating scale for the standard chronological resume

A. In the standard chronological resume, client presents a detailed, clear and concise summary of qualification and employment history. Format is easily accessible with the most relevant information highlighted. Headings are chosen to accurately present and summarise information. Spelling, grammar and use of expressions are correct. Equivalent Australian professional terminology is used. Client has selected items and presented a level of detail that communicates with fellow professionals. Client used elaborated English and demonstrates an ability to adapt the language to specific purposes. Client also includes some elements designed to present self to advantage.

B. Client presents a standard chronological resume containing all the necessary information, with some attention given to use of headings and arranging and highlighting information to provide ease of access. Accurate spelling, grammar and use of equivalent Australian terminology are achieved after a number of redrafts. Layout needs some further modifications. Information is presented in predictable language and style. Usually in language of profession but perhaps not detailed enough to interest a fellow professional. Information selected is a reliable representation of the client but there is no evidence of ability to adapt material to specific purposes or to add in items to impress.

C. Client is unable to present information in a standard chronological resume, in a clear fashion which readily informs. Layout needs considerable modification. Random errors in spelling, grammar and expression still occur after revision. Australian equivalents are not always used. Technical and professional terminology is lacking. Language is non-specific and level of detail is inadequate. The overall effect is the creation of a negative impression of the client.

Rating scale for the short talk

A. Client demonstrates a high degree of preparation of the short talk, in selection and organisation of material and familiarity with the topic. Information is logically and coherently presented and objectively stated. Easy to understand; any accent does not interfere. Delivery is well pitched, audible and clearly articulated. Timing is well controlled. Presentation relevant and of interest to the audience.

B. Client usually demonstrates evidence of adequate preparation of the short talk in terms of selection and organisation of material. May not always be in control of the material as organisation may be imprecise or client is unfamiliar with the topic. Client is able to be understood although may be experiencing some difficulties with pronunciation, vocabulary or use of English expressions. Timing is reasonably well controlled. Presentation is comprehensible and is followed by the audience.

C. Client experiences difficulty in the presentation of the short talk because of lack of preparation. Material is poorly selected and disorganised. Presentation is too long or too short. Client not always familiar with the topic and adds irrelevant details. Lacks ability to vary register. Difficult to understand because of pronunciation and/or inappropriate language use. Delivery may be dull and inaudible. Presentation is difficult to follow and fails to engage the audience.

Rating scale for the telephone call to obtain a duty statement

A. Client organises the information needed to make the call. Performs sequence of functions involved in making the call. Is able to demonstrate the use of some strategies to meet the demands of unpredictable elements.

Can request clarification. Can sustain the conversation with only a few hesitations. Is easy to understand; any accent does not interfere. Is pleasant and polite and achieves purpose.

B. Client organises the information needed to make the call. Performs sequence of functions involved in making the call. Usually has difficulty in responding to any unpredictable elements. May not have strategies to call on. Pronunciation may be difficult to understand at times. Choice of words and expression not always appropriate. Hesitates but without disrupting the conversation. Limited range of register. Achieves purpose in the end.

C. Client is not completely clear about the task. Cannot perform sequence of functions involved in making the call. Needs to ask for some repetition, or pauses to assimilate what is being said. Hesitates in giving responses and is only able to respond with some difficulty to standard utterances. Responses not always appropriate. Is difficult to understand because of pronunciation and word choice. Unable to vary register. In danger of not fulfilling purpose due to a break-down in communication.

Rating scale for the standard job interview

A. Client presents required documents and shows detailed knowledge of the position advertised, particularly the criteria for selection of required staff. Able to understand all questions, requesting clarification where necessary. Able to answer questions clearly and appropriately, giving accurate and detailed information related wherever possible to the selection criteria. Terminology and selection of detail is consistent with the professional field. Uses appropriately polite register. Communication is smooth and accent does not cause serious difficulty for the interviewer.

B. Client presents required documents and shows some knowledge of the position advertised, including the criteria for selection of required staff. Requires some questions to be repeated or restated. Able to provide adequate answers, however information may be stated in general terms rather than in language specific to the profession. Adequate detail, technical terminology and relevance to the selection criteria sometimes lacking. Able to make a simple request for clarification. Word choice may occasionally cause misunderstanding. Mostly uses appropriately polite register.

Pronunciation may cause some difficulty for the interviewer but not enough to prevent the interview from proceeding. Able to sustain the communication.

C. Client is unable to present all the required documents and shows little or no knowledge of the position advertised, nor of the criteria for selection of required staff. May have considerable difficulty in understanding questions/ Interviewer may have to repeat or restate a number of questions. Client may need to make several attempts to answer questions. Has difficulty in finding appropriate words and expressions to use. May use inappropriate register. Information may be sketchy, often irrelevant and unrelated to the selection criteria. Communication is laboured, mispronunciation and inappropriate word choice and register hamper the interview process. Client lacks strategies for requesting clarification. Interview is unable to proceed smoothly.

Appendix C

End of Course Certificate

Rating Scale for Completion of the English for Professional Employment Course

A. Client fully meets the objectives of tasks undertaken in the six-week course.

Has prepared a clear and accurate professional profile for potential work experience employers.

Has written a letter of application which provides a suitably impressive introduction to future employers.

Has prepared a well formatted resume which is readily accessible to employers and optimally represents the client as job applicant.

Has made a simple telephone call to obtain a duty statement for an advertised position.

Has delivered a short talk about own professional experience which is well organised, interesting and easily understood by the listener.

Has performed well at a simulated professional employment interview, by
- communicating smoothly with the interviewer;
- relating own skills and experience to employment selection criteria.

B. Client largely meets the objectives of tasks undertaken in the six-week course.

After revisions, has prepared a clear and accurate professional profile for potential work experience employers.

After revisions, has written a letter of application which provides a mostly positive introduction to future employers.

After revisions, has prepared a well formatted resume which is accessible to employers and positively represents the client as job applicant.

Has made a simple telephone call to obtain a duty statement for an advertised position.

Has delivered a short talk about own professional experience which is mostly well organised, interesting and easily understood by the listener.

Has performed reasonably well at a simulated professional employment interview, by
- communicating without too much difficulty with the interviewer;
- generally relating own skills and experience to employment selection criteria.

C. **Client meets only some of the objectives of tasks undertaken in the six-week course.**

(Objective met are indicated by a tick)

After revisions, has prepared a clear and accurate professional profile for potential work experience employers.

After revisions, has written a letter of application which provides a mostly positive introduction to future employers.

After revisions, has prepared a well formatted resume which is accessible to employers and positively represents the client as job applicant.

Has made a simple telephone call to obtain a duty statement for an advertised position.

Has delivered a short talk about own professional experience which is mostly well organised, interesting and easily understood by the listener.

Has performed reasonably well at a simulated professional employment interview, by
- communicating without too much difficulty with the interviewer;
- generally relating own skills and experience to employment selection criteria.

8 Classroom-based assessment in Intensive English Centres

John Grierson

Introduction

This chapter describes a study which investigated the nature and quality of the classroom assessment of teachers in secondary Intensive English Centres (IECs) in Australia. It draws on data from a survey of IEC teachers, interviews with some of the teachers, and a survey of IEC students.

The study revealed that the main purposes for which teachers assess students are diagnosis and feedback, and that the most frequent methods were those characterised by informality and spontaneity, such as observation and discussion, and the traditional methods of marking and correction. Students, on the other hand, rated class tests as their most preferred method of assessment.

The study concludes that teachers' assessment practices need to be informed by a theory of language use. It found evidence to suggest that the focus of and criteria for assessment were often narrow, with the possibility that significant components of language ability and skills in important domains of language use could be neglected in teaching and assessment. It also recommends that systematic procedures for observation be developed to complement teachers' informed assessments and to contribute to a record of learning.

Background: Intensive English Centres

There are nineteen Intensive English Centres in Sydney and Wollongong. Their role is to provide 'on–arrival English... for students of secondary school age with minimal proficiency in English and to develop their English language skills across the curriculum so that they can continue their education in a system where English is the medium of instruction' (Draft IEC Policy Statement, Multicultural Education Unit, 1990). Although there are policies on the maximum time students can stay in an IEC, the lack of clear criteria for determining when they can 'continue their education' means there is room for considerable difference between IECs in the criteria used to determine whether a student needs intensive instruction or should be transferred to mainstream.

The phrase 'so that they can continue their education' is a pointer to a deeper problem. It implies that there is a gap in formal education while students are in IECs, although IECs would claim that language development is central to success in schooling. The IECs' relative independence in designing curriculum and assessment can and often has resulted in responsiveness at the classroom and school level to learners' needs, unfettered by mandatory content, and has also led to experimentation in and thoughtful evaluation of pedagogy. But the lack of formal accountability for learning outcomes could lead to other results, including stagnation in teaching content and methodology and unfocused teaching programs.

There are signs that the relative independence of IECs may change. At both Federal and state levels economic difficulties have put pressure on education expenditure, and administrative reforms focusing on program effectiveness and efficiency have led on one hand to examination of how resources are allocated and on the other to calls for improved outcomes or productivity. An example of this demand for accountability and measurable outcomes can be seen in *The language of Australia* (1990), which called for changes in the funding of ESL programs, with proposed strategies that included:

1. Development of a framework 'in which Commonwealth funding... could be monitored against performance indicators'.

2. '(Assistance with) funding for the development of agreed assessment procedures, with particular emphasis on the ESL proficiency of school children' (Volume 1, 5.2.2:36). Volume 2 (69) contains the following implied criticism: 'It is difficult to assess the adequacy of outcomes of the ESL Program. There is no national ESL standard by which its effectiveness can be evaluated.'

The introduction by systems of state-wide assessment schemes such as the Basic Skills Test in NSW, and the Literacy Profiles in Victoria could be seen as both a demand for hard data on outcomes and a distrust of teachers' assessments.

It thus appears inevitable that IECs will have to conform to the demands of the educational and administrative reforms. System-wide instruments, such as those developed through the *ESL Development: Language and Literacy Project* (McKay, this volume) are likely to play a major role in this move towards greater public accountability.

Issues in classroom-based assessment

The recommendations made in *The language of Australia* (quoted above) indicated that funding bodies are interested in measuring ESL learners' proficiency in order to monitor and report outcomes for accountability purposes. Teachers on the other hand, are more likely to use assessment to measure progress and achievement, to motivate learners, to diagnose weaknesses and to inform the teaching process (Broadfoot 1987). This highlights the potential problems inherent in attempting to devise assessment systems aimed at providing information on both proficiency and achievement.

Proficiency and achievement

The distinction between proficiency and achievement, however, is becoming blurred. The kinds of communicative tasks learners undertake in the classroom constitute a part of their 'terminal' proficiency. In this context, Richards (1985), for example, notes that proficiency relates to 'observable and measurable behaviour' and 'is always referenced to the ability to perform real-world tasks, and implies degrees of skill'. Nunan (1987) also argues for a definition of proficiency that includes skill: 'proficiency refers to the ability to perform certain communicative tasks with a certain degree of skill'.

Brindley (1989:13–17) makes the link between proficiency and achievement by proposing a three-level conceptualisation of 'achievement'. At the first level, where the focus is on aggregated learner outcomes, achievement refers to the gains achieved by the learner in terms of 'overall proficiency', and assessment tends to be formal, results often being in the form of ratings on a scale. At the second level, 'achievement refers to the achievement of particular communicative objectives as part of a given course', so the focus is on 'functional proficiency' — 'the sorts of things people can do in the language'. Level 3 achievement 'refers to the achievement of particular objectives relating to the knowledge and enabling skills which are part of a particular course of instruction'.

Defining assessment criteria

The communicative needs of IEC learners relate particularly to the school setting in which they must understand and use language. However, assessment of this 'school' proficiency must take account of not only the distinctive and significant domains of language use within the school context, but also should be informed by a broader model of what it means to know a language. In this way it becomes possible to generalise beyond the specific contexts in which assessments are made (Bachman 1990). Criteria for assessment may then be derived from the domain specification and the features of language identified by the model. (See McKay, this volume, for an example of this approach.)

'Criterion' in language assessment can mean 'standard', such as 'native speaker ability' in a rating scale. However, in the context of classroom-based assessment, the most relevant sense is 'assessments which are based on sampling of a behavioural domain and which make explicit the features of this domain' (Brindley 1991:140).

Choice of appropriate criteria will be determined by the purpose of the assessment as well as by the type of learner and task. For 'Level 3' type achievement (Brindley 1989), for example, a criterion of (grammatical) accuracy may be sufficient for many purposes on the level of overall task achievement. On the other hand, the activities-based Australian Language Levels (ALL) Guidelines (Scarino et al. 1988) uses criteria such as 'successful completion of task' or 'use of communication strategies'. Affective criteria may also be included. The assessment scheme of the Primary Language Record (Barrs et al. 1988) uses criteria such as 'experience and confidence' which are influenced by considerations of child development. Brinton et al. (1989:199), focusing on assessment of specific academic writing tasks, use criteria related to functional skills in academic texts or discourse types, such as correct identification of 'vocabulary used to express contrast in scientific writing'.

Even when criteria are explicit, however, Brindley (1991:153) notes that 'the influence of (teachers') background and experience may be sufficiently strong to override the criteria that are given'. For example, he found that teachers using oral proficiency rating scales referred to 'criteria which are not contained in the performance descriptors at all, such as confidence' and that they tended to 'concentrate heavily on the assessment of some features of performance at the expense of others' (in this case the focus was frequently on grammatical accuracy).

Although it is often assumed that criterion-referenced assessment will have a useful diagnostic role, a number of studies have highlighted potential problems in specifying ability domains. The use of criterion-referenced assessment for diagnostic purposes was examined by Black and Dockrell (1984). It was found that domain definition was the key to teachers being able to construct diagnostic tools which were pedagogically useful and had content validity. However, they also noted a possible negative backwash effect on teaching of specifying outcomes which were easy to test rather than being truly most important. Rudman (1987) reviewed the research studies on the link between diagnosis and treatment. One of these studies, by Arter and Jenkins (1979) questions whether abilities to be measured could be defined precisely, whether diagnostic tasks were valid and reliable, and whether there was a match between diagnosis and learning. Another study by Yearney (1979) of diagnostic assessment in an introductory science class at university found that diagnosis and treatment had an impact on low-level rote-learning only — an unintended result.

Although it seems clear from these studies that implicit understandings of the domains of language use need to be informed by explicit criteria, it is also apparent that further efforts must be made 'to develop criteria and descriptors which not only reflect current theories of language learning and language use but which also attempt to embody multiple perspectives on communicative ability' (Brindley 1991:156).

Improving the quality of criterion-referenced assessment

Brindley's study of AMES teachers' assessment practices (1989) found problems in reconciling the general informality of their assessment with the expectations of administrators and learners for explicit information on outcomes. He recommends that greater emphasis be given to assessing learners' achievement of the communicative objectives of a course, using explicit criteria derived from a well-defined domain of ability. This would allow some formalisation and enable use of summative profiles of achievement, both of which would help meet the demands of stakeholders.

Stiggins and Bridgeford (1985) analysed teachers' performance and attitudes and the role of performance assessment in their classrooms. (Performance is defined as the demonstration of proficiency through the application of skills and knowledge.) More than three quarters of the teachers surveyed expressed concerns about the quality and use of assessment and its integration into teaching. The researchers found that quality control was indeed poor, with frequent incidence of teachers not informing learners of the criteria for assessment, or planning scoring procedures. The study recommends that greater attention be paid to assessment methods and quality control issues that affect learning, and that further research be done on informal assessment such as teacher observation.

The primary language record (Barrs et al. 1988) uses structured observation, through conferencing and tools such as diaries and miscue analysis of reading, to observe children's progress in language and literacy. This is then recorded in a cumulative profile that can provide feedback to teachers and information to parents. The PLR also provides qualitative judgements that complement Standard Assessment Tasks under the National Curriculum. In Australia, the Australian Language Levels (ALL) Guidelines (Scarino et al. 1988), and the ESL Framework of Stages (McKay and Scarino 1991), provide numerous examples of curriculum-linked and criterion-referenced assessment activities and tools for observation and recording. Their context is the teaching of languages other than English (LOTE) and general ESL, respectively, and IEC teachers would need to consider such approaches in the light of the particular content-based orientation of their programs.

Although there have been significant advances in profiling and reporting schemes, a lot more work needs to be done to establish the validity and reliability of the assessment tools used.

Withers (1986 and 1989) notes that little attention has been paid to the validation of profiles and other monitoring strategies. In this regard, some pertinent questions (Withers 1986:328) of particular relevance to IECs, where students stay a relatively short time, include:

- *What value is there in short-term profiles, given the sequential nature of much learning and the 'leaps of knowledge' which often characterise achievement?*

- *How detailed about skills acquisition can a profile be without being unwieldy or unworkable?*

The criteria used by IEC teachers to assess achievement will depend on their content objectives as well as language objectives. Nevertheless, the proficiency goals of IECs make it imperative that a model of communicative language use inform both teaching and language assessment. Bachman's (1990) model of Communicative Language Ability, although aimed at providing a framework for development and validation of tests of proficiency rather than achievement, also has the potential for informing teachers of what is meant by language competence and validating their own assessments. It can do this by attempting to define the full range of abilities required for communicative language use. These include:

- language competence (consisting of organisational competence and pragmatic competence, the latter including those abilities employed to interpret and use the language in socially appropriate ways);

- strategic competence (the ability to make efficient use of language abilities by interpreting discourse and matching it with knowledge held in memory about the world or language); and

- the psychophysiological mechanisms used in listening, speaking, reading and writing.

Figure 1 shows a possible application of the Bachman model for classroom use. In this tool, aspects of organisational and pragmatic competence are identified. The teacher can use this as a tool for observation and diagnosis.

The intended use of Bachman's framework for diagnosis and observation makes it important to identify contextual features which will determine or limit the particular abilities which can be observed. The identification of context gives the tool something in common with formats for writing assessment based on a systemic functional model of language use (see Mincham, this volume).

Task/activity: Participants: Topics:	never/rarely 0	sometimes 1	often 2	frequently 3	almost always 4	Notes
Grammar • uses wide range of syntactic structures (e.g. tense forms, question forms, clause complexes) • uses structures accurately						

Discourse
• utterances are cohesive
• utterances are extended
• is able to
  – initiate topics
  – maintain/develop topics						

Functional • uses range of functions appropriately/effectively (ideational, manipulative, heuristic, imaginative)						
Sociolinguistic • shows sensitivity to register (topic, roles) • speech sounds natural						

Figure 1 Checklist/observational tool for assessment of communicative ability in spoken discourse

While the Bachman framework is specifically designed to describe communicative ability, Systemic Functional Linguistics (Halliday 1985) provides a model of language behaviour or use in context (rather than abilities). It has already had considerable influence in assisting teachers to identify the generic structure and language features of the curriculum genres or text-types of school subjects. Its main influence has been in the teaching of writing, but through the concept of Register (elaborated as Field, or the topic of discourse, Tenor, the relationship between the participants, and Mode, the role language [spoken or written] is playing) it has also contributed to the teaching and assessment of spoken language in different contexts and for different purposes (e.g. Hagan et al. 1993).

The study

The study on which this chapter is based is in three parts: a survey of teachers' assessment practices (itself in two parts); a survey of IEC students; and interviews with a sample of surveyed teachers. The surveys and interviews were conducted in the second half of 1990.

The survey of teachers: part one

The first part of the survey (Appendix A) set out to collect general information on teachers' experience and approaches to teaching and assessment. The following is a brief summary of the results.

Teachers' experience

Half the teachers surveyed (twenty-four out of forty-eight) described themselves as English or language teachers (three of them with another teaching area). Eight had less than one year IEC teaching experience, seven had one to two years, eleven had two to five years, and twenty-two had over five years experience.

Importance of program content

Table 1 below shows that of three given elements of possible program content, 'Using language for a purpose' (which could be called a 'communicative approach') ranked above 'Teaching components of language' and 'Subject knowledge/skills'.

Element	Rank			
	1	2	3	Total
Subject knowledge/skills	14	19	12	46
Teaching components of language (e.g. grammar)	9	17	21	46
Using language for a purpose (e.g. to inform)	32	7	8	46

Table 1 Rank importance of possible elements of program content

Assessed activities

The assessment activities were categorised according to the activity-types described in the Australian Language Levels (ALL) Guidelines, i.e. informational, interactional and aesthetic. The types of activities identified by the sample were indicative of a content area-based curriculum, with strong emphasis on informational skills (obtaining, using and giving information). There were also a very large number of exercises described which focused on components of language or skills which were stepping-stones to broader activities.

There were comparatively few examples of 'aesthetic' activities. Activities involving the use of literature (e.g. novels, plays, poetry) were generally structured rather than creative. For example, an activity requiring learners to 'read a short story and attempt comprehension questions', implies that a creative response is dependent on a high level of language and cultural knowledge. Activities involving 'interacting and discussing' also appeared under-represented. It may be, however, that many of these activities were done collaboratively in groups (see below).

Decision-making

Table 2 (below) shows the responses to the questions concerning the organisation of student work. Decision-making on content and method of work was generally teacher-controlled, some teachers indicating that this was essential with younger and less able learners. There were comments that method was more negotiable than content.

Element	Present in this number of activities*					As % of total no. of activities
	0	**1**	**2**	**3**	**4**	**(n = 191)**
1. Decision making						
• solely by teacher	4	5	11	14	14	65
• student–teacher agreement	16	18	12	1	1	28
• solely by student	37	8	3	0	0	7
2. Student grouping						
• individual	5	17	12	10	4	45
• small groups	2	17	17	8	4	47
• whole class	25	12	6	4	1	21**
3. Intended audience						
• teacher	16	11	5	6	8	38
• whole class	7	21	11	6	1	35
• group	14	19	10	2	1	27
• student him/herself	15	12	8	8	3	35
• outside group	36	9	1	0	0	6
• other	42	4	0	0	0	2**
4. Time for completion						
• less than 1 period	16	10	9	6	7	39
• 1–2 periods	8	17	12	6	5	40
• more than 2 periods	23	15	7	1	2	21
5. Difficulty						
• easy	18	23	4	0	1	20
• moderate	1	7	20	13	5	60
• difficult	19	19	7	1	0	20
6. Students knew activity would be assessed	9	7	4	10	18	61

* The numbers in the columns refer to teacher/survey forms.
** The totals greater than 100% indicate that teachers had more than one form of grouping or more than one intended audience for an activity.

Table 2 The organisation of student work

Student grouping

Small groups were the favoured form of classroom organisation.

Audiences

The audience for student work was almost exclusively within the class (teacher or students). The only outside audience identified was a Year 11 class.

Time allowed for assessment

The duration of assessed activities was relatively short: thirty-nine per cent were intended to be completed in less than one (forty to fifty minute) period, and forty per cent in one to two periods.

Perceived difficulty of assessment

Teachers rated sixty per cent of assessment tasks as moderately difficult, twenty per cent as easy and twenty per cent as hard. Some noted that the level of difficulty reflected level (within the IEC) and ability.

Information given to students on assessment

In sixty-one per cent of activities, students knew they were to be assessed. When students did not know, the assessment was likely to be more informal (Table 2).

The survey of teachers: part two

The second part of the survey, questions 12–16, relates to teachers' perceptions of the importance of assessment in the teaching program, the purposes of assessment, and the frequency and usefulness of methods of assessment. The results are set out in Tables 3, 4 and 5.

Assessment in the teaching program

From Table 3 below, it can be seen that the ongoing preparation and ongoing programming all rate very highly on a scale from 0 to 5. 'Pre-topic planning' and 'final evaluation' are seen as quite important with means of 4.0 and 3.7. 'Assessment for class placement' has the lowest mean of 3.61, though the high standard deviation indicates a range of opinions on this element, as indicated further on.

There are some differences when the data for 'time spent' is examined. (The means are calculated on averages from the survey, '1–2 hours' averaged at 1.5, '3–5 hours' at 4, and '5+ hours' at 6.) Teachers spent most time on 'ongoing programming', with a little less on 'materials preparation' and 'ongoing assessment'.

'Ongoing assessment', perhaps surprisingly, was rated the most important element of the teaching program with a mean of 4.48. One wonders whether there is a 'halo effect' in a survey about assessment which tends to increase the importance attached to it.

Teachers spent the least time on 'assessment for class placement' and 'final evaluation'.

The categories used in the survey may distort the true picture, however. One teacher wrote: 'I spent much more time producing materials than giving formal marks. 5+ hours can't show the distribution — should be 5–10 – 15–20'. Furthermore, informal assessment is probably unplanned, whereas time spent on other aspects of course design is often time spent at home or in the staffroom.

Some teachers commented that assessment for class placement was irrelevant to their program, or involved little of their time. One teacher wrote: 'Depends very much on the group you are looking at. Some classes are set — students needn't be placed'. For reception classes, however, assessment for placement is considered very important, two teachers saying most time was spent on it. One of them commented: 'Assessment is part of the Reception Programme which runs for 2+ weeks and is a major focus of that programme'. Many IECs do not have reception programs, and this may account for the wide range of scores given class placement (reflected in the comparatively high standard deviation of 1.63).

Other comments made in the survey reflect the diversity of classes and levels taught from term to term and changing emphases. Comments included:

> *With beginners I find more relevant 'ongoing student assessment' in English. With advanced classes I find it important to evaluate at the end of the topic.*

and

> *A class with less English requires far more planning and materials preparation.*

A teacher who rated 'ongoing assessment' as most important wrote:

> *Although I consider assessment for class placement and ongoing student assessment to be very important, my colleagues do not generally share my views and neither does the school have an assessment policy or a coordinated assessment strategy. Therefore I do not spend much time on assessment as there seems little point.*

Element	Perceived Importance		Time Spent (hours)	
	Mean	S.D.	Mean	S.D.
Assessment for class placement	3.61	1.63	2.76	1.07
Pre-topic planning	4.00	1.22	3.59	0.84
Ongoing programming	4.32	0.87	4.66	0.87
Materials preparation	4.40	0.75	4.27	0.84
Ongoing assessment	4.48	0.73	4.20	0.78
Final evaluation	3.70	0.91	2.67	0.66

n = 48

Table 3 The teaching program: the importance and time spent

The purposes of assessment

Table 4 below sets out the results of Question 13, where teachers were asked to rate the importance of different purposes of assessment. 'To diagnose strengths and weaknesses and set further learning objectives' ranked highest with a mean of 4.52. 'Feedback to learners', 'feedback to teachers', and 'general proficiency' also rated very highly. The low ranking of 'placement' parallels its relatively low importance (Table 3) in the teaching program. Also rated as less important (though still with means of 3.41 and 3.28) were 'to indicate learners' subject/content knowledge' and 'to provide information to others, e.g. other teachers, parents'.

The low ranking of 'indication of subject knowledge' probably indicates that subject content is generally regarded as providing a context for language learning rather than as knowledge to be learnt for its own sake. The low ranking of 'providing information to others' could be due to lower parent/community demands for accountability for IECs. This may be in part a consequence of parents' lack of English, and in part because the IEC is seen as providing preparation for high school rather than an examinable curriculum.

One teacher who gave 'readiness for high school' the lowest ranking commented that 'readiness… is not the reason we send students to high school', a reference to the fact that time spent in an IEC, rather than 'readiness' or proficiency, is often the determining factor in students exiting.

Element	Mean	S.D.	Rank
Placement	3.29	1.73	8
Feedback to learners	4.31	0.87	3
Feedback to teachers	4.34	0.81	2
Diagnose strengths & weaknesses	4.52	0.66	1
Indication of suject knowledge	3.41	0.92	7
Providing information to others	3.28	1.11	9
Readiness for High School	3.80	1.32	5
General proficiency	4.11	0.90	4
Achievement	3.67	1.19	6

Table 4 Purposes of assessment

Methods of assessment

The list of assessment methods in Question 14 was adapted from that used in Brindley (1989). Standardised tests were not listed because they are mainly used in IECs by counsellors, very rarely by teachers. The results are displayed in Table 5 below.

Element	Frequency			Usefulness		
	Mean	S.D.	Rank	Mean	S.D	Rank
Observation	4.50	0.75	1	4.52	0.76	1
Marking/correction	3.96	1.07	2	3.95	1.07	3
Recycling	3.32	1.43	4	3.83	0.97	4
Teacher/student discussion	3.42	1.33	3	4.11	0.97	2
Peer discussion	2.78	1.50	5	3.45	1.19	5
Self-assessment	1.85	1.58	9	2.95	1.60	9
Short tests	2.69	1.61	6	3.21	1.35	6
Objective tests	2.48	1.42	7	2.95	1.40	9
Teacher journal	1.91	1.83	8	3.05	1.64	8
Learner journal	1.77	1.89	10	3.13	1.67	7

Table 5 Methods of assessment

Informal methods (observation, discussion, marking, correction and recycling) were most frequently used, with 'observation' having the highest frequency with a mean of 4.5. Teacher-constructed tests — 'short tests' and 'objective tests' — were ranked 6 and 7 with means of 2.69 and 2.48. 'Self-assessment', 'teacher journals' and 'learner journals' were not commonly used for assessment. The only other forms of assessment added by teachers were: 'highlighting of positive features in writing' and 'lexical chains to assess appropriate field'.

There was a high correspondence between teachers' perceptions of usefulness of the methods and the frequency of their use. However, although the rank is similar in each case, the rating for perceived usefulness for all but one item is higher than for frequency, indicating that teachers may be prepared to try methods they have not used. The greatest differences between 'frequency' and 'usefulness' were for 'self-assessment', 'teacher journal' and 'learner journal'. A significant number of teachers gave no rating on the usefulness of 'self-assessment' (eight teachers) and 'learner journal' (nine). Some noted that they could not judge without having tried a method.

Most of the comments in this section of the survey related to self-assessment or recycling of work. The comments on self-assessment indicate that it was perceived primarily as a cognitive strategy without any form of recording, rather than as a formal assessment device, e.g.

> *I value it. Do students though?*

and

> *I would expect students to do a measure of self-assessment when they do homework but I don't have a method (yet) for accounting for this.*

Other comments acknowledged the potential value of self-assessment:

> *I should get students to self-assess more often.*

Some teachers highlighted the logistical difficulties in self-assessing in a second language. A teacher of beginners wrote:

> *Discussion and self-assessment is very frustrating because the students and I desperately want to communicate but the language barrier is a real deterrent.*

Some comments on recycling of work focused on its positive outcomes:

> *I have found that recycling of work with interim teaching and giving models (either oral or written — taken from other students' successful writing) has achieved very good results. (How to raise work from C to A.)*

Others noted that constraints of time and student numbers made recycling difficult:

> *We don't have much time to recycle work in content-area classes. I teach about 100 people, most assessment is done by students themselves with me and whole class immediately after finishing an activity. I only formally mark pieces of writing.*

Comparison of the use of assessment methods by English and other teachers

To determine whether there were significant differences in assessment methods, teachers were classified as teachers of 'English' or 'other' subjects. The results are set out in Tables 6 and 7.

Table 6 below (based on Question 11) examines the frequency of assessment methods in activities. It appears to indicate that the use of 'correction/marking' strategies is more frequent in English activities, while teachers of other subject areas are more likely to give 'oral feedback'.

Method	English (n = 26)		Other (n = 21)	
	Used in this % of all tasks	As % by method	Used in this % of all tasks	As % by method
Marking/Corrections	47.16	29.50	39.39	20.75
Oral feedback	47.16	29.50	61.90	32.70
Written feedback	27.88	16.87	33.00	17.61
Test	7.69	4.82	5.95	3.14
Self-assessment	7.69	4.82	17.86	9.43
Evaluation/discussion after completion	22.11	13.86	30.95	16.35

Table 6 Use of assessment methods by English and other teachers (based on Q11)

Table 7 (based on question 14) examines the frequency (0–6) of different methods. The rank orders correlated significantly (rho = .815, p < .01). The use of marking/correction is a little lower in other subjects, with a mean of 3.67 compared to 4.04, but the difference is not great. There is marked difference in the frequency of short tests, however. Their mean frequency among English teachers is 3.08, but among other teachers only 1.86 (with ranks of 5 and 9 respectively). Table 7 also indicates that English teachers are more likely to use tests, but the difference was not great.

Another clear difference in Table 7, is that learner journals are more frequently used by English teachers. Although Table 7 indicates that English teachers use self-assessment almost as often as other subject teachers, this conclusion is not warranted on the basis of the figures in Table 6, where they appear to use it considerably less. This raises doubts about the interpretation by respondents of the frequency categories.

Discussion of results

On the basis of the overall survey results there is some evidence to suggest that teachers of subjects other than English are less likely to use marking/correction strategies. This may indicate a greater concern with content and meaning than with form, but the small sample makes it difficult to draw firm conclusions. One possible explanation is that subject teachers (other than English) are more likely to use summative tests. There is some evidence from the interviews for this. The survey did not specifically seek information on the use of summative tests, however, so the issue cannot be resolved with certainty.

Concerns with assessment

More than half the teachers responded to Question 15 (Do you have any major concerns with assessment?). The most frequent cause for concern was time. Comments included:

> *To be effective it needs to be ongoing, persistent and regular and needs feedback time with individual learners to be of value. This may work if two teachers were in the class at all times but I can't do it all! (i.e I don't want to abbreviate my program to do it.)*

> *Lack of time to accurately assess students due to numbers in class.*

Method	English (n = 26)		Other (n = 21)	
	Mean	**Rank**	**Mean**	**Rank**
Observation	4.31	1	4.62	1
Marking/correction	4.04	2	3.67	2
Recycling	3.23	4	3.00	4
Teacher/student discussion	3.50	3	3.67	2
Peer discussion	2.85	6	2.57	5
Self-assessment	1.85	9	1.90	8
Short tests	3.08	5	1.86	9
Objective tests	2.61	7	2.00	6
Teacher journal	1.73	10	1.95	7
Learner journal	2.35	8	1.05	10

rho = .815

Table 7 Frequency of use of assessment methods (based on Q. 14)

Some inexperienced teachers were unsure of what and how to assess:

> *My focus in teaching ESL has not been on assessment. I'm continually watching, observing and assessing but not in a structured way. This is because I'm not sure how to.*

> *I think it is very important. However I need to clarify my own ideas and develop a more effective assessment system.*

Concerns with the validity and effectiveness of assessment practices were also common:

Yes, to ensure that what is being acquired by the student during the teaching procedure is the subject of the assessment. All too often what is assessed is not what has been taught!

Yes. From what I have seen, teachers mainly correct spelling and grammar errors — giving little guidance in how to achieve high standards of functional language or different appropriate generic structures.

Students need to be aware of assessment of tasks so they will attempt to take more seriously (unfortunately) that IECs are 'real' learning centres.

Assessment of language ability is inconsistent. Post Reception class and everywhere focuses more on written skills than aural/oral skills.

Comments on the use of tests revealed widely differing points of view. Some teachers called for standardised testing, one calling for the introduction of tests:

... as a means of regulating a student's progress through the levels and on to high school, possibly based on principles of second language acquisition and informed by a consensus view of staff as to an individual's achievement and performance.

The other teachers who called for standardised testing, however, questioned how it could be done, especially across all IECs. One suggestion was:

Perhaps there could be some standard learning/progress system for teachers to recognise and comment on a student record card at various stages.

There were some negative comments on the role of teachers' marking and correction:

Throughout the learning process marking seems a necessary evil in terms of time and effectiveness.

My students are more interested in assessment than me and respond very strongly to it. My colleagues mostly assess in the formal red pen way and create an environment where marking and discipline are linked.

Finally concerns were expressed by some teachers that assessment practices could be misleading or misused:

> *It's always relative — perhaps can give students 'false' ideas of achievement in the secure setting of IECs, compared to HS.*

> *Often marks on rolls don't reflect strengths of some students.*

> *If assessment methods are just tests, then assessment does not properly indicate how well the student is performing.*

General comments on the role of assessment

Teachers responding to Question 16, which called for general comments on the role of assessment, repeated many of the concerns of Question 15. Some teachers were concerned that misuse of assessment could harm students' self-confidence and the secure environment of an IEC:

> *It has to be done in such a way that students can achieve and so that their self-confidence does not suffer.*

> *Clash between preparing students for high school (a fairly rigid system with strict marking), and trying to do the opposite in an IEC (i.e. provide a non-threatening, positive environment for students to gain confidence in mastering a new language).*

> *Tests should be kept to a minimum. Non-threatening methods of assessment best.*

Generally, however, the attitude to assessment was positive. Teachers recognised its value in assessing their own teaching ('it is most useful for re-assessing teachers' own objectives') and in learning more about their students ('it allows both teacher and student to be aware of what students think about their learning and what their goals are'). The importance of using and passing on information was often stressed:

> *Teacher liaison is important… as actual testing… is difficult at the best of times. So on the job assessment has to be performed and information relayed.*

> *Needs to be ongoing, skills/content-based as well as language-based, needs to be transferable so that other institutions can make use of it.*

Once again, a few teachers commented on their perceptions of how others assessed and on how to make assessment more explicit:

> *Assessment is generally too haphazard and teachers lack skills and measurement tools.*

> *Students benefit if they have specific features to work on. This means **teaching** them in the first place — which necessitates the teacher recognising the **language demands** of the task and building that language focus into the lesson.*

In response to both Questions 15 and 16 teachers commented on the need for flexibility in adapting assessment practices to different classes. The notion that the time constraints of IEC teaching impose limitations on the teacher's assessment practice received further comment:

> *Due to the high turnover of students, the necessary shortness of programs, entry of new students into class — assessment is on the run, i.e. it is built-in — weekly collection/correction/bi-weekly spelling tests/objective questions coupled with the work.*

The survey of students

Thirty-three students from four IECs in the Metropolitan East and South West Regions were surveyed on the methods of assessment used in their country of origin and in the IEC. The main purpose of the survey was to establish to what extent student responses corresponded with what teachers said about their assessment practices. A copy of the survey is included in Appendix B.

The student group was composed of twenty-one Vietnamese, three Yugoslavs, two Chileans, two Lebanese, one Egyptian, one Pole, one Swede, one Pakistani, and one Nicaraguan. They had between five and twelve years of schooling, with an average of 9.27 years.

The small size of the sample means one has to be cautious about drawing conclusions from the survey. Nevertheless, some rough generalisations can be made.

Table 8 below shows the results of the question regarding the frequency of different types of assessment in IECs. In general, it confirms the findings from the teacher survey on frequency of assessment methods. Seventy-three per cent said tests were used sometimes rather than often, whilst frequency of correction of mistakes was rated as 'often' by sixty-seven per cent. The common emphasis teachers attached to feedback is supported by the figures in 'teacher discusses work with you' (sixty-four per cent 'often') and 'teacher writes advice or comments in your book' (seventy per cent 'often'). It is interesting that the figures fall a little for two other items ('teacher tells you what you need to do better' and 'teacher tells you what you do well'). This may support the concerns expressed by some teachers that assessment is often putting marks on paper without having a clear idea of how to raise the level of students' work. The figures for 'self-assessment' and 'peer-assessment' also support the findings in the teacher survey that the use of student self-assessment is relatively uncommon.

A comparison of this data with that on assessment in students' countries of origin (shown in Table 9) shows that tests are used less frequently in the IEC, while

Method	Never	%	Some-times	%	Often	%	Preferred methods	Rank
Tests or examinations	1	(3)	24	(73)	8	(24)	16	1
Marking/correction	0		11	(33)	22	(67)	11	4
Teacher/student discussion	0		12	(36)	21	(64)	14	2
Written advice/comments	0		10	(30)	23	(70)	6	5
Teacher tells student what needs to be done better	0		14	(42)	19	(58)	12	3
Teacher tells student what has been done well	0		17	(52)	16	(48)	1	6
Self-assessment	6	(18)	19	(58)	8	(24)	0	7
Peer-assessment	6	(18)	20	(61)	7	(21)	0	7

Table 8 Assessment methods used in students' IECs

there was little difference in the frequency of mistake correction or telling students how to do better or what was done well. Teacher discussion with students was less frequent in the country of origin than in the IEC, which may reflect cultural differences in the teacher–student relationship. Students rated the frequency of self-assessment and peer-assessment as much lower in their country of origin, which probably shows that IEC teachers have in fact gone some way towards encouraging learner responsibility for assessment.

Students were also asked to select the two best ways teachers could assess them. There was a strong preference for teacher-directed methods, with 'tests' ranking highest (sixteen mentions), followed by 'teacher–student discussion' (fourteen mentions) and 'correction' (eleven mentions). It is unrealistic to infer that students would see themselves as equal partners in a discussion, but the choice of teacher–student discussion as the second most preferred method probably indicates that students want to be involved in the assessment process, rather than be just passive recipients of corrections. No students chose either self- or peer-assessment as a preferred method. Only one student preferred teacher advice on

Method	Never	%	Sometimes	%	Often	%
Tests or examinations	0		14	(42)	19	(58)
Marking/correction	0		11	(33)	22	(67)
Teacher/student discussion	1	(3)	20	(61)	12	(37)
Written advice/comments	1	(3)	23	(70)	9	(27)
Teacher tells student what needs to be done better	0		16	(48)	17	(52)
Teacher tells student what has been done well	0		19	(58)	14	(42)
Self-assessment	18	(55)	12	(30)	3	(9)
Peer-assessment	14	(42)	19	(58)	0	

n = 33

Table 9 Assessment methods used in students' countries of origin

what was done well — most preferred correction, written advice or comments, and being told what needed to be done better.

The findings of this brief survey are similar to surveys of adult students (Alcorso and Kalantzis 1985; Brindley 1984), reported in Brindley (1989). Brindley's survey of fifty adult learners showed a 'tendency to insist on the value of formal methods of assessment. Most learners interviewed had been educated in educational systems where testing played a prominent role. They consequently expected progress tests…' (Brindley 1989:41).

Summary

The student survey supports the evidence of the teacher survey that IEC teachers tend to rely in their assessment on traditional strategies such as marking and informal feedback. It also indicates that more innovative strategies such as self-assessment and peer-assessment are being used, although less frequently. However, they were not preferred methods for any of the students. The survey further indicates that the major difference between student expectations and teacher practices is in the use of formal assessment methods such as tests. Students wanted more formal assessment than teachers appeared to be giving.

Interviews with teachers

In order to gather more substantive information on teachers' attitudes and practices, thirteen of the surveyed teachers were interviewed for about fifteen minutes each. The interviews were aimed at eliciting information about their teaching orientation, their views on the purpose of assessment, and the type of assessment they favoured.

Teaching orientation

Teachers tended to identify their teaching as falling into one of four approaches, loosely labelled as grammatical/structural, subject knowledge and skills, communicative, or genre, although there was considerable overlap between these categories.

The 'communicative' approach was described in the following ways emphasising the motivational role of classroom activities:

I do a lot of communicative activities, because... the kids have got to have that confidence...

(Teacher C)

Now I'm very much a communicative teacher... (the implications for the classroom are) often a topic approach rather than a grammatical approach, interest, seeing that the students are interested... any method... to make the children function in the new language.

(Teacher G)

I encourage a lot of discussions in my class. I've got a lot of pair work... I see myself as a communicative teacher.

(Teacher M)

Genre-based approaches were not seen as incompatible with the communicative approach. Teacher B commented that:

(the genre approach is) conducive to a whole lot of other approaches as well, like the whole language approach, the communicative approach... (it is) a good shorthand short-cut approach.

However, the point was made that communicative approaches could benefit from the structure of genre-based teaching. In this regard, Teacher H commented on deficiencies in the way people have interpreted 'communicative':

I do believe in a communicative approach and I link that in with my work in genre, but... a lot of people have taken up a communicative approach without having much knowledge of... what language needs to be developed and encouraged, and some people have taken talking and communication to be enough on its own.

The teaching orientation was closely related to the level of training. The teachers with post-graduate qualifications in ESL (TESOL Certificate, Grad.Dip. TESOL, RSA Certificate, MA in Applied Linguistics) described their approach as communicative, genre-based or both. The others were more likely to emphasise grammar, although one of them (Teacher K) said development of thinking and problem-solving skills was also important.

Perceived purposes of assessment

The most frequently mentioned purpose of assessment was to provide feedback to teachers and learners. This feedback was seen as an integral part of the communication and dialogue which accompanies teaching:

> *To find out if the kids are understanding what's going on in the lesson, then I ask them all the time. Like it's not a mechanical thing when I say 'Did you understand that?' It's a subconscious thing where I'm just making sure... it just comes into the teaching, just comes in... and I'm always walking around just looking to see what they're doing, how they're going, just giving a helping hand.*
>
> (Teacher D)

> *I feed off the students and they feed off me. I see what they're interested in and I work on that. I like to point things out to them that they might not have noticed themselves.*
>
> (Teacher L)

> *You look at the person who's giving an answer to see that he or she knows what he's on about.*
>
> (Teacher M)

> *... providing students with a reaction from me about what they're doing, giving them advice about how they can, maybe, do it a little better... I talk to all my students at least twice a lesson. Everybody in the class gets some sort of reaction from me.*
>
> (Teacher B)

Some commented on the diagnostic role of feedback:

> *... assessment is also so you can gauge students' strengths and weaknesses from the tests. If it's something which is very important to them, and they haven't mastered, they are going to need more reinforcement, and you're just going to have to change your strategies...*
>
> (Teacher M)

Teacher C saw diagnosis and follow-up not as a planned strategy, but as an occasional targeted response to an identified need:

Say I've given them a piece of writing and I find there's a lot of errors being made — the same errors made by a lot of students. I can... focus on that skill that they don't understand. Depends on the task... But not every time'.

Whereas Teacher M focused on the need for responsive variation in teaching strategies, Teacher A emphasised the need for teachers to be able to show students how to improve:

When you've got that assessed, show them, and say, okay, this is at, say Level C, how do you get this up to an A? or at least a B+? How do we go from here? And this is what I don't think is done enough.

Only two teachers mentioned the role of assessment in needs analysis and planning. Teacher H commented:

... to a large extent what you're doing should be driven by the kinds of assessment that you're doing. When I started off the last unit of writing that I did, the first thing I did was to get the students to do some writing and I used various means of assessing that... I see that as some form of needs analysis to get the unit started, and then ongoing assessment from that. Assessment is one of the most important tools for deciding where to start and where to head and how quickly to get there.

Teacher K emphasised the role of assessment as a mechanism for checking what had already been taught or learned:

People also tend to fall into an assumption that once something is covered at one level, therefore students know that and they never have to touch it again... if a group of students come to me and I'm told 'They're at Level 4, Level 5 or whatnot' I will try and check whether they know things they're supposed to have covered...

Focus of assessment

Language
One of the aims of the interviews was to identify those elements of language focused on by teachers in their assessment. In this regard, there was a consistent focus on grammatical competence as a criterion for assessment, even among teachers who described their teaching as 'communicative'. Teacher M, for

example, spoke of testing language on the basis of 'ability to communicate', but gave the following example: 'If you're emphasising, for instance, past tense, you'd be looking out that students have learned the past tense'. Teacher J said she marked writing on an overall impression, but then said: 'Like if they're telling a story or something, I have to check, it has to be in the past'.

Some teachers, on the other hand, were more concerned with the overall communicative effect of student work. Teacher G, for example, referred to 'language competence' and said of writing assessment: 'The overall thing I'm looking for is fluency and communicability, not necessarily grammatical corrections, unless, of course, I set that as an objective'. Teacher K indicated that successful communication of purpose was the first consideration: 'I tend to take a functional approach. I try to teach them various functions. How do I assess that? Well if they've acquired the basis of that, I would have a look at structural things, grammar things as well'.

The interview data, however, did not reveal much explicit recognition of dimensions of communicative competence other than grammatical. Considerations of sociolinguistic or illocutionary competence were rarely mentioned. This lack of awareness of the pragmatic dimension of language ability can have unfortunate consequences as in the case of one teacher who wrote 'Good introduction' in response to this written dialogue:

Hello George, it's nice to meet you.

Oh thank you.

'Thank you' is an inappropriate response to the greeting, and an awareness of the sociolinguistic dimension of language ability may have led this teacher to consider a different comment and teaching strategy.

The teachers who had adopted a genre approach used the concept of generic structure to establish content and criteria for assessment. By mapping out in detail the schematic structures and linguistic features of the genres they were teaching, they were able to establish objectives for teaching and detailed assessment criteria. One of these teachers, H, also spoke of the interdependence of ongoing and summative assessment. Activities such as matrices were used 'to see whether they were building that field knowledge…' and information from that assessment would inform the next stage of teaching. Then, the initial piece of writing used for needs analysis was compared with the final piece, 'and from that I was able to see how much each of them had learnt... how much progress they'd made...'. The explicit communication of assessment criteria to students was another feature of the genre approach.

Subject content

Some teachers were concerned with assessment of subject content, sometimes together with language assessment. Teacher E commented thus on the use of summative tests in science:

> *I test their ability to write English and express themselves as well as some knowledge of the content area, but that's not really my first aim. I suppose in a way I need to know that they have understood what we are doing, but... it's really more English-based than content-area-based.*

Later, she invokes the role of grammar in written expression:

> *I have to admit (grammar) does come into it because it's not really a high school standard if the grammar is really bad.*

The importance of content-area learning or knowledge is highlighted in the following statement:

> *I think they do need to know a little by rote, especially in chemistry, otherwise they can't continue on with the unit.*

Teacher E also spoke of the 'need to know that they have understood'. 'Understanding' was linked by some teachers to subject content or concepts, and by others to language use. Teacher C reported that:

> *'I like to give subject tests... In some ways it's just to see how much the kids have understood... a way of them revising, as well as me having a look at how much they've understood, how well they use the language for instance'.*

Assessment methods

Ongoing, informal, observational assessment was the most commonly used form of assessment, primarily because of its perceived immediacy as a means of giving corrective feedback to students and monitoring their comprehension and performance. There was a clear preference for formative over summative assessment, although the use of tests was not uncommon. Teacher A questioned the value of tests but also provided evidence of 'quality control':

> *If you do it at the end and off they go, what's the purpose of it?... (but) if I give them a test, I say, for example, you get ten points for content and ten for language... so that the students will know exactly where their marks are going to come from.*

Teacher G, who described his teaching as 'communicative', was the only teacher to feel a need for more testing:

> *Nor do I do enough frequency of tests... But I know the only way I'm going to do it is to have better pre-planning and write the test into my actual objectives.*

A unit test supplied by this teacher was very strongly weighted towards content and word knowledge. Thirty-five out of forty marks were allocated to true/false questions and matching of words with definitions — an indication that the tag 'communicative' does not necessarily indicate a communicative orientation to assessment.

Caution about the value of 'red pen' correction was common, even among 'traditional' teachers. For example, Teacher J commented:

> *They get upset when they find a lot of marking. So I've found it's always better... to check it either orally, or do it first orally and then they write it down and they check it themselves.*

Summary

The interview data reveal that teachers place a good deal of importance on the role of assessment as a means of communication. They want their assessment to be appropriate and useful, and they use a wide range of strategies, mostly informal and unsystematic. However, there is some evidence to suggest that the criteria which form the basis of their assessments are based on a restricted view of communicative language ability. There also appears to be limited use of explicit and systematic procedures for classroom observation. As a result, assessment frequently becomes something which is done as an afterthought or on the spur of the moment rather than an activity which is integrated into the teaching program.

Conclusion

The results of the survey reported in this chapter suggest that the assessments teachers carry out in their classrooms are frequently informal and undertaken primarily to provide feedback to learners and to guide teachers in planning to cater for strengths and weaknesses. Because of the informality of these practices, it could be argued that there is not much to be learnt from studying them. However, the insights gained from a study of teachers' assessment practices can be very helpful in improving the quality of teaching and learning. In particular, it is evident from this study that there is room for innovation and development in the use of tools for systematic classroom observation, based on models of language use, which can contribute to a pedagogically useful record of learners' progress and achievements. (See above for a suggestion as to how the Bachman framework (1990) could be used as a starting point.) There is also room for experimentation in non-traditional methods such as self- and peer-assessment, which may be helpful in developing learner autonomy (Cram, this volume).

The survey reported on here revealed that much classroom-based assessment narrowly focused on the mechanics of language use and thus was capable of giving only a very limited picture of learners' abilities and skills. It also identified the need to spell out in detail the components of communicative language ability and the tasks associated with these components in the content-based but language-oriented classrooms of the IECs. However, the study also shows that practical considerations of time are sometimes as significant as teachers' knowledge in determining the quality and relevance of assessment. Nevertheless, it seems reasonable to conclude that definitions of language ability and domains of language use by IEC learners, and the identification of criteria for teaching and assessment which are referenced to these abilities and domains, would allow teachers and learners to be better informed about their goals and achievements. The explicit identification of the goals and content of learning in this way would lead to a relevant and responsive curriculum. Until these innovations in classroom-based assessment are generally practised, however, teachers will be unable to provide to each other, to learners and to parents substantial evidence of the content and quality what is learned. At the same time information about learning would be a valuable complement to any externally-designed assessment of language proficiency that may be introduced to ESL.

Acknowledgements

I would like to thank all those teachers who gave their time to complete the survey and be interviewed.

References

Alcorso, C. and M. Kalantzis. 1985. *The learning process and being a learner in the AMEP.* Paper prepared for the Committee of Review of the Adult Migrant Education Program. Wollongong: Centre for Multicultural Studies.

Arter, J.A. and J.R. Jenkins. 1979. Differential diagnosis — prescriptive teaching: a critical appraisal. *Review of Educational Research* 49:517–556.

Bachman, L.F. 1990. *Fundamental considerations in language testing.* Oxford: Oxford University Press.

Barrs, M., S. Ellis, H. Hester and A. Thomas. 1988. *The primary language record.* London: ILEA/Centre for Language in Primary Education.

Black, H.D. and W.B. Dockrell. 1984. *Criterion-referenced assessment in the classroom.* Edinburgh: Scottish Council for Research in Education.

Brindley, G. 1984. *Needs analysis and objective setting in the Adult Migrant Education Program.* Sydney: Adult Migrant English Service.

Brindley, G. 1989. *Assessing achievement in the learner-centred curriculum.* Sydney: National Centre for English Language Teaching and Research.

Brindley, G. 1991. Defining language ability: the criteria for criteria. In S. Anivan (ed.) *Current developments in language testing.* Singapore: Regional Language Centre.

Brinton, O., M. Snow and M. Wesche. 1989. *Content-based second language instruction.* New York: Newbury House.

Broadfoot, P. 1987. *Introducing profiling: a practical manual.* Basingstoke: Macmillan Education.

Department of Employment, Education and Training (DEET). 1990. *The language of Australia: discussion paper on an Australian literacy and language policy for the 1990s.* Canberra: Australian Government Publishing Service.

Hagan, P., S. Hood, E. Jackson, M. Jones, H. Joyce and M. Manidis. 1993. *Certificate in Spoken and Written English.* Sydney: Adult Migrant English Service NSW and the National Centre for English Language Teaching and Research.

Halliday, M.A.K. 1985. *An introduction to functional grammar.* London: Edward Arnold.

McKay, P. and A. Scarino. 1991. *ESL framework of stages.* Melbourne: Curriculum Corporation.

Nunan, D. 1987. The ghost in the machine: an examination of the concept of language proficiency. *Prospect* 2, 2:153–169.

Richards, J.C. 1985. Planning for proficiency. *Prospect* 1, 2:1–5.

Rudman, H.C. 1987. Testing and teaching — two sides of the same coin? *Studies in Educational Evaluation* 13:73–90.

Scarino, A., D. Vale, P. McKay and J. Clark. 1988. *Australian language levels guidelines.* Canberra: Curriculum Development Centre.

Stiggins, R. and N. Bridgeford. 1985. The ecology of classroom assessment. *Journal of Educational Measurement* 22, 4:271–286.

Withers, G. 1986. Profile reports — a typology and some caveats. *Studies in Educational Evaluation* 12:325–334.

Withers, G. 1989. Validity and reliability — issues in the assessment of LOTE/ESL. A paper prepared for the *NAFLaSSL Conference*, Sydney, December.

Yearney, R.H. et al. 1979. The effects of diagnostic prescriptive instruction and focus of control on the achievement and attitudes of university students. Paper given at the annual meeting of the *National Association for Research in Science Teaching*.

Appendix A

Survey of IEC teachers

Part One

1. How many years have you taught intensive language classes?
    (please circle)

    less than 1 year   1–2 years   2–5 years   5+ years

2. What is your main teaching (subject) area in the IEC?

    _____

3. Please number in order of importance the following statements of
    possible content of a program in your subject.

    [   ] subject knowledge/skills
    [   ] components of language (e.g. grammar, word knowledge)
    [   ] using language for a purpose (e.g. to inform, discuss, express
           opinions)
    [   ] other (specify) _____

    Comments_____

    _____

    _____

Student Work and its Organisation

4. Assessed activities — please write brief descriptions of up to 4 student
    tasks/activities which you assessed during the past 3–4 weeks in your
    main teaching area.
    e.g 'Read a story, make notes and write a paragraph.'
         'Do an experiment and give an oral report.'

Task 1 _____

Task 2 _____

Task 3 _____

Task 4 _____

(please tick)	Tasks			
	1	2	3	4
5. Decision-making on **what** work is to be done and **how**				
solely by teacher				
student–teacher agreement				
solely by student				
6. Student grouping for the work				
individual				
small groups				
whole class				
7. Audience or focus for the work				
teacher				
whole class				
small group				
student her/himself				
outside group				
other				
8. Time allowed for completion of the work				
short (less than 1 period)				
moderate (1–2 periods)				
long (more than 2 periods)				
9. Difficulty				
easy				
moderate				
hard				

Student Assessment

(please tick)	Tasks			
	1	**2**	**3**	**4**
10. Students knew beforehand that the task was to be assessed.				
11. Methods of assessment correction/marking..................				
oral feedback given				
written feedback given				
test given				
self-assessment...............				
evaluation/discussion of task by class after completion				
other...............				

Part Two

This part relates to assessment in a whole program, topic or unit of work.

12. **The Teaching Program**
    Please indicate how important you consider the following aspects of teaching to be, and approximately how much time you typically spend on them (or, spent on them last term) in a topic/unit of work in your main subject area.

    (Importance: 0 = not important at all; 5 = very important)

(please circle)	Importance	Time spent (hrs)
Assessment of students		
for class placement	0 1 2 3 4 5	0 1–2 3–5 5+
Pre-topic planning	0 1 2 3 4 5	0 1–2 3–5 5+
Ongoing programming		
(lesson planning)	0 1 2 3 4 5	0 1–2 3–5 5+
Materials preparation	0 1 2 3 4 5	0 1–2 3–5 5+

(please circle)	Importance	Time spent (hrs)
Ongoing student assessment		
(e.g. marking, feedback)	0 1 2 3 4 5	0 1–2 3–5 5+
Final evaluation of		
topic/unit of work	0 1 2 3 4 5	0 1–2 3–5 5+

Comments_____

_____

_____

13. **The Purposes of Assessment**

Please indicate how important you consider the following purposes of assessment to be.

(Importance: 0 = not important at all; 5 = very important)

(please circle)	Importance
to place students in class	0 1 2 3 4 5
to give learners feedback on progress	0 1 2 3 4 5
to give teachers feedback on learners progress	0 1 2 3 4 5
to diagnose strengths and weaknesses and set further learning objectives	0 1 2 3 4 5
to indicate learners' subject/content knowledge	0 1 2 3 4 5
to provide information to others e.g. other teachers, parents	0 1 2 3 4 5
to indicate readiness for high school	0 1 2 3 4 5
to indicate levels of general language proficiency (Listening, Speaking, Reading, Writing)	0 1 2 3 4 5
to indicate the students' achievement of course objectives	0 1 2 3 4 5

Comments_____

_____

_____

14. **Methods of Assessment**
    Which of the following methods did you use in your main subject in your
    most recent completed topic, unit of work or program?
    How useful did you find them?

    (Frequency: 0 = not used; 5 = used very frequently)
    (Usefulness: 0 = not useful; 5 = very useful)

(please circle)	Frequency	Usefulness
observation of students in		
typical class activities	0 1 2 3 4 5	0 1 2 3 4 5
marking/correction of work	0 1 2 3 4 5	0 1 2 3 4 5
recycling of work (e.g. for		
revision after comment)	0 1 2 3 4 5	0 1 2 3 4 5
discussion (teacher–student)	0 1 2 3 4 5	0 1 2 3 4 5
peer conferencing/discussion	0 1 2 3 4 5	0 1 2 3 4 5
student self-assessment	0 1 2 3 4 5	0 1 2 3 4 5
regular short tests		
(e.g. spelling, dictation)	0 1 2 3 4 5	0 1 2 3 4 5
objective tests (e.g. true/false,		
multiple choice)	0 1 2 3 4 5	0 1 2 3 4 5
teacher journal (teacher writes		
about what happens in class)	0 1 2 3 4 5	0 1 2 3 4 5
learner journal (learner writes		
about what happens in class)	0 1 2 3 4 5	0 1 2 3 4 5
other (specify)_____		
_____	0 1 2 3 4 5	0 1 2 3 4 5

Comments_____

_____

_____

15. Do you have any major concerns with assessment?

_____

_____

_____

_____

16. Do you have any general comments about the role of student assessment in intensive language classes?

_____

_____

_____

_____

Appendix B

Survey of IEC students

1. Country of origin _____

2. Years at school in that country (e.g. 6 years) _____

3. How did your school in your country of origin assess your work?
   (Put a circle around one number e.g. 1 ② 3)

	Never	Sometimes	Often
tests or examinations	1	2	3
correction of mistakes	1	2	3
teacher discussed work with you	1	2	3
teacher wrote advice or comments in your book	1	2	3
teacher told you what you needed to do better	1	2	3
teacher told you what you did well	1	2	3
you had to assess your own work (e.g. gave yourself a mark)	1	2	3
you assessed other students (e.g. gave them a mark)	1	2	3

4. How are you assessed in the IEC?

tests or examinations	1	2	3
correction of mistakes	1	2	3
teacher discusses work with you	1	2	3
teacher writes advice or comments in your book	1	2	3
teacher tells you what you need to do better	1	2	3
teacher tells you what you do well	1	2	3
you assess your own work	1	2	3
you assess other students	1	2	3

5. What are the best ways teachers can assess you?
   (Choose 2 from the list above) _____

   _____

9 Criterion-based assessment: a classroom teacher's perspective

Margaret Gunn

Introduction

In recent years, Commonwealth and state governments in Australia have placed increasingly heavy emphasis on the need for education and training programs to demonstrate their public accountability through explicit and detailed reporting of program objectives, content and outcomes. This move has forced educational institutions to examine their assessment and reporting practices in order to meet the information requirements of the various audiences to whom they are accountable.

This chapter outlines an attempt to come to terms with these demands for accountability in the context of the Adult Migrant English Program (AMEP). It describes a classroom-based project in which a small group of teachers set about devising, implementing and evaluating a set of assessment procedures for adult immigrant learners of English which it was hoped would satisfy the information requirements of the various stakeholders within the Program.

Background to the Project

The Adult Migrant English Program (AMEP)

The AMEP is one of the largest Government-funded immigrant English language programs in the world, with a projected budget of $440 million from 1993 to 1997. Recently, in response to increasing demands for accountability, the Program has undertaken extensive reviews of its curricula, task design, methods of program evaluation, materials, teacher training, and educational and placement services. In such a climate, it was inevitable that issues of assessment of learning outcomes would figure prominently. Not surprisingly, the principal object of attention has been the language gains made by learners of learners as they exit a predetermined period of tuition.

Assessment concerns in the AMEP

In the mid to late 1980s, research studies into the AMEP curriculum revealed a number of concerns related to assessment (Campbell et al. 1986; Colman 1989; Brindley 1986, 1989). Amongst these were:

- a perceived lack of coherence in program objectives within and across States (Campbell et al. 1986);

- the lack of formally accredited courses articulating to mainstream education and training (Lipa 1993);

- a lack of 'fine-grained' assessment procedures suitable for measuring learners' attainment of objectives (Campbell et al., op. cit.);

- a lack of explicit information on learner outcomes that could be used to inform parties outside the Program of learners' progress and achievement (Brindley 1989).

The findings from these studies drew attention to the pivotal role of classroom assessment within the Program. However, in a climate in which the importance of documenting outcomes was being increasingly highlighted, it was not surprising that some teachers felt it was their work, rather than that of their students, which was under investigation — a situation not unique to AMEP teachers (Popham 1980).

The pressure for assessment: meeting the needs of different audiences

The pressure for assessment, however, did not seem to teachers to be coming solely from above but, rather, from four different directions. First, it came from students and ex-students alike who wanted documentary evidence of their language achievement in the AMEP. Learners had variable expectations of educational practices, and the lack of accredited evidence of their course participation frequently surprised and disappointed them. Teachers, too, regretted being unable to supply formal recognition of the learners' achievements.

Secondly, the teachers themselves were attempting to provide substantive evidence of learner outcomes for each other, not only to support decisions about student allocation to language activities but also to facilitate continuity between classes.

Thirdly, administrators were anxious to have tangible evidence to account for expenditure and to demonstrate program effectiveness. Although it was unclear precisely in what form such information would be required over and above statistical evidence of enrolment numbers and language proficiency levels in terms of ASLPR ratings (Australian Second Language Proficiency Ratings) (Ingram and Wylie 1984), teachers felt that they would inevitably be called upon to provide other kinds of explicit information on student outcomes.

Finally, teachers knew that employers, training advisers and other interested parties outside the program would be likely to require evidence of an applicant's immediate past language learning activities and the extent of his/her capacity to operate in English.

The need to demonstrate learners' achievements was not confined, however, to the time they exited a Program. In the AMEP there are frequent transitional points throughout the Program at which assessment is required.

The teacher who is trying to document and assess a learners' progress through the system is thus faced with two key questions:

- How can the classroom teacher best demonstrate the learners' achievements, both during and at the culmination of a period of study?

- What form should this evidence take, so that each 'stakeholder' can identify the true nature of learners' achievement?

It was on the basis of these questions that a project brief was formulated to investigate the development and implementation of classroom assessment procedures in adult ESL classrooms.

Issues in second language assessment: a practitioner's view

In order to set the context in which the project was undertaken, it is useful to consider some of the issues which face the classroom teacher seeking to devise and implement an assessment system to meet the needs of the various stakeholders in a language program.

A number of language testers have observed that many classroom practitioners find the area of assessment to be obscure and problematic (Stevenson 1985; Hughes 1986). In choosing the kind of assessment system to adopt we had to consider three recurring problems which regularly confront teachers. These are the problems of establishing the purpose for assessment, defining the audience and then choosing or developing appropriate tools and procedures.

The purpose of assessment: issues of ideology

One of the thorniest problems in language assessment is defining the nature of what is to be assessed: that is, language proficiency. This amounts to asking the question posed by Spolsky (1985): 'What does it mean to know how to use a language?'

A construct as complex as language proficiency is extraordinarily difficult to define, however, as numerous authors have pointed out. For this reason, Rea (1985) notes a 'fuzziness' surrounding the field of language proficiency assessment which according to Brindley (1986:38) is due to 'the lack of sound empirically-based theories of language learning' to underpin assessment.

The confusion and 'fuzziness' surrounding the construct of proficiency exist not only at the theoretical level. At a more practical level, the *purpose* of assessment is often unclear to teachers. In a climate in which there has been an increasing focus on assessment as a means of reporting outcomes to external stakeholders, the prime *educational* purpose of assessment has tended to become obscured (see Bachman 1990:291).

It is here that two metaphors help to re-establish this purpose:

> *Assessment is to educational and instructional goals as maps are to travellers (sic) and their destinations.*
>
> (Richard et al 1991)

> *Assessment is a celebration of learning.*
>
> (Broadfoot 1991)

The first quotation highlights the goals of instruction, or more specifically, the goals held by learners who subject themselves to the rigours of learning. A map is primarily of use to the traveller; it is of mere curiosity value to the armchair critic. In a sense, the teacher is a fellow traveller, a guide, aware of the possible destinations and committed to enabling the traveller to reach the preferred destination. Such an image helps the teacher put the demands of the stakeholders into perspective. Assessment of learning is chiefly the domain of the learner and teacher. The concern of the administrators or funding agencies should be the total teaching environment, not solely the proficiency outcomes of the learners. On the other hand, the learner's chief concern should be to exercise the language skills they have acquired in situations beyond the classroom.

The second quotation, that 'assessment is a celebration of learning', appears almost flippant compared with the seriousness of the wider issues. Yet Broadfoot's vigorous optimism is timely, because it refocuses attention on the learner and the learning process itself, rather than on the difficulties inherent in assessing language proficiency or on measurement considerations. In fact, this view reflects the key notion of responsiveness to learners' needs which has been a central tenet in the AMEP (Campbell et al. 1986). It also brings the classroom teacher back to the audience to whom they feel primarily accountable: that is, learners themselves (Brindley 1989).

Determining the audience for assessment outcomes

If the purposes for assessment are unclear, there is a chance that inappropriate assessment procedures may be used. This in turn, may mean that assessment information may be misused or misunderstood. In order to avoid this, it was necessary for us to consider the assessment instruments currently used in the AMEP in relation to the audiences they were intended to inform.

At the time the project was undertaken, the main assessment tool of most AMEP classroom teachers, the Australian Second Language Proficiency Rating Scale

(ASLPR) was widely used for assessment and reporting. The scale represents a convenient means of summarising assessment outcomes in a single figure which can be referenced to a set of behavioural descriptors. As such it seemed suitable for the purposes of teachers and administrators where those administrators were familiar with the operation of a language program. Unfortunately, the mere existence of the scale tended to confirm the assumption that this single piece of evidence could satisfy all of the stakeholders in the program.

However, as Campbell et al. (1986) point out, while the ASLPR fulfils the purpose of providing broad indicators of overall gain for funding bodies who require this type of information, it cannot provide very detailed information on individual achievement relative to course objectives which is what teachers and learners are interested in. It cannot, in other words, be used to fulfil the two purposes of diagnosis and reporting simultaneously (Alderson 1991).

This confusion of purpose exemplified by the use of the ASLPR seemed to us to account for a substantial amount of the confusion and frustration about assessment that exists in the AMEP, not only amongst the project group. In our investigation of teachers' assessment procedures, we encountered a wide range of assessment tools, proficiency descriptors, grids and graphs. Yet it was rarely made clear for whom the information yielded by these instruments was intended or how it was to be used.

It should be noted, however, that at the time the project began, the demands of funding agencies were general rather than specific[1] and the need to satisfy learners and fellow teachers was much more pressing. The expectation that all four stakeholders could be satisfied with one piece of evidence was, nevertheless, still present.

The problem of assessment methods

Since behaviourist theories of language acquisition were first challenged, it has become apparent that language learning is complex and multidimensional and language testers have argued that models of language ability should also reflect that complexity (Bachman 1990). Assessment of language proficiency, by extension, involves long and careful deliberation to determine to what extent individuals can use the language to achieve their communicative goals.

Subjectivity in assessment

From a layperson's point of view, however, it is hard to see why assessment has to be so complicated. People are constantly making judgements about the clarity and appropriateness of what others say and how they say it. Native speakers make frequent evaluations of non-native speakers' ability to use the target language. In some circumstances, such judgements may have the power to determine a non-native speaker's access to employment or training programs.

Although this type of subjective anecdotal opinion alone would not be considered by language testers to be acceptable as assessment evidence, it is not difficult to find examples of more formal language assessment which look remarkably 'subjective'. An example is the Interview Scale taken from Carroll and Hall (1985). This scale consists of nine Bands or proficiency levels, ranging from 'non-speaker' (Band 0/1) to 'expert speaker' (Band 9). Contained in the descriptors are phrases which expose the subjective standards of the assessor. A person is placed on Band 9 because of 'a slight non-native accent', and a capacity to speak and interact 'authoritatively'. This clearly implies that an accent is a disadvantage, while a 'non-authoritative personality' precludes the learner from achieving 'expert' status. Further, the ambience of the encounter between assessor and learner is of significance in moulding the assessor's judgement. If the speaker 'demonstrates a dependence' on the interviewer, or if there are 'noticeable inaccuracies and inappropriacies', then 'the interview is not a rewarding experience' (for the interviewer, one assumes), primarily because the encounter 'requires tolerance from listener' (Band 4 — Marginal Speaker).[2]

'Objective' methods of assessment

While there are clearly problems in basing formal statements of learner achievement on subjective judgements methods which could be seen to be at the other extreme of the subjectivity-objectivity continuum, are equally open to question. Assessment methods emanating from behaviourist theory, that implied, for example, that it was appropriate to quantify a learner's performance by determining the frequency of error in utterances, have been rightly judged as too narrow in scope and unlikely to engage the classroom teacher. They do not readily provide the types of answers about the learner's achievement that the teacher (or others) are likely to ask.

Rado and Reynolds (1989) observe, 'language learning is a complex process in which regression is as integral a part as progress. Successful language learning is essentially cumulative.' The classroom teacher, more than any other stakeholder, recognises this complexity, being required at times to account for a learner's diminished performance, while recognising the full gamut of variables constraining this performance, such as learners' personal circumstances, cultural, educational, or economic background, motivation, personality, aptitude and so on, each of which may influence observable behaviour. Clearly, the phenomenon of language cannot be distilled into a mere set of facts available for learners to memorise. For this reason assessment inevitably involves a degree of oversimplification.

Standardised tests

Standardised tests have been influential in shaping expectations of what 'language assessment' should look like. Large scale international tests such as TOEFL (Test of English as a Foreign Language) and the International English Language Testing System (IELTS) test have been widely used to determine levels of proficiency particularly amongst pre-tertiary applicants in the US and Europe. Such tests vary in their 'communicativeness'. While some use mainly 'indirect' methods such as multiple choice reading and listening, others incorporate a face-to-face speaking component.

For purposes of classroom testing, general advice for the writing of language tests is readily available to teachers (Heaton 1975; Carroll and Hall 1985), as are explicit guidelines for the testing of a variety of curricular components such as vocabulary, cloze and pronunciation (Madsen 1983). Courchene and de Bagheera (1985) examine practical and theoretical decisions that can affect test construction — providing a decision maker's checklist designed to lead to a more valid and reliable evaluation of learners' communicative performance.

However, such tools are not widely used in the AMEP. Brindley (1989:29) surveyed 131 AMEP teachers and found that of the nine reportedly favoured assessment methods in current usage, 'standardised tests' or 'teacher-made tests' were used by less than ten per cent of respondents with high or very high frequency. Unfamiliarity with standardised tests is given (1989:28) as a reason for their infrequent use, but it is also worth noting that almost ninety-three per cent of respondents expressed a strong antipathy towards their use.

This suggests that Australian adult ESL teachers may have developed a suspicion of any materials, not least assessment materials, which derive from outside the context in which the learner may reasonably expect to use the language. They are also aware of the potential for a standardised test to exercise a negative effect on the curriculum and of the well documented risks of 'teaching to the test'. This distrust of standardised tests reflects the rapid changes which have occurred over the last twenty or so years, in particular with the implementation of the communicative curriculum (Melrose 1991:1–16). As numerous authors have commented, testing has tended to lag behind the curriculum and communicative curricula can be easily sabotaged by the introduction of a non–communicative test (Shohamy 1993).

Assessment methods in the AMEP

But if 'tests', standardised or teacher-made, are out of favour, what methods are used for assessment? Brindley's (1989) survey of AMEP assessment practices indicated that learners' behaviour was being assessed primarily informally as it occurred in the classroom, rather than being 'deliberately stimulated to allow specific observation of that behaviour' by the assessor (Tuckman 1975:3).

Such results from Brindley's enquiry were perceived as a source of concern by those responsible for guiding the AMEP towards greater accountability since non–intrusive, informal observation, undertaken either by the learners themselves or by others, does not yield information in an explicit or standardised form. This makes public accountability very difficult and precludes any systematic control, which conventionally takes the form of providing evidence for the validity and reliability of the assessment procedures and outcomes (Bachman 1990:238–291).

Summary

Hazards, then, could be identified in each of the assessment methods familiar to the project group. Level descriptors were sometimes highly subjective and difficult to apply consistently; experimental methods were narrowly focused and of no immediate relevance to practitioners; standardised tests were artificial and inappropriate to the context in which the learners were expecting to operate and, like teacher-made tests, needed to be analysed for their validity, reliability and authenticity.

The problem thus remained of choosing assessment procedures which could be used to obtain information about learners' achievements which was concise, objective, fair and accessible to the relevant stakeholders.

Criterion-based assessment: a way forward?

In an attempt to reconcile the differing demands for information on the part of the different audiences within the AMEP, Brindley (1986, 1989) proposed criterion-based assessment as a means by which learner-outcomes from learner-centred curricula could be demonstrated.

Referred to variously as 'criterion-referenced' and 'criterion-based', the essential feature of this type of assessment is that the learner's performance is interpreted by reference to predetermined criteria. A dual process is involved: (a) establishing the criteria and (b) determining the standards of performance.

This approach to assessment is in marked contrast to norm-referenced assessment, which has dominated the assessment scene until relatively recently. Norm-referenced assessment is concerned with the performance of a particular group of learners, and the distribution of scores across the group. The nature of the individual's performance becomes evident only when it is compared directly with that of the others in the group.

The two terms, 'criterion-referenced' and 'criterion-based' are not entirely interchangeable (Wylie 1992). 'Criterion-referenced' is derived from the US context, where, according to Popham (1980:531), the practice emerged as a 'repudiation of traditional testing methods'. He states:

> The distinctive attribute of a criterion-referenced test is the vastly improved precision with which it describes the behavior being assessed.

In the US, however, criterion-referenced tests tend to remain closely identified with formal procedures. This does not mean that test content drives instruction, however. The classroom teacher teaches towards the domain of abilities being measured by the test, rather than the test items themselves (Popham 1980:531–533). Glaser and Nitko (Hughes 1986:32) summarised the matter this way:

> *A criterion-referenced test is one that is deliberately constructed to yield measurements that are directly interpretable in terms of specified performance standards… they must be established prior to test construction… and the purpose of testing is to assess an individual's status with respect to those standards.*

'Criterion-based assessment' is the term more commonly used in general education in Australia, indicating a less rigorous identification with the psychometric orientation of much of the US foreign language testing tradition. Criterion-based assessment is predicated upon clearly defined course objectives, formulated expressly in response to learner-expressed needs. From these, tasks are devised, and, as in criterion-referenced assessment, competency criteria are established and predetermined standards of performance are identified.

For the purposes of this paper, the term 'criterion-based' assessment will be used, because the assessment processes undertaken by the project group do not all conform to Tuckman's definition of 'test' (1975:3), in which learners are required to 'undertake tasks devised deliberately to stimulate behaviours which are then closely observed'. The methodologies employed in the project mirrored those described by Brindley (1989:29) where formal 'test-like' instruments were substantially avoided.

Despite the obvious attractions of criterion-based assessment, they are not without their problems (Skehan 1984; Brindley 1991). Though aware of these problems, some researchers maintain a high level of optimism. Sadler (1986), speaking from the perspective of one involved in criterion-based assessment in foreign language teaching in secondary schools, commented:

> *As we are finding out, the theory of a standards-based (i.e. criterion-based) assessment is disarmingly simple but the practice is extraordinarily difficult. But having got this coveted ball into our court, we are going to see where we can hit it to maximise the good effects.*

The Project

Aims

In a similar vein, we embarked on the project with the aim of exploring the use of criterion-based procedures in the AMEP context. The purpose of the project was to determine the feasibility of criterion-based assessment procedures in on-going, general English language courses.

Specifically, its aims were:

a) to determine the impact on teachers, learners and the curriculum, of implementing criterion-based assessment in the Program, and
b) to examine the nature of the accountability demanded by external audiences, and a consider a suitable response.

Defining terms

Much of the assessment terminology used in the project has been discussed previously in this chapter. However, in order to clarify the basis on which our assessment procedures were developed, it is worth briefly revisiting some of these.

'Criterion-based assessment' has been preferred to 'criterion-referenced' assessment, because the practices undertaken in this account of assessing second-language learning are eclectic rather than 'test-like'.

'Language proficiency' is used to refer to a summative description of what the learner can do in particular circumstances. However, judgements about learner proficiency can only refer to the learner's likely performance in a real-life situation, given that the circumstances are often a projection of the assessor's knowledge of the target society (Richards 1985).

'Communicative competence' refers to the learner's knowledge of the rules of the language as well as the learner's ability to demonstrate appropriate language use in context (Hymes 1972). Despite Canale and Swain's assertion (1980:5) that the two are usually dichotomised, it is difficult in this project to sustain a distinction between 'communicative competence' and 'communicative performance'. The terms 'competence' and 'performance' could be applied respectively to 'knowledge about the language' and 'use of the language' but the term 'communicative' is taken as neutralising any distinction, each then representing evidence of the learners' use in real-life situation of what they have acquired while learning. To demonstrate this validly, a range of performance tasks need to be assessed or sampled, using a variety of instruments and procedures (Brindley 1986:11).

In a similar way, *'achievement'* indicates that learners can demonstrate acquired competencies, that their communicative performance is evidence of language gain either in terms of overall proficiency (general ability as evidenced by a test score or rating on one or more skills), functional proficiency (ability to perform specific tasks) or structural proficiency (ability to manipulate the language system) (Spolsky 1985).

Such constructs, however, are subject to review, and this in fact has occurred, particularly in the light of recent national developments in assessment[3]. The notion of 'language competency' has now gained prominence within the AMEP with the introduction of competency-based curricula and accreditation procedures. Competencies are intended course outcomes stated in terms of knowledge, learning strategies and linguistic skills (Hagan et al. 1993:5). In this respect a language competency embodies elements of both communicative competence and communicative performance.

Participants

Initial discussion about the project occurred during a state-wide professional development seminar in early 1990. At regular intervals throughout the year, most teachers contributed to subsequent seminars on assessment. Thus, staff became familiar with many of the issues as well as models of assessment procedures.

Two teachers were given the task of trialling criterion-based methods of assessment, one to teach, the other to report. For this, a test class was selected. Designated a 'lower intermediate' class, (ASLPR 1- to 1), the class ran for an eleven week term, fifteen hours per week. There were twenty-one learners with an age range of nineteen to forty-one years, who represented ten different language groups. Their educational background ranged from minimal schooling to post-graduate university study and consequently, they had a variety of occupational skills and goals.

Approach

Figure 1 (p. 252) conceptualises the approach to assessment of the classroom teachers in the project group. It demonstrates the nature of the relationship between communicative language testing, teaching and learning and shows the links between the student's language needs and the response of the language teaching institution.

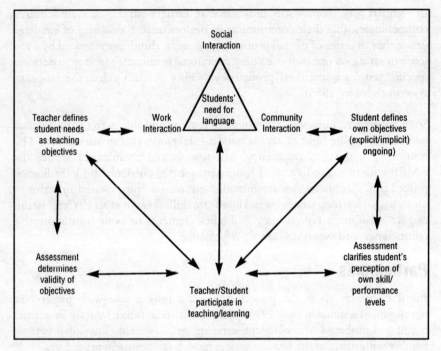

Figure 1   Relationship between communicative language assessment, teaching and learning

A statement which attempted to summarise the intentions and expectations for the project was formulated thus:

> *Criterion-based assessment practices will require teachers:*
>
> - *to identify key competencies needed by learners to perform communicative tasks inside and/or outside the classroom;*
>
> - *to specify standards by which degrees of proficiency can be identified;*
>
> - *to determine learners' performance levels through carefully devised tasks; and*
>
> - *report these to learners and/or peers and/or external audiences.*

Undertaken within the scope of the professional development program across the state, this trialling will provide an indication of the feasibility of implementing criterion-based assessment as standard practice.

Adapting assessment procedures

Of the many assessment tools which teachers examined, three were found to be of particular relevance. The first was a profile sheet, Thompson's Progress Profile for pre-nursing training (Thompson 1986) which was reprinted in Brindley (1989:96–97). Here, four general areas under scrutiny, 'communication', 'practical and numerical', 'social' and 'decision making' were nominated, then abilities appropriate to each were enumerated. A sequence of 'can do' statements were then ranged across the page, with a narrow space stretching as a continuum beneath these statements. This space was shaded to indicate the extent of the student's achievement.

The second procedure used were the guidelines for establishing performance criteria developed by the Royal Society of Arts (1988, 1989). Here, a formula is offered for the production of performance criteria. It consists of:

• a profile sentence — which identifies the nature of the task being assessed;

• performance criteria — providing 'can do' statements of the learner's ability;

• a statement demonstrating consistency of the learner's performance in a variety of contexts;

• a statement indicating constraints operating on the learner and the performance standards required;

• examples of contexts — indicating where the task will be undertaken; and

• examples of appropriate evidence which would represent the outcome of learner activity.

Thirdly, documents from the ALL project, (Scarino et al. 1988) served to stimulate experiments in assessment. Learner self-assessment diaries (Brindley 1989:90) in particular, became immediately popular as an assessment tool.

Documents like the National Curriculum Frameworks (1989) had guided the development of an environment in which the 'cornerstones' of curriculum development — needs analysis, objective setting, task design and implementation, assessment and evaluation had been well established. These Frameworks had therefore been instrumental in determining our understanding of 'clearly-defined objectives' — taken to indicate 'specific objectives' (National Curriculum Project — New Arrivals Framework 1989:10) which were the foundation of each course. The 'standards of performance' — the second facet of determining criteria — were derived on the basis of practitioners' experience with the ASLPR proficiency descriptors, and also from experience in recognising the language components which made communicative tasks increasingly complex.

Deciding what to test

The assessment project set out to develop a range of assessable tasks which represented what learners were actually doing, or hoping to do, in their day-to-day lives. In this way assessment procedures could be closely linked to the curriculum and its intended outcomes.

Ten types of activity or skills, were identified which enabled the assessor to focus, within reason, on the discrete use of each of the four macro-skills. Of necessity, the number was quickly reduced to five. These were:

1. extracting information from a written text (assessing aspects of reading);

2. asking and answering questions (with the focus on interactive speaking);

3. written communication (assessing a range of relevant writing tasks);

4. telephoning (assessing specialised listening and speaking skills);

5. socialising (assessing casual conversation).

The next step was to define in detail the content domain of each task and to specify the end points of an ability scale which could be used to describe a learner's standard of performance.

A grid was thus drawn up (see Figure 2 p. 255) which tabulated the five activities or skills in the left column and specified five sets of conditions — in effect, tasks

CLIENT'S NAME: _____

SKILLS   CONDITIONS

Extract information from a written text	Recognise text types: • bus timetable; • advertisement; • letter; • street sign.	Extract essential information from: • a familiar bus timetable; • ads; • traffic signs; • appointment cards.	Get the gist of: • a newspaper account of a topical event; • an information letter from service provider, e.g. Hydro, RACT.	Identity: • key information; • register; • inference in: a) a newspaper article; b) a business letter.	Analyse vocational text.
	← WITHIN THE CLASSROOM →		← BEYOND THE CLASSROOM →		
Ask and answer questions	Between teacher/ student and student/teacher — ask and answer simple questions about ID.	Ask and answer questions about time and money.	Carry out simple transactions. Ask directions.	With native speakers — ask for clarification and obtain information. Respond to all of the above.	Interview (face to face). Seek or give an opinion.
Written communication	Write shopping list (ten common items) understand-able to native speaker. Provide ID information on e.g. blood test form.	Write a short note to a child's teacher. Fill out a blank form. Greeting card.	Write an appropri-ately worded letter to a teacher (info should be clear) OR write a short informal letter to a native speaker.	Write a short (one page) business letter with appropri-ate register, layout and information.	As in 4 — task more complex e.g.: • applying for a job; • responding to a service provider about a public issue.
Telephone skills	Provide appropriate initial response to telephone call (name, number).	Give a simple message: 'Can't come to school today'.	Manage more complex exchanges, e.g. making appointment, etc.	Take down a message from the phone.	Leave a message on an answering machine.
Socialising	Respond face to face in predictable areas including greetings, farewells, offering limited personal information.	Can initiate simple face to face conversations and respond to more detailed personal questions.	Enter and exit conversations appropriately. Make sensible exchanges of information within the school context.	Has a range of polite forms and is able to socialise on the phone.	Able to negotiate when making arrangements; can discuss the weather; give detained personal information.
GENERAL COMMENTS					

TEACHER'S NAME: _____

Figure 2 Student Record Sheet

of increasing difficulty, at which this skill could be assessed. Parallel lines beneath each task allowed the assessor to shade the level of proficiency achieved (cf. Thompson 1986).

Data collection

A timetable was prepared for administering eight assessment tasks envisaged as necessary for the course. Following Brindley's findings, (1989:29) a variety of methods were employed in developing assessment tools. Teacher-made tests were not included, although the teacher concerned occasionally practised this form of assessment.

Two of the tasks were to be on-going, requiring teacher observation and informal discussion with learners. These were Task 1, *socialisation*, which was made possible during semi-structured conversation classes with native speakers who came as guests to the Centre each week, and Task 2, *asking and answering questions* which was to be assessed in regular small group or informal classroom discussion.

The remaining six tasks were:

Task 3: making an appointment on the telephone;
Task 4: writing an apology;
Task 5: reading an advertisement and appointment card;
Task 6: telephoning to leave a message (re-assessing the competencies in Task 3);
Task 7: reading a newspaper article and a business letter (expanding the range of genres introduced in Task 5);
Task 8: writing formal letters: (i) a complaint and (ii) making a reservation.

The assessment data was intended to be recorded in three ways:

1. Figure 2 was to be used as a record sheet for each student throughout the course. In fact, such skills are relevant to second-language learners throughout the AMEP's general language courses. Given the range of competencies indicated horizontally, it was suggested the sheet could apply to learners throughout their time in the Program.

2. For the purposes of the trial, a 'Record of Assessment Procedure' was devised (see Figure 3 p. 257) requiring the teacher to record the specific

Record of Assessment Procedure   Date: _____

Target Group:

Objective of Assessment Task:

Criteria

1.
2.
3.
4.
5.

Methodology

a) Preparation:

                                         Time: (teacher's + class) _____
b) Implementation:

                                         Time: (teacher's + class) _____
c) Analysis:

                                         Time: (teacher's + class) _____

                                         Total Time: _____

Results: (brief description of learners' performance against criteria)

Any changes needed in the process?

                    Signed: _____ (Teacher)

Figure 3 Record of assessment procedure

Task Objective					
Name (Class list)	1	2	3	4	5

Figure 4 Grid for recording achievement

objectives of the task, the descriptors establishing criteria, details of preparation, implementation and analysis procedures as well as the class and teacher time expended. Provision was also made for comments on outcomes and improvements needed.

3.   The trial teacher added a grid (see Figure 4 p. 258) which enabled her to keep a graphic record of each student's achievement on an unspecified scale of 1–5 for each assessment task. This could be described as maintaining a 'normative' eye on the class, but it also provided information which affected teaching practice, highlighting the variable needs of learners.

Discussion

Time involved in assessment activities

Table 1 (p. 260) indicates teacher time required for each assessment task.

These statistics do not differentiate between the teacher's contact hours and hours spent out of class in preparation or analysis of assessment tasks. If say, twenty per cent of the preparation hours in Table 1 are allocated to introducing the tasks (2.3 hours), one hundred per cent to implementation (22.5 hours) and ten per cent to reporting back to the learners (0.9 hours) then teacher time devoted to assessment comprised 25.7 hours or 21.4% of the total contact time of 120 hours.

When confronted with the finding that over twenty per cent of face-to-face teaching time was spent in actual assessment tasks, the teacher commented that this was a fair reflection of her practice. It was not the only form of assessment undertaken, however. Students' work was regularly collected for marking and in addition, a summative assessment in the form of an ASLPR level for each macro-skill was still required at the end of the course. This would have made the total time spent on assessment substantially greater.

The assessment tools: an evaluation

The student record sheet shown in Figure 2 represents an attempt to devise a framework that would provide standardised achievement levels for all general

Task Number	Preparation#	Implementation	Analysis	Total
1	4	6	n/a*	10
2	n/a	12¥	2	14
3	1	1	1	3
4	2	0.5	1	3.5
5	1.5	0.5	1	3
6	1	0.5	2	3.5
7	1.5	1	1	3.5
8	0.5	1	1	2.5
Total Hours	**11.5**	**22.5**	**9**	**43**

\#   Preparation includes both teacher time before class and time spent with
learners explaining the Assessment Task.

*   Analysis occurred simultaneously, as assessment involved observation.

¥   Teacher-directed 'Class talk' e.g. weekend talk, preparation for Wednesday
conversation class, discussion on topical issues etc. were all vehicles for Task
2 assessment: Asking and answering questions.

Table 1 Time taken in Assessment Tasks

English classes within the Centre, if not the state. It was designed to be transported
between classes; that is, one teacher could use the framework to indicate to her
successor the level of achievement reached by an individual student.

However, dissatisfaction with this framework arose soon after the trialling had
begun. In particular there were severe conceptual problems associated with the
so-called 'conditions'. These were later seen to serve variously as a checklist of
increasingly complex tasks; specifications of competencies required to perform
tasks; examples of varying modes in which a task may occur; or a test of
familiarity with different genres. Nowhere was there a statement of criteria in
a form that might have been expected, given previous interest in the RSA
performance criteria (RSA 1987, 1988).

For all its perceived shortcomings, the grid was not entirely ineffective,
however. One teacher observing the trial indicated that she found the sheet a

valuable resource, mainly because it suggested a variety of tasks, and there was considerable satisfaction for herself and her beginner learners in shading across the columns to show task achievement.

Determining criteria

Determining the criteria for task performance turned out to be the hardest problem. Unfortunately, the warnings which abound in the literature were unheeded. As Brindley (1986:16) comments:

> *Defining adequate criteria for assessing communicative performance... still remains one of the most pressing problems facing language testers.*

We discovered only through practice how difficult it is to specify criteria for task performance in a clear and unambiguous way.

The Record of Assessment Procedure (Figure 3) which had been distributed to teachers state-wide, required them to devise criteria for their own assessment tasks. Here it was interesting to note that the way in which they did this turned out to be a function of their experience. Those teachers familiar with the ASLPR descriptors were able to find appropriate terminology to describe the development of learner competencies in a sequential way. Other teachers, however could only specify individual tasks of increasing complexity.

In attempting to address some of these problems inherent in specifying criteria for task performance, a range of approaches invite further exploration. The RSA ESL Profile Certificate (1988), for example, spells out in detail the essential features of performance which need to be observed under a series of useful headings which include the nature and consistency of the performance, the conditions under which it takes place as well as examples of contexts and appropriate evidence. Other models which break down particular skills into their components, such as Dickinson's Oral Skills Evaluation Sheet in Brindley (1989:82), could also be usefully adapted. This model could apply across many levels of proficiency and for many tasks where speaking proficiency is being assessed.

It would also be possible to draw on more complex theoretical frameworks of language ability such as that proposed by Bachman (1990:253) to systematically describe elements of performance in assessment tasks. This framework presents a detailed description of the components of language competence which are called on in any communicative act. Bachman (1990:255) suggests that his framework can be used to develop context-free generic criteria for each macro-skill. Such an approach, however, while theoretically interesting, was not feasible in the light of the resources available to the project and thus will not be further explored in this chapter.

Outcomes of the Project

The need to demonstrate accountability in a language teaching program such as the AMEP was the initial impetus for this and several other state-based projects which simultaneously were investigating learner assessment. This present project focused on determining the feasibility of criterion-based assessment in an on-going, general language course in order to determine its impact on teachers, learners and the curriculum, and consider a suitable response to external audiences, should their demands become more specific in the future.

As foreshadowed, the outcomes were not as conclusive as we would have hoped. However, the project generated a number of helpful insights which may be summarised as follows:

1. Participation in the trialling of criterion-based assessment proved a stimulating experience for the teacher concerned. The Records of Assessment (Figure 4) regularly contained references to the impact of the exercise on her classroom practice, for example, helping her identify the cultural components of a task which may disadvantage some learners, revealing hitherto hidden learner problems which warrant closer teacher attention. She commented:

    It (the trialling experience) kept me on focus (i.e. in relation to the objectives). Because the assessment was carried out regularly, (as opposed to a terminal or exit assessment) I was constantly aware of devoting time equally to the areas being assessed — these areas can be equated to the four macro-skills with a functional-communicative base. It also made me much more mindful of function rather than content. i.e. Why teach this? How useful is it? In what way is the learner better able to handle discourse of the various

> *situations? However, in retrospect, I realise there was not time for revision tests as such, content/grammar etc. I'm enjoying having time now (subsequent course) to catch up on this and as is almost predictable, the students are showing a preference for the right/wrong system.*

2. Determining criteria for the language proficiency envisaged for learners is an overwhelming task for most classroom practitioners. The development of generic criteria for each macro-skill would allow practitioners to approach criteria-based assessment with greater insight into the components of competency and to able to track and record their learners' language development more systematically.[4]

If teachers are required to prepare criteria for separate assessment tasks, regardless of the macro-skills being tested, then criterion-based assessment will continue to consume substantial non-contact time, and this may well provoke resentment, if not aggravate confusion and weariness.

3. On the basis of the findings of this project, there is evidence to suggest that the learners' need-to-know may be grossly exaggerated, especially where there is an expectation of continuing access to language courses. The trial group was invited to view and discuss the graphic depiction of their performance as indicated on Figure 4, but only two out of the twenty-one students accepted. One could perhaps infer from this·that factors such as learner's unfamiliarity with criterion-based assessment models affected their expectations of results. On the other hand, adult learners require clearly defined goals, and offering them knowledge of the specific criteria against which their proficiency is to be judged has been found to be a major stimulus to learning (Dickinson 1987). However, it is important to note that in order for lower-level learners to gain maximum benefit, assessment criteria would need to be accessible to learners in translation or expressed in sufficiently simple English (Lewis 1990). In this way it is likely that in time, learners will come to value access to explicit information on assessment criteria and their learning outcomes.

4. The adoption of criterion-based assessment procedures appears to have had a positive impact on the curriculum. Evidence from this study indicates that the imperatives of determining objectives, devising relevant tasks which promote learner interaction and interest, and assessing learner performance

in objectives-driven tasks constitute a formula for disciplined, accountable curricula.

5. It is highly unlikely that information gathered on individual achievement could be used for communicating information to stakeholders outside the Program if it were not available in aggregated form. Demonstrating learner's achievement to an external enquirer, say, employer, or representative of the funding agency, (in the case of the AMEP, a Government official), would be extremely problematic from a logistical point of view since, strictly speaking, it would involve providing eight records of performance as in Figure 4, along with the summative assessment in the form of the shading on the grid (Figure 2). Reporting in this form would involve supplying a substantial volume of paper relevant to each learner and in any case the resulting information might well be uninterpretable to a non-specialist.

Defining the stakeholders' requirements

The issues canvassed above reinforce the necessity of clarifying the information requirements of each of the audiences in the Program in order to determine the form in which assessment information is provided (Brindley 1989:158).

To this end, towards the end of the trialling period, teachers simulated the demands and expectations of stakeholders in the Program, recognising that each stakeholder made vastly different demands.

It was agreed that learners were likely to want positive comments about their personal qualities, as well as documented evidence of their ability to write English and interact with Australian native speakers, so that an employer would not refuse them on the grounds of their language proficiency.

Teachers recognised that they would be happy to divulge positive evidence about a learner's attitude and personal qualities, but they would be selective about negative features. They were willing to supply information about the learner's language abilities as they related to the needs of the workplace if the external audience were the employer. However, they commented that the 'shelf-life' of such information was likely to be limited. This created considerable concern, as teachers felt that an outdated document could misrepresent both the learner's proficiency and the work of the teaching institution.

Employers were assumed likely to require evidence of an applicant's literacy and numeracy. In addition, they would want to ensure the person's pronunciation was intelligible. They would be concerned with the external appearance and personal habits of the applicant and that their qualifications were appropriate for the job. Therefore, teachers thought that evidence of educational background, health, commitment, initiative and adaptability would all be sought.

The group decided that in the present political climate, funding (governmental) agencies would be particularly interested in the employment or re-training success rate of learners from the language program. They would have little interest in the details of the individual assessments undertaken, although they would wish to ensure valid assessment methods were employed in the program.

Such a simulation helped to clarify purpose and direction. Clearly it is incorrect to assume that teachers would have to provide detailed evidence of individual learner proficiency gains to funding agencies. Nor can language teachers presume to report on learner details which are beyond the domain of language ability. However, teachers can certainly report to their colleagues, and the materials developed in the trial serve that purpose adequately. Learners also could benefit from increased familiarity with the criteria and performance standards against which their language proficiency is being assessed.

However, the need remains for a system which would allow achievement to be reported in an aggregated way without oversimplifying or misrepresenting the nature of the language learning process. The ASLPR is increasingly vulnerable to being used as the single official measure of language gains, because it appears so simple and 'clean'. The challenge for the AMEP is to find ways of providing complementary supporting evidence which fairly and accurately reflects the complexity of learners' individual achievements in the Program.

Notes

1   Since July 1991, changes to the arrangement between the Federal Government Departments of Social Security and Education, Employment and Training have required the AMEP to provide statements of the language proficiency of selected clients. These are then used in determining

educational or training opportunities. Simultaneously, intensive reformulation of AMEP policy and curricula has been occurring.

2   Paragraphs which represent descriptors of different levels of proficiency are to be found in the ACTFL Provisional Proficiency Guidelines (1986), which resemble the ASLPR descriptors. Terminology of the kind found in Carroll and Hall's Interview Scale is not replicated in either of these scales.

3   Proposals from the 'Learner Pathways Project' (Lipa 1993) indicate that the aim of learning activities in the AMEP is to assist participants 'to achieve levels of language competency that will enable them to attain their educational, vocational and social goals *as they relate to national priorities'*. What is emerging is a specification of what a learner must demonstrate in order to gain access to a variety of services provided by Government and semi-government agencies. The risk therefore of conflating concepts of *communicative competence* and *performance* in the present project is acknowledged, especially if, as is being suggested by these developments, the external stakeholders have specified their demands to the point of superseding all others.

4   Since this project was completed such statements have become available in the form of the language competencies described in the *Certificate of Spoken and Written English* (Hagan et al. 1993). However while these provide useful overall statements of learning outcomes, teachers will still have to develop their own criteria for ongoing informal assessment of task performance in the classroom.

References

Alderson, J.C. 1991. Bands and scores. In J.C. Alderson and B. North (eds) *Language testing in the 1990s*. London: Modern English Publications and the British Council.

Bachman, L.F. 1990. *Fundamental considerations in language testing*. Oxford: Oxford University Press.

Brindley, G. 1986. *The assessment of second language proficiency: issues and approaches*. Adelaide: National Curriculum Resource Centre.

Brindley, G. 1989. *Assessing achievement in the learner-centred curriculum*. Sydney: National Centre for English Language Teaching and Research.

Brindley, G. 1991. Defining language ability: the criteria for criteria. In S. Anivan (ed.) *Current developments in language testing*. Singapore. Regional Language Centre.

Broadfoot, P. 1987. *Introducing profiling: a practical manual*. London: Macmillan Educational.

Broadfoot, P. 1991. *Assessment: a celebration of learning*. Australian Curriculum Studies Association Workshop Report No. 1. ACSA.

Campbell, W.J. et al. 1986. *Towards active voice*. Report of the Committee of Review of the Adult Migrant English Program. Canberra: Department of Immigration and Ethnic Affairs.

Canale, M. and M. Swain. 1980. Theoretical bases of communicative approaches to second language teaching and testing. *Applied Linguistics* 1, 1:1–47.

Carroll, B. and P. Hall. 1985. *Make your own language tests*. Oxford: Pergamon.

Colman, J. 1989. Where are we now? How did we get here? *Interchange* 13.

Courchêne, R.J. and J.I. de Bagheera. 1985. A theoretical framework for the development of performance tests. In P.C. Hauptman, R. le Blanc and M.B. Wesche (eds) *Second language performance testing*. Ottawa: University of Ottawa Press.

Dickinson, L. 1987. *Self-instruction in language learning*. Cambridge: Cambridge University Press.

Hagan. P., S. Hood, E. Jackson, M. Jones, H. Joyce and M. Manidis. 1993. *Certificate in Spoken and Written English*. Sydney: Adult Migrant English Service NSW and the National Centre for English Language Teaching and Research.

Heaton, J.B. 1975. *Writing English language tests*. Sydney: Longman.

Hughes, A. 1986. A pragmatic approach to criterion–referenced foreign language testing. In M. Portal (ed.) *Innovation in language testing*. Proceedings of the US National Foundation for Educational Research (NFER) Conference, April. Windsor, Berkshire: NFER — Nelson.

Hymes, D.H. 1972. On communicative competence. In J.B. Pride and J. Holmes (eds) *Sociolinguistics*. Harmondsworth: Penguin.

Ingram, D.E. and E. Wylie. 1984. *Australian second language proficiency ratings (ASLPR)*. Canberra: Australian Government Publishing Service.

Lewis, J. 1990. Self-assessment in the classroom: a case study. In G. Brindley (ed.) The *second language curriculum in action*. Sydney: National Centre for English Language Teaching and Research.

Lipa, L. 1993. *Learner pathways in the Adult Migrant English Program*. Sydney: National Centre for English Language Teaching and Research.

Madsen, H.S. 1983. *Techniques in testing*. Oxford: Oxford University Press.

Melrose, R. 1991. *The communicative syllabus: a systemic-functional approach to language teaching*. London: Pinter Publishers.

National Curriculum Frameworks. 1989. *New arrivals: initial-elementary proficiency*. Sydney: National Centre for English Language Teaching and Research.

Popham, W.J. 1980. Educational measurement for the improvement of instruction. *Phi Delta Kappan* April:531–533.

Rado, M. and C. Reynolds. 1989. Progression in language curriculum: sequence or expansion? *Australian Review of Applied Linguistics* 12, 1.

Rea, P.M. 1985. Language testing and the communicative curriculum. In Y.P. Lee, C.Y.Y. Fok, R. Lord and G. Low (eds) *New dimensions in language testing*. Oxford: Pergamon.

Richard, P. et al. 1991. The essential role of assessment. *Adult Learning* 2, 7.

Richards, J.C. 1985. Planning for proficiency. *Prospect* 1, 2:1–5.

Royal Society of Arts. 1988. *Practical skills profile scheme.* London: Royal Society of Arts.

Royal Society of Arts. 1989. *English as a second language — dual certification.* London: Royal Society of Arts.

Sadler, D.R. 1986. *ROSBA's family connections.* Discussion Paper 1. Queensland Board of Secondary School Studies.

Sadler, D.R. 1987. Specifying and promulgating achievement standards. *Oxford Review of Education* 13, 2.

Scarino, A., D. Vale, P. McKay and J. Clark. 1988. *Method, resources and assessment. Australian language levels guidelines, Book 3.* Canberra: Curriculum Development Centre.

Shohamy, E. 1993. *The power of tests: the impact of language tests on teaching and learning.* Washington, DC: The National Foreign Language Center.

Skehan, P. 1984. Issues in the testing of English for specific purposes. *Language Testing* 1, 2.

Spolsky, B.A. 1985. What does it mean to know how to use a language? An essay on the theoretical basis of language testing. *Language Testing* 2, 2.

Stevenson, D. 1985. Pop validity and performance testing. In Y.P. Lee, R. Lord, A.C. Fok and G. Low (eds) *New Directions in Language Testing.* Oxford: Pergamon.

Thompson, P. 1986. *Student assessment: a handbook for TAFE teachers.* Melbourne: Nelson Wadsworth.

Tuckman, B.W. 1975. *Measuring educational outcomes: fundamentals of testing.* New York: Harcourt Brace Jovanovich.

Wylie, E. 1992. Criterion–based assessment: tasks for teachers, tasks for students. Address delivered to a seminar *Criterion-based assessment* sponsored by the National Languages and Literacy Institute of Australia and LOTE, Department of Education, Tasmania, April.

10 Self-assessment: from theory to practice. Developing a workshop guide for teachers

Barbara Cram

Introduction

In second language classrooms, **assessment** is concerned with 'what the student does' (Brindley 1989:3). It also involves consciously 'obtaining and interpreting information about the knowledge and understanding, or abilities and attitudes' of the learner (Rowntree 1977:4). **Self-assessment**, which is that part of assessment carried out by learners (Holec 1985; Dickinson 1987), involves learners in discovering what they know and what they feel as well as what they can do. Variously termed 'self evaluation', 'self rating', 'self testing', 'self appraisal' and 'self control' (Oskarsson 1984:7), the practice of self-assessment has been presented by many authors as advantageous to both learners and teachers (e.g. Holec 1985; Dickinson 1987; Cohen 1994).

One of the most important characteristics of self-assessment (SA) is the sharing of responsibility for assessment decisions between the teacher and the learner. However, the concept of self-assessment has not been readily embraced by language teachers, partly because of the current emphasis on formal testing in language classrooms and partly because of the perception that learners will find self-assessment difficult. Many studies have considered the value of self-assessment as an alternative to formal testing, either for course placement (von Elek 1982; le Blanc and Painchaud 1985; Kenny and Hall 1986; Ready-Morfitt 1991) or for determining language proficiency levels (Oskarsson 1984; Jafarpur 1991). Several studies have described the benefits of SA to learners (e.g. Blanche 1990; Lewis 1990), but there has been little detailed analysis of how learners feel about SA or about how teachers might introduce self-assessment into their programs.

The first section of this paper examines the characteristics of self-assessment and provides the rationale for the introduction of SA into learner-centred programs. Particular emphasis is placed on the benefits of SA to learners. In the second section a description of a training workshop for teachers is presented. Through an analysis of the various dimensions of assessment, teachers are guided in the choice of self-assessment tools which would be appropriate for learners in their programs. The final section considers the degree of difficulty of various self-assessment procedures and explores what learners are being asked to do when they assess their own gains.

Throughout the paper the emphasis will be on the application of self-assessment to gains made by adult learners of English as a second language. However, the analysis would be adaptable to a variety of foreign language learning situations.

Potential problems with self-assessment

The introduction of the learner centred curriculum has brought about major changes in the nature of second language programs (Nunan 1988; Brindley 1989). One significant change has occurred in the relative status of teachers and learners (Parkinson and O'Sullivan 1990), with teachers being encouraged to share both power and responsibility in the classroom with learners.

Teacher attitudes

The enhanced role of the learner in second language teaching is now fairly well accepted, but teachers still appear reluctant to 'lose their control' over assessment (Blue 1988:100). This may reflect teachers' unfamiliarity with collaborative assessment procedures or their concern for assessment accuracy. However, as Heron (1988:85) comments, the resistance of teachers to sharing responsibility for assessment may prevent the adoption of a collaborative approach to teaching and assessment.

> *Assessment is the most political of all the educational processes: it is the area where issues of power are most at stake. If there is no staff-student collaboration on assessment, then staff exert a stranglehold that inhibits the development of collaboration with respect to all other processes.*

Heron maintains though, that:

Once varying mixtures of self, peer and collaborative assessment replace unilateral assessment by staff, a completely new educational climate can be created.

Learner attitudes

Ironically, one of the principal obstacles to the introduction of self-assessment may be the attitudes of learners themselves. Many learners also continue to cling to traditional power roles. Just as they have looked to teachers to determine 'what they need to know', some learners still prefer that teachers measure 'how much they have learnt'. Others may feel that they lack the linguistic knowledge and skills required to assess themselves, and learners with poor English language skills may feel threatened by self-assessment (Lewis 1990). In addition, learners with no experience in self monitored learning may not be familiar with assessment standards or assessment procedures.

To discover more about learners' attitudes towards self-assessment, immigrants starting an intermediate level employment-related course were asked to give their views on the practice of learner self-assessment. One wrote:

As a learner we have to fit in, but sometimes I don't know what... I need, and that's why the teacher have always to correct the mistakes. If I don't agree with the teacher, that's OK, it doesn't matter, but I need that correction from the teacher.

This appeal for 'correction' reflects a widespread concern about the 'accuracy' of self-assessed results. Several authors have explored the reliability and validity of self-assessment (see Oskarsson 1984; Blanche 1988; Rolfe 1990; Wilkes, this volume). These studies have typically investigated the 'extent to which learners' estimates of their own language skills are consonant with independent "objective" criteria such as test results and teacher evaluation' (Oskarsson 1984:31). While the results of some of these studies show quite high correlations between test results and self-assessment, in general, the 'accuracy' of SA appears to vary according to the type of assessment carried out, learner characteristics such as language proficiency, academic record and career aspirations, and the degree of training they have received in self-assessment.

Privacy

The issue of 'accuracy' raises the question of whether self-assessment activities should be 'private' (records kept by the learner for the learner's personal use) or 'public' (records perhaps kept by the learner but available for use by the teacher). Private records could be considered to be the more 'accurate' because learners have no reason to record biased observations or measurements. On the other hand, public records which are shared with the teacher would generally form part of a larger assessment program, and learners may be tempted to overestimate their achievements. As Heilenman (1990:194) argues, however, the fact that 'self-reports may contain response error is not a reason to reject them out of hand', as the benefits of self-assessment are considerable.

Advantages of self-assessment

Since it is considered that students involved in setting learning objectives should also be involved in 'deciding on the most appropriate ways to achieve them' (Brindley 1989:9), it is also probable that learner cooperation in designing programs is 'not likely to make much headway... without some measure of self-assessment' (Heron 1988:85). Assessment is ideally a shared process (Kohonen 1991), with teachers and learners making joint decisions about the types of gain to be assessed, the tools to be used to analyse gains and the standards required for 'success' in each area of assessment (Nunan 1988).

The Modern Languages Project of the Council of Europe has been dedicated to the development of a learner-centred, needs-oriented language learning system. Research undertaken in this area by members of the Council has played a crucial role in raising language teachers' awareness of self-assessment opportunities in language learning programs (Blanche 1988:76). The advantages of self-assessment, as described in this and other research, are outlined below.

SA gives learners greater control over their learning

Holec (1985:142) argues that a learner should know 'at all times whether, on the one hand, his performances correspond to what he was aiming at, and on the other hand, whether he has made any progress towards his chosen objective'. Learners who are able to define a starting point and describe their goals can then develop the skills needed to monitor their performance in the light of these goals (Ellis and Sinclair 1989). Extended self monitoring provides continuous feedback on what learners are achieving and enables learners to define strategies for future action. Learners practising self-assessment have enormous control over both what and how they learn. They are able to adapt their learning to meet changing conditions and can thus ensure that they are following the path that they have chosen (Holec 1985:143).

SA enhances learner awareness of the learning process

The enhancement of self-awareness which results from self-assessment practices has been documented by Stanton (1988:121), who writes:

> My experience... has been that self-evaluation is of immense educational value to students. Through consultation with other learners and tutors about their self-assessments, students learn how to evaluate themselves realistically. By doing so, they also learn a great deal about themselves as individuals.

Other authors report an increased awareness of the learning process as a result of SA practices (Ferst and Wright 1990; Ellis and Sinclair 1989; Dickinson 1987). In a study by Ferst and Wright (1990) a 'progress perception program' was introduced to help students become aware of improvements they had made in their language performance. Students were asked not only to assess their abilities in several language areas but also to evaluate previous learning experiences in the light of their current feelings about their progress. They were then placed in a program which guided their observations of the processes involved in the development of understanding of, for example, word formation and function. As a consequence of the program, students expressed an increased awareness of the complexity of factors involved in language learning.

Learners who understand the process of learning are also better able to understand evaluation processes. Learners undertaking comprehensive self-assessment are involved in the selection of assessment criteria, in determining acceptable standards of performance and in deciding the types of assessment task to be implemented (Holec 1985:151). As a consequence of their involvement, learners develop an understanding of their own skills 'profile' as well as their language proficiency level. This knowledge can then be used to diagnose strengths and weaknesses at both specific and general levels (Brindley 1989; Sheerin 1989; Ready-Morfitt 1991).

For example, Ready-Morfitt (1991) describes two Canadian studies in which SA is used as a screening pre-test to help learners decide whether they are ready to sit for a standardised university test. As a result of the pre-test, students are able to identify their strengths and are able to work on their weaknesses before they attempt the formal test. In the language classroom, self-assessment exercises based on test items appearing in a particular proficiency test could be introduced to help learners understand the measurement devices used in the test, the elements of 'proficiency' being tested and the level of proficiency required for success (Holec 1985; Ferst and Wright 1990).

Although SA practices in second language classrooms are most commonly applied to the assessment of language, SA is also valuable in the assessment of non-linguistic gains. The introduction of competency-based standards into many industries and educational programs in Australia paves the way for the development of progress profiles and rating scales that could be productively adapted for the self-assessment of vocational competency. Once progress profiles defining the knowledge, skill and attitude requirements for a particular vocational level have been established, potential workers will be able to self-assess their current level of competence and develop strategies for raising the level to that required by employers (see Gonczi et al. 1990; Masters and McCurry 1990).

SA encourages autonomous learning

The term 'autonomous learning' is generally given to that part of learning which is 'carried out in the absence of a teacher' (Heidt 1979, quoted in Oskarsson 1984:4). Such autonomy implies learner responsibility for decisions of both learning content and process (see, for example, Hunt et al. 1989). Self-assessment is therefore more than 'the end action in a problem-decision-solution sequence'; it is a continuous, 'cyclical self-checking' activity carried out on the learner and by the learner, often independently of external authorities (Hunt et al. 1989).

The cyclical nature of SA results in continuous advancement of learner autonomy. As Dickinson (1987:136) states:

> *Decisions about whether to go on to the next item, exercise or unit, decisions concerned with the allocation of time to various skills, decisions concerned with*

> *the need for remedial work, are… key matters in any learning program, and if*
> *we are to persuade learners to take responsibility for their own learning, then this*
> *must include responsibility for being involved in, and eventually making,*
> *decisions such as these.*

Self-directed learners working in one subject area tend to transfer their learning to other subject areas and to subsequently carry on their learning outside the classroom (Ellis and Sinclair 1989). Self-assessment practices enable learners to establish their own criteria for judging the accuracy and appropriacy of their performance (Dickinson 1987:151; Brindley 1989:60). These practices and criteria can then be used to continue self-monitoring after a course of formal instruction.

SA alleviates the assessment burden of teachers

As well as reducing the learner's dependence on the teacher for the evaluation of his/her progress, self-assessment carried out in collaboration with the teacher can reduce the teacher's total assessment burden. Traditionally, assessment systems have been characterised by a 'numbers-driven inflexibility based on marks obtained by formal or semi-formal examinations' (Hunt et al. 1989:211). If learners and teachers were to survive this system, they also had to become numbers-driven. The recent trend away from the quantifiable, product-driven language curriculum is reflected in the acceptance by stakeholders of qualitative assessment outcomes and reports on non-linguistic gains. These might include gains in learners' knowledge of the workplace, gains in vocational/academic skills and changes in confidence and motivation. Much of the data for a report on non-linguistic gains can thus be collected by learners themselves.

Since self-assessment activities contribute to the development of learner confidence, self-esteem and motivation (Dickinson 1987; Ferst and Wright 1990; Jafarpur 1991), teachers are able to devote more time to specific problem-solving and individual support. Blanche (1988) cites eight studies in which SA practices appeared to increase learner motivation, and von Elek (1982) reports on the curiosity and motivation that SA arouses in learners. Kenny and Hall (1986:457) based their self-assessment questionnaire on the principle that 'learner autonomy is a vital and highly motivating educational force to be used positively'. And teachers claim anecdotally that learners who are self confident and motivated are far more focused than those who are unsure of why they have come to the classroom.

Based on the principles of self-assessment outlined above, the following section provides a guide aimed at assisting teachers to introduce self-assessment into a language learning program.

Training workshop for teachers

The Training Workshop which is entitled *'Which self-assessment tool is appropriate for a particular assessment situation?'* presents a framework from which teachers can choose self-assessment tools for programs with particular requirements. This choice requires participants to take a number of key factors into account:

- purpose of assessment;
- types of achievement to be assessed;
- major stakeholders involved in the program;
- learner characteristics;
- constraints of the learning environment;
- level of achievement to be assessed;
- role of self-assessment in the program;
- training procedures required.

Selection of tools and procedures

The workshop is designed to be used with groups working on specific programs, but it is also adaptable for teachers studying independently. It involves a combination of input and activities based on the Framework described in Figure 1.

Readers firstly identify the learning program in which they would like to introduce self-assessment. Then they are guided through each element of Figure 1. Following discussion of each of the questions they are asked to complete a series of tasks according to the needs of the program they have identified. The final task is to nominate the self-assessment activities which would be suitable for this program using Tables 1 and 2.

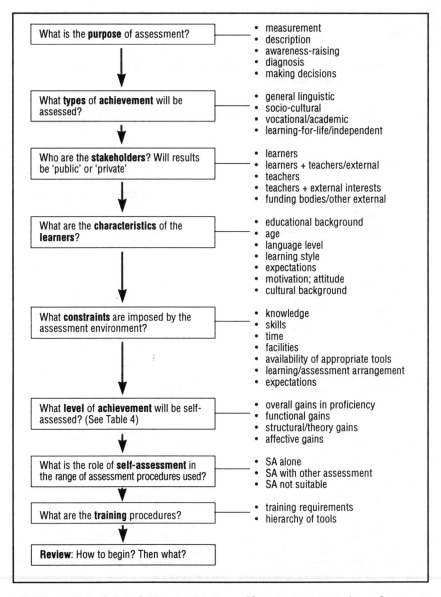

*Figure 1 How do we choose appropriate self-assessment procedures for our
programs?*

Task 1

a. Reflect: What does the term 'self–assessment' mean to you?
Discuss with colleagues.

b. Reflect: What are your feelings towards self–assessment?
Discuss with others; make notes.

c. Study the variety of self–assessment tools listed in Table 1. Mark the
assessment tools that you have previously used with learners. Note the
self–assessment tools you would like to implement in your next
program.

Questionnaires:
- true/false
- scales e.g. mark a point between 1 and 7
- short answers

Description and reflection:
- diaries and journals
- self-reporting: introspectively, retrospectively
- observation of or interviews with peers
- guessing a grade immediately after completing a test

Progress profiles:
- progress cards, objective grids, contracts
- portfolios/collections of work
- learner-kept records of achievement
- recycling or redoing work and making comparisons
- self-graded profiles of achievement

Self-rated rating scales:
- formal e.g. ASLPR; competency standards, placement profiles, confidence/self-esteem scales
- informal e.g. class-developed scales for assess-ment of seminar presentations etc.
- computer based rating scales (when available)

Tests:
- learner-produced e.g. cloze; using checklists to mark an essay or a videotaped interaction
- teacher-produced e.g. self-placement tests, sample tests, past exam papers with answer key
- externally produced e.g. past exam papers with answer key
- computer tests e.g. CBELT, CBT, CELA
- continuous progress tests with answer key

Table 1 Assessment tools suitable for self–assessment

Self Assessment Tools	Purpose					Type of Achievement				Stakeholder					Learner Characteristics							Constraints/ Learning Arrangement					Levels of Achievement				Role of Self-Assessment		
	Measure	Describe	Develop Awareness	Diagnose	Make Decisions	Linguistic	Socio-Cultural	Vocational/Academic	Learning for Life	Learners	Learners + Teachers	Teachers	Teachers + External	External	Language Level H	Language Level L	Education H	Education L	Cultural Background	Learning Style	Self-Concept	Limited Time	Poor Environment	Independent Learning	Classroom	Distance	Proficiency	Function	Structure	Affective	SA Alone	Some SA	SA Unsuitable
Questionnaires	✓	✓	✓	✓	✓	✓	✓	✓		✓	✓	✓	✓		✓	✓ *	✓		#	#	#	✓	✓	✓	✓	✓		✓		✓	✓	✓	
Description and Reflection		✓	✓	✓	✓	✓	✓	✓	✓	✓	✓				✓	✓ *	✓	✓	#	#	#	✓	✓	✓	✓	✓		✓		✓	✓	✓	
Progress Profiles	✓	✓	✓	✓	✓	✓	✓	✓	✓	✓	✓	✓	✓	✓	✓	✓ *	✓	✓	#	#	#	✓	✓	✓	✓	✓		✓	✓		✓	✓	
Self-Rated Rating Scales	✓		✓	✓	✓	✓		✓							✓		✓		#	#	#			✓	✓	✓	✓	✓	✓		✓	✓	
Self-Marked Tests	✓		✓	✓	✓	✓		✓							✓	✓ *	✓		#	#	#			✓	✓	✓	✓		✓		✓	✓	

* in first language   # training required

Table 2 Inventory of SA tools

Figure 1 (p. 279) defines the framework for the selection of tools and procedures for self-assessment. Each section will now be described in detail.

Purpose of self-assessment

The major purpose of self-assessment is to provide the opportunity for learners to develop an understanding of their own level of skill, knowledge or personal readiness for a task in relation to their goals. This level will often be compared with a previously determined level and incorporated either into a summative report of gains made during a course or into a cumulative record of learner achievement (see Brindley 1989). Dickinson (1987:15) considers SA to be most desirable when it is used as part of formative assessment, where SA outcomes can provide feedback to learners. For example, learner profiles of both functional and affective gains could be developed through self-assessment. Cumulative assessment records could then be used by learners to diagnose strengths and weaknesses or to make decisions about future action.

Task 2

Describe a current program or a program in which you are planning to implement self-assessment.

Consider the purpose(s) of assessment in this program.

Types of achievement

The four types of achievement that second and foreign language teachers assess are:

- **general linguistic gains**, including improvements in general proficiency, communicative competence and knowledge of linguistic structures;

- **academic and/or vocational gains**, including improvements in professional or technical competency, standard letter writing or essay writing skills and knowledge of appropriate academic or employment systems;

- **social and/or cultural gains**, including improvements in social skills and knowledge, and gains in socio-cultural understanding;

- **gains made in independent learning skills**, including accessing information, self-correction and other skills which enable learners to continue learning after the program.

The distinction between the four types of achievement would generally be discussed early in a teaching program, especially during the goal-setting phase. For the introduction of self-assessment, teachers are encouraged to show linkages between the four types of achievement but to allow each type of achievement to be assessed separately.

Task 3

Consider these questions:

a. Which types of achievement are of most concern to the learners in my program?

b. When learners begin self-assessment, what information should they collect? What will they do with this information?

Major stakeholders

In learner-centred programs, there are several stakeholders who have an interest in assessment outcomes. These include:

- **learners**, who wish to understand what they can do in real terms;

- **teachers**, who wish to place learners in appropriate programs, to quantify learner progress or to evaluate the effectiveness of learning programs;

- **administrators** and funding authorities, who require details of course outcomes;

- **external users**, who require descriptions of learners' skills and knowledge at entry and on exit.

Stakeholders differ in their assessment needs and in the type of information they require. However, all are concerned with program 'accountability'. This results in a dilemma common to learner-centred classrooms: how to provide accountable data to administrators and funding authorities and at the same time involve learners in their own assessment?

While we do not suggest that self-assessment will ever replace formal assessment, SA can provide useful data to learners and teachers, and can play a significant role even when quantifiable data is required for external bodies.

Task 4

Consider these questions:

a. Who are the major stakeholders in my program?

b. What type of information do these stakeholders require?

c. How much of the information could be achieved through self-assessment?

d. How much of this information could be kept privately by students and how much should be made public?

e. Given the constraints from Task 3, which SA tools would best provide the required information?

Record your conclusions on Table 3.

Characteristics of the learners

The educational and linguistic background of learners determine the degree and type of self-assessment that can be used in a program. In addition, characteristics such as learners' age, cultural background, expectations, learning style, motivation and attitude towards the target language may have an impact on SA results (Oskarsson 1984; Blanche 1988).

Major Stakeholders	Possible Information Requirements	Information which could be obtained through self-assessment. Results public or private?
Learners	What can I do? What do I know? What have I achieved? How do I feel? Am I coping? What should I do next?	
Learners and Teachers	How are learners progressing? Are all learners ready for next course? Are learners becoming more independent? Should the learning program be adapted?	
Learners and External Users	What have learners achieved? Should changes be made to program structure?	
Teachers	What do learners feel they have achieved? Have learners gained in skills/knowledge? Have learners' attitudes changed?	
Teachers and External Users	Have learners gained in skills/knowledge?	
Administrative and External Users	What has the program achieved? Was the program cost-effective?	

Table 3 Self-assessment tools: major stakeholders

Culture, which may be defined as 'a way of seeing, a way of perceiving, and a way of behaving on the basis of that perception' (McOmie 1990:177), is thought to affect the way learners rate their achievements. Deckert (1989) found that students from the Middle East tended to assess their performances overly high while those from East Asia assessed their performances markedly low. Such differences are attributed to cultural differences in the 'skill of estimating, in perception of personal performance, or in inclination to disclose one's true self-assessments' (Deckert 1989:132).

Differences in learners' reported motivation, learning effort and feelings towards the target language were recorded in the DLIFLC study conducted by Blanche (1990). Personal characteristics were found to affect the accuracy of self-assessments, but the results could not be used to predict the impact of these characteristics in other programs. Similarly, a study by Ready-Morfitt (1991) found a link between personality factors and under- or over-estimation of achievement, but the results should not be generalised to other assessment situations. Reid (1987) and Dirksen (1990) have used self-reporting learning styles inventories to ascertain whether there is a correlation between learning style and country of origin. While some differences in style correlate positively with country of origin, it does not appear to be possible to make predictions about the behaviour of individual students. However, if we were to study the relationship between learning style and self-assessment, we might expect that learners with an 'analytical' learning style, or those who like to find their own mistakes, would feel more comfortable with SA than the more 'authority-oriented' learners who expect the teacher to explain everything to them (see Willing 1989, 1991).

While data collected on the effect of learner characteristics on self-assessment outcomes provide generalisable conclusions, most studies concur that SA reliability is maximised when learners are trained in self-assessment techniques (Deckert 1989; Hunt et al. 1989; Mangelsdorf 1992). In addition it is important that characteristics which may limit a learner's involvement in self-assessment (such as literacy level, L2 proficiency, specific needs and goals and previous learning experiences) are taken into account when SA is introduced.

Task 5

Consider these questions:

a. What are the most common characteristics of the learners in my program?

b. Are there other characteristics which could influence the way self-assessment is implemented?

c. What restrictions are there on the introduction of SA?

d. Which tools would best suit these learners?

Constraints in the learning environment

Constraints in the learning environment can also limit the degree to which self-assessment can be introduced. Some of the constraints which are common in language classrooms are:

- **time** limitations;

- **inflexibility** in the environment: physical limitations, teacher or institutional resistance;

- **unavailability** of self-assessment tools in a form that is appropriate to a particular group of learners;

- **learning arrangement**: ratio of classroom-based to independent learning.

When time is limited or the learning environment is inflexible, teachers may like to begin with the more reflective forms of self-assessment. These include questionnaires, which can be designed so that learners' self reflection provides valuable feedback to the teacher; progress profiles, which can double as a form of continuous goal-setting; and descriptive/reflective tools such as oral reporting or diaries and journals, which are used to promote authentic communication.

Examples of self-assessment materials such as questionnaires, rating scales, tests and skills profiles are readily available in the literature (see samples in Oskarsson 1984; Brindley 1989; Lewis 1990). However, since goal setting and assessment are closely interwoven, self-assessment procedures would generally have to be adapted by teachers to suit the needs of particular groups of learners. In many cases adaptation would consist of changing the wording of questions or adapting the tasks represented in progress profiles. In other cases such as the preparation of rating scales, an entire document may have to be developed.

Further limitations to the implementation of self-assessment may emanate from the learning arrangement, or the amount of contact learners have with a teacher. For example, learners in independent or distance programs work mainly alone, while those studying in a classroom alternate between working alone, with peers or with a teacher. Other learners may not use a teacher at all, and may learn mostly from friends, family and mentors. The value of group support in self-assessment has been reported in several studies (Heron 1988; Mangelsdorf 1992; Underhill 1992). When group work is incorporated into the initial training stages, group support can raise learners' confidence and thus contribute to the development of positive attitudes towards SA processes. Where learners are working alone, descriptive/reflective tools and progress profiles are recommended in the initial stages.

Task 6

Consider these questions:

a. What are the main constraints affecting my program?

b. Would changes in the learning arrangement facilitate the introduction of self-assessment in this program?

c. Are there particular tools which would be more or less suitable in this environment?

Levels of achievement

As outlined previously, the four **types** of achievement that we assess are linguistic gains, academic/vocational gains, socio-cultural gains and gains in independent learning skills. Within each type of achievement, four different **levels** of assessment can be identified. For example, information may be required on whether gains are:

- **overall gains in proficiency**, e.g. speaking;

- **gains made in areas of functional language skill**, e.g. obtaining information by telephone;

- **gains made in understanding or knowledge** of the formal language system, e.g. understanding of tenses;

- **changes in awareness or attitude**, e.g. gains in confidence.

The concept of 'levels of achievement' is used by Brindley (1989:13-17) to describe the different types of assessment information that are required at different levels of program operation. Brindley's 'Level 1' achievement refers to gains made by the learner in terms of 'overall proficiency'. Assessment is formal and consists mainly of standardised tests which provide a summative record of the achievement of a particular skill as a result of a course of instruction. Results are quantifiable and are used by external stakeholders as well as by teachers and learners. Tools recommended for self-assessment at the 'overall proficiency' level include self-marked rating scales and tests with answer keys.

Brindley's 'Level 2' achievement refers to the learner's achievement of 'particular proficiency-related objectives as part of a given course' (ibid.:15). Assessment is semi-formal, using standardised criterion-related achievement tests or records such as profiles of achievement. The results provide continuous assessment of a learner's 'functional' ability to perform real-world tasks. Possible self-assessment tools for use at Level 2 include progress profiles, self-rated rating scales, reflective exercises and questionnaires.

'Level 3' achievement refers to the learner's achievement of 'specific objectives relating to knowledge and enabling skills taught in a particular course' (ibid.:15). Assessment here focuses principally on the language code and is mainly informal and descriptive, using discussion, observation, verbal feedback and class tests. The results provide continuous feedback to teachers and learners and are used for the analysis of 'structural' needs as well as for increasing learner motivation. Tools recommended for self-assessment at Level 3 include progress profiles, self-rated rating scales and computer tests.

The fourth level of achievement refers to the affective gains made by learners, particularly in the areas of confidence and motivation. This level of achievement is not included in Brindley's framework for describing achievement, but assessment of affective gains would be informal and descriptive, with the results of most interest to learners and teachers. Affective gains are most suited to self-assessment, and the use of questionnaires and descriptive/reflective procedures is suggested by a number of authors (Holec 1985; Oskarsson 1989).

The relationship between types and levels of achievement is depicted in matrix form in Table 4a. This table also provides examples of questions which learners might ask as they assess their achievements against their predetermined goals.

Task 7

Consider these questions:

a. What are the objectives of the learners in my current program?

b. Which types and levels of achievement will be assessed?
   Which of these are suitable for self-assessment?

c. Which tools would be most appropriate for the self-assessment of these types and levels of achievement?

Task 8

Using Table 4b fill in the questions that you or your learners would like to consider. Do not fill in more than five boxes at this stage.

Levels of Achievement	Areas of Achievement			
	General Linguistic	Socio-Cultural	Vocational/ Academic	Learning for Life/ Independent
Proficiency (overall gains)	Have I reached a higher level of proficiency in: • reading • writing • listening • speaking?	Do I 'fit' better into the local sub-culture?	Am I able to cope better in the academic/ vocational area that I plan to pursue?	Have I developed strategies for life-long learning? Am I a more indepen-dent learner?
Practice (functional gains)	Can I carry out (Task X) better? e.g. obtain information by telephone	Do I behave more appropriately in both formal and informal situations?	Can I carry out academic or vocational tasks more effectively? e.g. write a letter using a computer	Have I improved my: • research skills • independent learning skills • ability to diag-nose strengths?
Theory/ Structural (gains in knowledge, understanding)	Have I increased my knowledge of the structure of English? e.g. tenses	Have I increased my knowledge of Australian customs? e.g. gender roles, educational practices	Have I increased my knowledge of educational or vocational practices in this country? e.g. career pathways	Have I increased my knowledge of: • learning strategies • services and how to access them?
Affective (gains in motivation, confidence)	Am I more confident when I use English?	Am I more confident in my social interactions?	Am I more confident that I can achieve my educational/ vocational goals?	Am I more motivated to continue learning independently after the course?

Table 4a Types of gain which can be self-assessed

Levels of Achievement	Areas of Achievement			
	General Linguistic	Socio-Cultural	Vocational/ Academic	Learning for Life/ Independent
Proficiency (overall gains)				
Practice (functional gains)				
Theory/ Structural (gains in knowledge, understanding)				
Affective (gains in motivation, confidence)				

Table 4b   Which gains do learners want to assess for themselves?

Role of self-assessment in the program

Another factor to consider when choosing SA tools and processes is the proportion of self-assessment in the total assessment program. One of the advantages of SA is that it is complementary to other forms of assessment. While it may replace some established assessment practices, it should be implemented as part of a balanced learner-centred program. In his discussion of the 'limits and possibilities of self-assessment', Dickinson (1987:138) considers that a 'high degree of self-assessment' would be characterised by an environment in which learners have a choice about assessment practices, the self-assessment is formative and learners are involved in and trained for SA tasks. 'Limited self-assessment', on the other hand, would be characterised by an environment in which learners have little control over or participation in total assessment.

In the SA framework presented here, the role of self-assessment will be determined firstly by the purpose of assessment and then by the other characteristics of the program as described in this paper.

Task 9

Consider the degree of SA expected in the assessment program. Will this affect the choice of SA tools?

Task 10

Summarise the results of this workshop in Table 5 (below).

Training procedures

The Training Workshop enables teachers to identify the assessment needs of language learners and to consider the role of self-assessment in a program. This section focuses on conditions for the **implementation** of self-assessment in second language programs. Three areas of teacher responsibility are addressed: creation of a supportive environment; implementation of a learner training program; and sequential introduction of self-assessment activities.

Name of Program: _____

Purpose of Program: _____

_____

Suitable Self-Assessment Activities
Questionnaires:
Description and Reflection:
Progress Profiles:
Self-Rating Scales:
Tests/Other Activities:

Table 5 Planning for self–assessment

Creating a supportive environment

The environment recommended for learners undertaking self-assessment is positive and supportive (Underhill 1992) as well as reasonably predictable and familiar (Porter 1991). In such an environment learners would be encouraged to debate the advantages and disadvantages of learner assessment, and to propose strategies for becoming more involved. Teachers would offer regular guidance and encouragement to learners as they accepted greater responsibility for assessment decisions. In addition, teachers would place high value on independent thought and action; learners' opinions would be accepted non-judgementally and external rewards would be minimised (Underhill 1992). Teacher feedback would thus highlight the usefulness of learner assessment in language learning.

To reduce learner anxiety and maintain a high level of motivation, self-assessment would be introduced gradually, beginning with tasks which reflected learners' skills and experience (Young 1991). Training would also be implemented, aiming to replace the 'external motivation' created by teachers with 'internal motivation' and learner self-direction (Skehan 1991).

Implementing a learner training program

In the literature concerned with the psychology of thinking, there is considerable interest in the way learners internalise 'rules'. Current research in educational psychology sustains the operational theories of Piaget, Wertheimer and Dewey, which propose that rules do not exist *a priori*, but 'are derived from experience and arise in the course of development' (Bolton 1972:35). In second language research, operationalism is sometimes termed 'experiential learning' (see Kohonen 1992) in which learners pass through cyclical stages of learning: practising a new skill, reflecting on performance, developing a concept about this performance and then applying the new concept to future learning.

Other second language research refers to this area of learning as 'metacognition' (Dickinson 1987; Skehan 1991). In a discussion of individual differences in second language learning, Skehan (1991:291) describes the importance of 'metacognitive strategies', or strategies 'that have a planning, directing, or monitoring role and that require the learner to stand back from the direct learning and consider how the direct learning itself can best be managed'.

Learner training for self-assessment would not assume prior knowledge of SA operations, therefore, but would provide a series of experiences and opportunities for reflection so that learners could 'operationalise' self-assessment concepts. Depending on the skills of learners, the training program would include practice in organising, in discussing achievements, in making decisions, in describing peer and personal performances and in comparing performances with external standards.

Training components to develop associated knowledge and attitude domains would also be provided. For example, students learning to assess their linguistic gains would require a working knowledge of the target language and an understanding of the rules of that language (Alderson 1991). They would also need some experience with the interpretation of the pragmatic value of utterances within the target culture. Exercises requiring decisions about the 'appropriacy' of expressions and gestures in different circumstances could then be added (Willing 1989).

Even with careful planning, the process of change is likely to take time, as learners entering a second language program hold predetermined values and expectations. In predicting the likelihood of resistance to change, Underhill (1992:72) writes:

> Development is a holistic process, development in one part of a human system (whether a group or an individual) affects other areas of the system. Resistance is a natural and inevitable response. Habits have to be unformed. Beliefs have to be challenged. Norms have to be questioned. Hidden values and attitudes have to be made explicit. The desire to change arising in one part of the system may be met by an equal resistance to change from another part of the same system.

Resistance to self-assessment may also vary with the cultural and educational backgrounds of learners. Blanche (1990) has found that the results of self-assessment could be affected by learners' prior educational and academic experiences as well as by the expectations of other learners, peers and parents. However, a training program which provides guided experience with self-assessment can minimise the impact of background and expectations and can improve the accuracy of self-assessment results (Blanche 1990; Bradshaw 1990; Heilenman 1990).

Sequencing of self-assessment activities

When introducing any new knowledge or skills, teachers generally begin with what is known and build upon it. Similarly, when introducing self-assessment, teachers would begin with activities that learners can already do. Throughout the training program, new knowledge and more complex skills would be added according to the 'likelihood of mastery' by a particular group of learners (Tomlinson et al. 1988:164).

A suggested sequence of self-assessment activities based on a model published by Cram (1992), is summarised in Table 6. The exercises are primarily reflective, requiring learners to 'explore their experiences in order to lead to new understandings and appreciations' (Boud et al. 1985:19). Initial exercises (Stage 1) are designed to raise learner awareness by asking them to reflect on something they have done well or to consider a problem they are having. As part of the reflective process, learners would discuss the topic informally with a classmate or colleague. Teachers would monitor the discussions to ensure that they were supportive and non-judgemental, but would not comment on the subject of the discussion. Thus learners would build up confidence in expressing how they felt about an experience and, at the same time, benefit from sharing in the reflections of others.

Following this (Stage 2), learners are taken through exercises which help them clarify their feelings. For example, questionnaires and activities requiring the selection of options (e.g. Willing 1989) could be used to help learners become more aware of their learning style and priorities. Questions with a 'yes/no' option would be introduced first as these are considered to be less cognitively demanding than those in which learners must choose from a 5-point or 7-point scale (Heilenman 1990).

For the introduction of problem-solving (Stage 3) collaborative activities are recommended to minimise the anxiety levels of learners. Building on the experiences of Stage 1, pairs of learners might discuss what they fear most about common tasks such as asking for transport directions. They could then form groups to discuss the most common fears and explore the reasons behind these fears. The results could then be shared with other groups and learners could suggest classroom activities that would help them cope with 'fearful' situations. By working in pairs and then in groups, learners start to 'feel comfortable about becoming more aware of their actions and attitudes', and can then allow change

Stage	Activities
Stage 1 Raising learner awareness	discussing with peers
Stage 2 Clarifying feelings	deciding between options (e.g. yes/no questionnaire; then questionnaire with a numbered scale)
Stage 3 Collaborative assessment	small group problem-solving with discussion and/or conclusions recorded
Stage 4 Individual reflective assessment	keeping a diary; completing a self-reflection sheet after discussion with peers
Stage 5 Diagnostic assessment	group strategy planning; action planning
Stage 6 Assessment of real-world performance	developing simple skills profiles and rating scales for self- and peer-assessment
Stage 7 Integrating skills, knowledge and practice	making value judgements against external standards; using externally produced language rating scales and competency scales
Stage 8 Assessing learning	reflecting on learning styles and achievements, and developing action plans for future learning

Table 6 Sequence of self-assessment activities

to follow (Underhill 1992:77). By working collaboratively to solve one kind of problem, learners also develop the confidence to work independently on other problems (O'Loughlin 1991; Mangelsdorf 1992).

Activities for practising individual reflective assessment are then introduced (Stage 4). Learners could be encouraged to keep a personal diary or to write regularly for a portfolio. Reflection sheets could also be completed after particular events or experiences. Whether or not this information is to be shared with the teacher, learners would be encouraged to report on how they felt as well as on what they had done. In practising reflective assessment, perhaps through the development of a portfolio, learners can develop the capacity to 'judge the quality of their work and reflect on growth' (Paulson and Paulson 1990:8). The emphasis would be on 'utilising positive feelings' during reflection while becoming aware of and removing any 'obstructive feelings' which limited growth (Boud et al. 1985:29).

The analysis of experiences can also be managed in group strategy discussions (Stage 5). Building on the knowledge and skills gained from previous stages, groups of learners could discuss a difficult situation such as applying for a job by telephone. The group would first collate learners' fears and develop collective strategies for overcoming them. Group members would then adapt these strategies for their own circumstances. Finally, learners would each apply for a job by telephone and would report on their experiences to the group.

Learners may then benefit from a checklist or profile with which to assess their experiences (Stage 6). Continuing with the telephone interview example, a skills profile sheet could be developed (see, for example, Chang [1991] and Clarkson and Jensen [1992]). This would enable learners to distinguish separate elements of the telephone call (e.g. degree to which the message was understood by the listener; degree to which the learner understood the speaker etc.), while attending to their feelings about the experience as a whole.

Advanced learners, who are about to leave 'ESL' education and join mainstream employment or study, should also gain experience in assessing themselves against externally produced scales (Stage 7). Examples of language proficiency scales include the ASLPR Self-Assessment Rating Scale for Speaking Ability (Wylie 1985, reproduced in Brindley 1989:66) and the self-assessment questionnaires used for course placement (e.g. le Blanc and Painchaud 1985). Self-assessment scales for non-linguistic knowledge and skills could also be developed from competency documents and/or course syllabuses.

Finally (Stage 8) learners consolidate the skills they have learned throughout the program by assessing themselves as learners. This would involve reviewing the self-assessment exercises already completed, reflecting on achievements, considering the implications of learning style and then developing strategies for future learning.

Conclusion

The introduction of self-assessment in second language programs necessitates a shift in the attitudes and activities of teachers and learners. Initial self-assessment exercises involve learners in self reflection, in order to assist them to become aware of their feelings about experiences with language. It is through sharing their experiences with their peers, that they gain confidence in articulating these feelings.

Further training in self-assessment helps learners to become more aware of their strengths and weaknesses and to accept greater responsibility for assessment decisions. As a result, they are able to take control of their learning and to develop individual action plans for continuing their learning outside the classroom.

The benefits of self-assessment, however, may not be immediately apparent to teachers or learners. Resistance may occur as a result of the maintenance on traditional power roles or from misunderstandings and unfamiliarity with self-assessment procedures. The workshop presented in this paper provides a framework for training and offers suggestions for the graded introduction of self-assessment exercises. This framework highlights the fact that self-assessment cannot be introduced without considering the needs and abilities of learners at different times as well as the internal and external restraints imposed on the program.

As we have seen, self-assessment encompasses the range of assessment procedures which are practised by learners. These procedures are, however, only a part of the totality of the assessment which is carried out. Self-assessment should be seen as a complement to the assessment carried out by teachers and peers. Numerous research studies have shown that the main beneficiaries are learners, who gain knowledge, skills and an understanding of the learning process. However, as learners take greater responsibility for their learning, and become more independent, teachers, too, will reap considerable personal and professional benefit.

Acknowledgements

I would like to thank Geoff Brindley of NCELTR and Linda Ross of AMES NSW for their useful comments on the first draft of this chapter.

References

Alderson, J.C. 1991. Language testing in the 1990s: how far have we come? How much further have we to go? In S. Anivan (ed.).

Anivan, S. (ed.) 1991. *Current developments in language testing*. Anthology Series 25. Singapore: SEAMEO Regional Language Centre.

Bickley, V. (ed.) 1989. *Language teaching and learning styles within and across cultures*. Hong Kong: Institute of Language in Education.

Blanche, P. 1988. Self-assessment of foreign language skills: implications for teachers and researchers. *RELC Journal* 19, 1:75–93.

Blanche, P. 1990. Using standardised achievement and oral proficiency tests for self-assessment purposes: the DLIFLC study. *Language Testing* 7, 2:202–229.

Blue, G.M. 1988. Self-assessment: the limits of learner independence. In A. Brookes and P. Grundy (eds).

Bolton, N. 1972. *The psychology of thinking*. London: Methuen and Co. Ltd.

Boud, D. (ed.) 1988. *Developing student autonomy in learning*. London: Kogan Page.

Boud, D., R. Keogh and D. Walker. 1985. Promoting reflection in learning: a model. In Boud et al. (eds).

Boud, D., R. Keogh and D. Walker (eds). 1985. *Reflection: turning experience into learning*. New York: Kogan Page.

Bradshaw, J. 1990. Test-takers' reactions to a placement test. *Language Testing* 7, 1:13–30.

Brindley, G. 1989. *Assessing achievement in the learner-centred curriculum*. Sydney: National Centre for English Language Teaching and Research.

Brindley, G. (ed.) 1990. *The second language curriculum in action*. Sydney: National Centre for English Language Teaching and Research.

Brookes, A. and P. Grundy (eds). 1988. *Individualisation and autonomy in language learning*. ELT Documents 131. London: Modern English Publications, British Council.

Chang, A. 1991. Learner self-assessment as a tool for developing job-seeking skills. *Interchange* 17:20–21.

Clarkson, R. and M-T. Jensen. 1992. *Inter-rater reliability on an EPE rating scale*. Melbourne: RMIT.

Cohen, A.D. 1994. *Assessing language ability in the classroom*. Second edition. Boston: Heinle and Heinle.

Cram, B. 1992. Training learners for self-assessment. *TESOL in Context* 2, 2:30–33.

Deckert, G.D. 1989. Cultural background and self-assessment tendencies in an ESL classroom. In V. Bickley (ed.).

Dickinson, L. 1987. *Self-instruction in language learning*. Cambridge: Cambridge University Press.

Dirksen, C. 1990. Learning styles of mainland Chinese students of English. *IDEAL* 5:29–38.

Ellis, G. and B. Sinclair. 1989. *Learning to learn English: a course in learner training*. Cambridge: Cambridge University Press.

Ferst, P. and J. Wright. 1990. My English is not improving. *Practical English Teaching* 10, 4:29.

Gonczi, A., P. Hager and L. Oliver. 1990. *Establishing competency-based standards in the professions.* Canberra: Australian Government Publishing Service.

Heilenman, L.K. 1990. Self-assessment of second language ability: the role of response effects. *Language Testing* 7, 2:174–201.

Heron, J. 1988. Assessment revisited. In D. Boud (ed.).

Holec, H. 1985. Self-assessment. In R. Mason (ed.).

Hunt, J., L. Gow and P. Barnes. 1989. Learner self-evaluation and assessment — a tool to autonomy in the language learning classroom. In V. Bickley (ed.).

Jafarpur, A. 1991. Can naive EFL learners estimate their own proficiency? *Evaluation and Research in Education* 5, 3:145–157.

Kenny, B. and D. Hall. 1986. Self-assessment as an alternative to testing. *Proceedings of the First International Conference on Trends in Language Program Evaluation.* Bangkok: CULI.

Kohonen, V. 1991. Foreign language learning as learner education: facilitating self-direction in language learning. Paper given at *Council of Europe Symposium,* Zurich.

Kohonen, V. 1992. Experiential language learning: second language learning as cooperative learner education. In D. Nunan (ed.).

le Blanc, R. and G. Painchaud. 1985. Self-assessment as a second language placement instrument. *TESOL Quarterly* 19, 4:673–687.

Lewis, J. 1990. Self-assessment in the classroom: a case study. In G. Brindley (ed.).

Low, G.D. 1988. The semantics of questionnaire rating scales. *Evaluation and Research in Education* 2, 2:69–81.

McOmie, W. 1990. Expanding the intercultural perspective. *Cross Currents* xvii, 2:177–183.

Mangelsdorf, K. 1992. Peer reviews in the ESL composition classroom: what do the students think? *ELT Journal* 46, 3:74–84.

Mason, R. (ed.) 1985. *Self-access and self-directed learning in Australia.* Melbourne: Council for Adult Education.

Masters, G.N. and D. McCurry. 1990. *Competency-based assessment in the professions.* Canberra: Australian Government Publishing Service.

Nunan, D. 1988. *The learner-centred curriculum.* Cambridge: Cambridge University Press.

Nunan, D. (ed.) 1992. *Collaborative language learning and teaching* Cambridge: Cambridge University Press.

O'Loughlin, K. 1991. Assessing achievement in distance learning. *Prospect* 6, 2:58–66.

Oskarsson, M. 1984. *Self-assessment of foreign language skills: a survey of research and development work.* Strasbourg: Council for Cultural Cooperation.

Oskarsson, M. 1989. Self-assessment of language proficiency: rationale and applications. *Language Testing* 6, 1.

Parkinson, L. and K. O'Sullivan. 1990. Negotiating the learner-centred curriculum. In G. Brindley (ed.).

Paulson, F.L. and P.R. Paulson. 1990. How do portfolios measure up? A cognitive model for assessing portfolios. Union, WA: Paper presented at *Aggregating Portfolio Data Conference.*

Porter, D. 1991. Affective factors in the assessment of oral interaction: gender and status. In S. Anivan (ed.).

Prodromou, L. 1992. What culture? Which culture? Cross-cultural factors in language learning. *ELT Journal* 46, 1:39–50.

Ready-Morfitt, D. 1991. *The role and limitations of self-assessment in testing and research.* Unpublished manuscript. Ottawa, Canada: Second Language Institute, University of Ottawa.

Reid, J.M. 1987. The learning style preferences of ESL students. *TESOL Quarterly* 21, 1:87–111.

Rolfe, T. 1990. Self- and peer-assessment in the ESL curriculum. In G. Brindley (ed.).

Rowntree, D. 1977. *Assessing students: how shall we know them?* London: Harper and Row.

Sheerin, S. 1989. *Self-access.* Oxford: Oxford University Press.

Skehan, P. 1991. Individual differences in second language learning. *SSLA* 13:275–298.

Stanton, H. 1988. Independent study: a matter of confidence? In D. Boud (ed.).

Tomlinson, B., P.E. Griffin, L. Martin and R.J. Adams. 1988. Developing an instrument to assess structural proficiency in English. *Prospect* 3, 2:157–173.

Underhill, A. 1992. The role of groups in developing teacher self-awareness. *ELT Journal* 46, 1:71–80.

von Elek, T. 1982. *Test of Swedish as a second language: an experiment in self-assessment.* Goteborg: Goteborg University.

Willing, K. 1989. *Teaching how to learn: learning strategies in ESL* (2 volumes). Sydney: National Centre for English Language Teaching and Research.

Willing, K. 1991. Learning how to learn: a review of current learner strategies publications. *Prospect* 6, 2:51–57.

Young, D.J. 1991. Creating a low-anxiety classroom environment: what does language anxiety research suggest? *The Modern Language Journal* 75, iv:426–437.

11 Learning pathways and the assessment process: a replication of a study on self- and peer-assessment in the ESL classroom

Michaela Wilkes

Introduction

Currently there is much attention being directed towards the notion of learner awareness of his/her own learning pathway, 'learning to learn' strategies and the fostering of an enabling discourse community in the classroom (see Zamel 1987; Nunan 1988, 1991; Candlin 1989). All such notions depend on learners objectively developing their own personal and cognitive resources and using them to interact with others in the classroom in a directed and co-operative manner. Underlying these skills are the learners' perceptions of their own language proficiency and their perceptions of the proficiency of their peers. Yet, do learners assess themselves and their peers realistically and to what extent can the teacher be instrumental in developing this awareness as the foundation for a pro-active learning community in the classroom?

One study which investigates these questions is presented in a paper titled *Self- and peer-assessment in the ESL curriculum* by Terence Rolfe (1990). The rationale behind Rolfe's study was an investigation of the extent to which official/ teacher-assessment of a learner accurately represented the 'reality' of the learner's own assessment. Literature in other studies reviewed by Rolfe suggested that realistic self-assessment was important in giving the learner control of his/her own learning. Rolfe extended this investigation to include peer-assessment which he reported as a useful form of assessment in other areas such as psychology and management.

In his study, Rolfe used the AMES Speaking Proficiency Descriptions (Brindley 1979) and an intuitive scale as the assessment tools. He found that learners tend to be too harsh in assessing themselves but that a 'consensus intuitive guess' by peers is likely to be as accurate as a single rating by an experienced and trained teacher using the defined AMES scale. If this is so, it provides valuable information to the teacher in terms of finding ways to make learners more aware of their own learning resources and goals.

Yet how generalisable are these findings to other settings and other scales? Given the psycho-social factors which often affect peer judgement of fellow learners, can peer-assessment really be considered as reliable as trained teacher-assessment? Or does this only apply to classrooms which have already developed an awareness of this learning process? In an attempt to throw further light on these questions, this paper presents a replication of Rolfe's study in another setting, a language centre in Melbourne, and with the use of another scale, the ASLPR scale (Ingram 1984).

Replication in research

Teresa Santos (1989:700) states that replication in applied linguistics research has many benefits:

> *Research is an accretive process; it is the accumulation and consolidation of knowledge over time. Replication of research confirms or calls into question existing findings; without it, a discipline exists of scattered hypotheses and insufficiently substantiated generalisations.*

Further, Santos claims that replication promotes communication among researchers, reminds researchers to be as critical as possible and enhances critical reading of reports.

With these points in mind, the aims of this replication study are:

- to replicate Rolfe's study and assess it generalisability across settings;

- to assess the extent to which joint peer-assessment is a reliable indicator in the classroom;

- to investigate the extent to which another scale, the ASLPR, reflects the 'psychological reality' of the learner;

- as an educative process, to involve the learners in their own assessment process and thereby make them more aware of their own learning pathways.

Rolfe's study

In his study, Rolfe (1990:172) investigated the extent to which the 'psychological reality' of the learner was reflected by the AMES Speaking Proficiency Descriptions:

> *The principal aim of the study was to determine if learners' ratings of their own oral proficiency and the oral proficiency ratings given to their peers were reliable with respect to oral proficiency ratings given by teachers… A secondary purpose was to involve learners in the assessment process and, as a by-product of that involvement, to inform them of their 'official' assessment.*

The assessments were carried out at an Adult Migrant Education Centre in Sydney. Five classes of learners, a total of sixty subjects with levels ranging from beginners to advanced, were involved. The learners were asked to rate their own speaking ability on an intuitive seven-point scale with only the end-points defined. They were also asked to rate their peers on a similar scale. Teachers were then asked to rate the oral proficiency of the learners using the defined seven-point AMES scale.

Data analysis

Self-assessment (SA) and teacher-assessment (TA) both consisted of single ratings and could be treated as raw data. Peer-assessment (PA) scores, however, were treated in two ways: as the mean of the score given by each learner (peer as rater) and the mean of the score given to each learner (peer as ratee).

For the purposes of Rolfe's study, the latter i.e. the mean of the scores given to each learner by peers, was considered more important.

Correlations between self-assessment, peer-assessment and teacher-assessment were then calculated for each class and for overall combinations of classes. Two

Spearman's Rho			
Class I **Self** **Peer**	**Self** (N=13)	**Peer** .564	**Teacher** .636 860**
Class II **Self** **Peer**	**Self** (N=12)	**Peer** .359	**Teacher** .222 .975**
Class III **Self** **Peer**	**Self** (N=9)	**Peer** .504	**Teacher** .163 .860**
Class IV **Self** **Peer**	**Self** (N=13)	**Peer** .589	**Teacher** .527 .764**
Class V **Self** **Peer**	**Self** (N=13)	**Peer** .659	**Teacher** .723* .659
Overall **Self** **Peer**	**Self** (N=60)	**Peer** .697*	**Teacher** .512** .807**

*p<.005   **p<.001

Table 1 Rolfe's study: Spearman's Rho correlations

types of correlation were used — Spearman's Rho for rank-order data and Pearson's r for parametric data. (See Table 1 for the Spearman's Rho correlations [Rolfe 1990:179], which are of most interest to this replication.) Scattergrams representing the tendency to agreement for the overall combinations were also given.

Results

1. Rolfe made the following observations comparing SA, PA and TA based on the raw data obtained:

    Peer as Rater vs Self-Ratings — learners gave themselves lower ratings than those they gave their peers. Learners, therefore, tend to under-rate themselves with respect to their peers.

    Peer as Ratee vs Self-Ratings — learners' self-ratings were, in forty-eight cases out of sixty, lower than the mean ratings given to the learners by their peers.

    Peer as Ratee vs Teacher Ratings — mean peer ratings were, in most cases, higher than ratings given by teachers. Peers, therefore, tended to be less critical than teachers.

    Self vs Teacher Ratings — self-ratings were in forty-three out of sixty cases, lower than teacher ratings. Learners tend to be more critical of themselves than are their teachers.

2. In correlating the data from the SA scores, the mean PA (as ratee) scores and the TA scores, Rolfe obtained the following information (see Table 1):

    Self–Teacher correlations — at class level there was only a tendency towards agreement, while at the overall level there was significant but weak agreement. SA was, therefore, not a reliable indicator of oral proficiency.

    Teacher–Peer (as ratee) correlations — at class level, the correlation coefficients were all significant (except for the lowest) and the overall correlation was highly significant, indicating mean PA was a potentially reliable measure of oral proficiency.

Self–Peer (as ratee) correlations — at class level, the self–peer ratings correlated weakly and were only weakly significant at the overall level.

Rolfe then concludes that SA is not a reliable technique for assessing oral proficiency — SA being too subject to affective factors. On the other hand, a consensus peer rating on an intuitive scale may be just as reliable as the trained teacher rating on a defined scale. In drawing these conclusions, Rolfe comments on the danger of using TA as the benchmark against which to compare both SA and PA, TA at times being scored too severely and also being subject to affective factors. Further, Rolfe points out that teacher–student interaction is rarely 'real-life', whereas peer interaction is likely to be more authentic thereby giving learners a more realistic picture of each other's ability. Finally, Rolfe calls for further training of teachers in using defined scales and greater involvement of the learners in their own assessment process to better enable them to develop their own 'yardsticks' for assessing self-proficiency.

This study

The hypothesis in this replication is similar to that of Rolfe's study i.e. to determine if learners' self-assessment of their oral proficiency and their peer-assessment of oral proficiency are reliable with respect to teacher-assessment of their oral proficiency. The hypothesis is, therefore, one of correlation between SA, PA and TA.

The subjects

Five classes (fifty-five learners) at a well-established and well-regarded English language centre in Melbourne were involved.

Class I (N=13): an AMEP EAP exit class of mainly European background, all hoping to do tertiary study in 1992. Entry level ASLPR 2+.

Class II (N=10): an ELICOS EAP class of mainly Asian background, all hoping to do tertiary study in 1992. Entry level ASLPR 2+.

Class III (N=11): an AMEP upper-intermediate class of mixed cultural background. Entry level ASLPR 2.

Class IV (N=6): an ELICOS upper-intermediate class of Asian background. Entry level ASLPR 2.

Class V (N=15): an ELICOS intermediate class of Asian background. Entry level ASLPR 1+.

Data collection

The data were gathered in the ninth week of a ten-week course in late September. A five-point rating scale was chosen for all assessments as the ASLPR scale used by teachers comprises five points. The scale was expanded to contain two intervals between points in order to correspond to the intervals usually given by teachers on the ASLPR scale. A third interval was later added to allow for even finer distinctions and to avoid tied rankings. The scale thus became a twenty-one-point scale in effect.

The learners were asked to rate their own oral proficiency (SA) and that of their peers (PA) on the undefined, intuitive five-point scale with zero representing zero proficiency and five representing native-like proficiency. The assessment was administered to the learners in the same standardised way as in Rolfe's study (see Rolfe 1990:172–173). The teachers were asked to rate the learners on the defined five-point ASLPR scale (TA).

Difficulties encountered in collecting the data for this study

- Class I deliberately marked themselves and their peers severely as they did not wish to exit from the centre five months before the new academic year was due to begin i.e. they wished to appear to be of low-level proficiency. Rolfe (1990:177) also noted this trend in his study.

- With the teachers, there was a lack of consistency in the use of the ASLPR scale — some teachers rated more severely than others.

- The use of three intervals between points on the scale was problematic as the finer distinction was found not to be practical and did not coincide with most teachers preferred intervals (e.g. 2, 2+, 3 , 3). Two intervals between points would have been more appropriate.

Data analysis

The data were analysed in a similar way to Rolfe's study. SA and TA scores consisted of a single rating. PA scores consisted of PA as ratee and PA as rater scores. The former, PA (as ratee), is of most interest to this study. Both PA (as ratee) and PA (as rater) scores were expressed as means of the scores given to and given by each learner. Individual class assessments and a combined overall assessment were calculated using the SA, PA (as ratee), and TA data.

Level of data

The scales used were not equal interval. The ratings were intuitive for learners and neither were teachers particularly consistent in their use of the scale.

The data in this study is not normally distributed and, therefore, the data should be ranked and a nonparametric test used. The weak tendency to agreement in the data can be seen visually in the overall SA, PA, TA relationships in the scattergrams in Figure 1. In using Pearson's r in his study, Rolfe treated his data as parametric — a reasonable step given the normal distribution of his data and the strong tendency to agreement in the overall scattergrams (Rolfe 1990:180). He does, however, express some reservations and also uses Spearman's Rho, the nonparametric equivalent.

There are two variables to be considered in each correlation:

• independent — the TA, as TA is the benchmark against which the SA and PA can be compared (although this is also questionable given the inconsistency of the TA rankings);

• dependent — the SA and PA. The relationship between the variables is dependent — the same learners being rated by themselves, their peers and their teachers.

Therefore, the statistics to be used is one of correlation for ranked data i.e. Spearman's Rho.

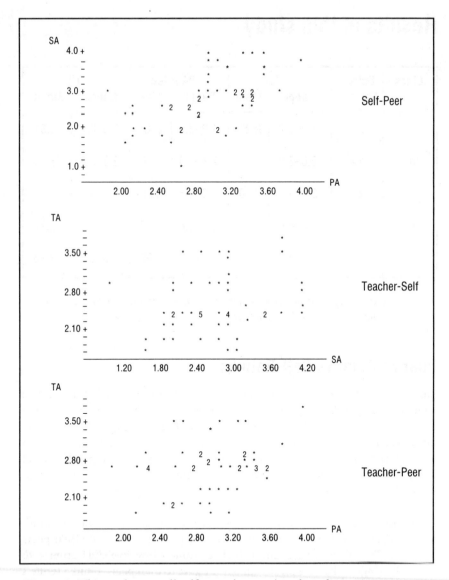

*Figure 1 This study: overall self, peer (as ratee) and teacher ratings —
scattergrams*

Results of this study

Class	Entry Range	SA		PA ratee		TA	
		Range	Mean	Range	Mean	Range	Mean
I	2+	1.0–3.0	2.25	1.9–2.9	2.42	2.5–3.5	2.81
II	2+	2.0–3.8	3.05	2.8–3.0	3.19	2.5–3.8	3.01
III	2	2.0–4.0	3.10	3.0–3.8	3.29	2.3–3.1	2.81
IV	2	2.8–4.0	3.28	2.9–3.6	3.37	1.8–2.5	2.27
V	1+	1.5–3.2	2.39	2.1–3.5	2.99	1.8–2.5	2.18

Table 2 This study: comparison of self, peer (as ratee) and teacher ratings and entry range for each class

Peer as Rater vs Self-Ratings

Similar to Rolfe's findings, the ratings given by learners to their peers (PA as rater) varied considerably. Some learners gave consistently high ratings while others gave consistently low ratings. As Rolfe (1990:177) suggests, this may be due to the lack of description on the SA and PA scales and may also be due to learners' lack of experience in judging others. Further, obvious psycho-social factors were in operation — in some cases a learner would give extremely high ratings to some peers and extremely low ratings to other peers.

In all classes, mean SA ratings were lower than mean PA (as rater) ratings indicating that learners rate themselves more harshly than they rate their peers (see Table 2). Only in fourteen individual cases (out of fifty-five) did learners rate themselves higher than the mean ratings they gave to their peers. Unlike Rolfe's study (1990:177), the data did not show that gross self under-raters were also gross peer over-raters.

Peer as Ratee vs Self-Ratings

Comparison of the mean PA (as ratee) ratings given by peers and the SA ratings is of interest to this study. Similar to Rolfe's study, in only fifteen cases out of fifty-five did learners rate themselves more highly than the mean peer rating given to them. This confirms the tendency for learners to under-rate themselves with respect to how their peers rate them. Affective factors, such as modesty, may come into play here.

Peer as Ratee vs Teacher Ratings

With the exception of Class I, the mean PA (as ratee) ratings given by peers were higher than the TA ratings in all but three cases. Like Rolfe's study (1990:179), this indicates that peers are more generous than teachers in assessing oral proficiency. In Class I, the exit class, the TA ratings were all higher (with the exception of one case) than the mean PA ratings. This is a reflection of the learners rating their peers harshly in order to give the impression the class needs to stay on at the centre and spend further time studying English.

Self vs Teacher Ratings

Learners tend to be more critical of themselves than are their teachers. In thirty-two cases out of fifty-five, SA ratings were lower than TA ratings. In comparison, Rolfe's study (1990:179) showed forty-three out of sixty which is noticeably higher and perhaps reflects the fact that learners in this study are less aware of and less critical of their own oral proficiency performance. In Class IV, all the learners rated themselves higher than the teacher rating. As mentioned above, this may indicate the teacher was rating severely, particularly as some TA ratings were lower than the entry level score (see Table 2).

Correlations: SA vs PA (as Ratee) vs TA

As mentioned previously, Spearman's Rho was calculated in this study as the data are not normally distributed and, therefore, not parametric. Table 3 shows the results of these correlations for the five classes and the overall combination.

The self–teacher correlations ranged from -0.117 to .516, none of which was statistically significant. This is similar to Rolfe's result (1990:180), although in this study the correlation coefficients are lower. This study's results can be seen visually in the self–teacher scattergram for the overall combination of classes (see Figure 1). From the scattergram, it is clear there is no good line of fit. Further, it is possible that Class IV reached a significant level of .516 because of the small class numbers only. SA does not appear to be a reliable indicator of oral proficiency when compared to TA ratings.

Spearman's Rho			
Class I	**Self**	**Peer**	**Teacher**
Self		-0.114	-0.117
Peer	(N=13)		.782**
Class II	**Self**	**Peer**	**Teacher**
Self		.239	.476
Peer	(N=10)		.612
Class III	**Self**	**Peer**	**Teacher**
Self		-0.016	-0.176
Peer	(N=11)		.802**
Class IV	**Self**	**Peer**	**Teacher**
Self		.880	.516
Peer	(N=6)		.677
Class V	**Self**	**Peer**	**Teacher**
Self		.625*	.292
Peer	(N=15)		.777**
Overall	**Self**	**Peer**	**Teacher**
Self		.586**	.204
Peer	(N=55)		.232

*p<.05   **p<.01

Table 3 This study: Spearman's Rho correlations

Similar to Rolfe (1990:181), peer–teacher correlations for the individual classes were higher, ranging from .612 to .802. The result is significant at the .01 level for Classes I, III and V. Unlike Rolfe's study, however, this strong tendency towards agreement at the class level was not reflected in the overall combination, having a correlation coefficient of only .204. The reason for this can be seen in the overall peer–teacher scattergram (Figure 1) which shows that, though there seemed to be agreement in some of the individual classes, when taken over a large group this relationship is non-significant — there is no one line of fit overall. It thus appears that mean PA may not be a reliable indicator of oral proficiency across all settings. Affective factors and lack of education in making proficiency judgements may be key reasons for this inconsistency in PA judgements.

The self–peer correlations ranged from -0.114 to .880, none of which was significant except for Class V at the .05 level and the overall combination at the .01 level. This is represented visually in the overall scattergram (see Figure 1). This is quite similar to Rolfe's findings (1990:181) on the class level. Unlike Rolfe's study, however, the relationship at the overall level is much stronger for the self–peer correlations than for the self–teacher and peer–teacher correlations. This stronger relationship may be due to the influence of the higher correlations in Classes IV and V. It must be remarked, however, that the correlation of .880 for Class IV was not statistically significant and may have been this high due to the small class numbers (N=6) only.

In summary, whereas Rolfe (1990:181) observes that PA ratings correlate highly with TA ratings and weakly with SA ratings at the overall level, this study indicates that both PA and SA ratings correlate weakly with TA ratings but are in statistically significant correlation with each other.

Discussion of the results of this replication

In his final discussion, Rolfe (1990:181–183) concludes that, while SA is not a highly reliable technique for assessing oral proficiency in terms of its agreement with TA, mean PA does appear to be reliable (with the exception of one class). This study does not support that conclusion. While showing a tendency towards agreement with TA at the class level, mean PA shows a weak and non-significant relationship with TA at the overall level, indicating a lack of consistency in overall PA–TA agreement. Neither do SA and TA correlate highly. Conversely, SA and PA correlate at a statistically significant level.

One possible reason for this is that the classes in this study have not had a strong or conscious policy of involving the learners in the assessment process and, as a result, the learners are not well-informed or critical judges of their own or their peers' oral proficiency levels. On the other hand, the classes in Rolfe's study may have had a more thorough background in involving the learners in the assessment process in the first place. It may also indicate that both SA and PA are affected by similar psycho-social motives and thus have more in common in comparison to the trained, defined judgement of the TA ratings.

Another possible reason is a lack of consistency in the TA ratings themselves — some of the teachers may have been inadequately trained in the use of the ASLPR scale and even trained teachers seemed to use different standards in applying the scale, this latter indicating ambiguity in the ASLPR scale itself (see McIntyre, this volume). A final possible reason may be differences between the ASLPR (this study) and AMES (Rolfe's study) scales. It may be that the AMES scale is more compatible in nature with intuitive scales. If this is so, it raises questions about the applicability and power of the ASLPR scale as a rating tool when it differs so widely from the consensus, intuitive 'yardsticks' which learners develop in assessing their own language proficiency and that of their peers.

Conclusion

In conclusion, this study does not support Rolfe's confidence in the reliability of mean peer-assessment and questions the generalisability of Rolfe's findings to other settings. It does, however, support his advocacy for (a) better training of teachers in applying assessment scales, in this case the ASLPR scale, and (b) involving the learner in the assessment process so that the learner is better able to judge his/her own proficiency and formulate more appropriate learning pathways and goals using this inbuilt yardstick.

References

Brindley, G. 1979. *Assessment of ESL speaking proficiency through the oral interview.* Sydney: Adult Migrant English Service.

Brindley, G. (ed.) 1990. *The second language curriculum in action.* Sydney: National Centre for English Language Teaching and Research.

Candlin, C.N. 1989. Language, culture and curriculum. In C.N. Candlin and T.F. McNamara (eds).

Candlin, C.N. and T.F. McNamara (eds). 1989. *Language, learning and community.* Sydney: National Centre for English Language Teaching and Research.

Ingram, D.E. and E. Wylie. 1984. *Australian second language proficiency ratings (ASLPR).* Canberra: Australian Government Publishing Service.

Nunan, D. 1988. *The learner-centred curriculum.* Cambridge: Cambridge University Press.

Nunan, D. 1991. *Language teaching methodology: a textbook for teachers.* Hemel Hempstead: Prentice Hall.

Rolfe, T. 1990. Self- and peer-assessment in the ESL curriculum. In G. Brindley (ed.).

Santos, T. 1989. Replication in applied linguistics research. *TESOL Quarterly* 23, 4:669–702.

Zamel, V. 1987. Recent research on writing pedagogy. *TESOL Quarterly* 21, 4:697–715.

Notes on contributors

Clare McDowell
Clare McDowell has been involved in TESOL for over fifteen years, recently specialising in the field of testing. She has worked extensively on the IELTS test, both in the area of training assessors and in item writing. She is Local Secretary for Cambridge EFL Examinations in Australia and is responsible for the delivery of their main suite exams. She consults on test design and development for a number of standardised public tests both within Australia and overseas. Her publications include articles on the assessment of speaking and she is the author of the self-instructional English preparation text *STEP Forward*, for the **step:** test.

Penny McKay
Penny McKay was the national coordinator of the NLLIA ESL Development: Language and Literacy in Schools Project. She has taught as a generalist in primary schools and as an ESL specialist in secondary intensive language centres and secondary schools. She was a National Project Officer for the Australian Language Levels Project and a lecturer/project consultant in the Centre for Applied Linguistics and Languages at Griffith University. Her PhD studies investigated the communicative orientation of teaching and learning outcomes in foreign languages in secondary schools. She is now a Lecturer in Language and Literacy Education at Queensland University of Technology.

Lexie Mincham
Lexie Mincham has worked in the ESL field since 1974 — as a teacher, principal of a secondary intensive language centre, consultant and project officer responsible for ESL assessment and evaluation. She is currently Manager of the ESL Program in South Australia. She contributed to the development of the assessment component of the NLLIA ESL Profiles Development Project in 1992, and in 1993 was a member of the writing team which developed the ESL Scales published by the Curriculum Corporation.

Chris Corbel
Chris Corbel is Curriculum Manager at AMES Victoria. He teaches Computer Assisted Language Learning on the MA Program in Applied Linguistics at the

University of Melbourne and is the author of *Computer enhanced language assessment* (NCELTR 1993) and of *From proficiencies to competencies* (NCELTR 1994).

Philip McIntyre

Philip McIntyre has worked with AMES since 1972, as an ESL teacher, teacher trainer, curriculum developer and materials writer. He recently gained a first-class Honours MA in Applied Linguistics from the University of Melbourne. His interest and work in the field of language assessment, specialising in ASLPR extends over fifteen years and he is currently delivering a program of moderation training for SIP assessors in various ESL providers in Victoria.

Geoff Brindley

Geoff Brindley is a Senior Lecturer in the School of English and Linguistics at Macquarie University and Research Coordinator in the National Centre for English Language Teaching and Research (NCELTR). He is the author of a range of publications on language proficiency assessment, second language acquisition and curriculum design.

Ruth Clarkson

Ruth Clarkson has been involved in ESL teaching for twelve years, firstly at the University of Technology in Lae, Papua New Guinea, and then at the Technisearch Centre for English Language Learning, RMIT University. Her main involvement has been in the teaching of EOP and prestudy skills courses with an emphasis on criterion-referenced assessment. The most recent of these was the NSW AMES Certificate of Written and Spoken English. These interests have led to participation in a number of NCELTR funded projects.

Marie-Therese Jensen

Marie-Therese Jensen is a Lecturer in TESOL at Monash University Faculty of Education. She has an interest in the assessment of second language proficiency from the point of view of the second language learner, as well as from that of the teacher and of the assessor. She has taught adult and secondary school learners of English as a second or foreign language in Australia, Great Britain, France. Germany and Japan. She has developed and trialled testing materials and rated candidates for both the OET and the IELTS test. She has also rated the spoken and written English of many adult migrants according to the ASLPR.

John Grierson

John Grierson is a Learning Support Lecturer at the University of Western Sydney, Macarthur. He is currently carrying out research into the oral and written feedback given by tutors to native and second language speakers on their university assignments. At the time the chapter was written he was a consultant with the New Arrivals Program of the Department of School Education.

Margaret Gunn

Margaret Gunn has wide experience in several facets of the Adult Migrant English Program (AMEP). She currently works in Hobart, Tasmania and completed an MA in Applied Linguistics through Macquarie University in 1992. Research interests include native speaker judgments of non-native speaker proficiency, and the relevance of competency criteria to public expectations.

Barbara Cram

Barbara Cram has contributed to a wide range of programs for adult migrants and overseas students over the past twelve years. While at NCELTR, she provided educational placement and referral support. At the same time, she carried out research into self-regulated language assessment. She is currently working as in instructional designer, developing materials for distance learners, at the Open Training and Education Network (OTEN) in Sydney.

Michaela Wilkes

Michaela Wilkes teaches English in Indonesia. Prior to this she was a Lecturer in English as a Second Language in the Faculty of Arts at Deakin University.